Adolescent Exposure to Violence and Adult Outcomes

Adolescent Exposure to Violence and Adult Outcomes

Results from the National Youth Survey Family Study

Scott Menard and Herbert C. Covey

LEXINGTON BOOKS

Lanham • Boulder • New York • London

Published by Lexington Books
An imprint of The Rowman & Littlefield Publishing Group, Inc.
4501 Forbes Boulevard, Suite 200, Lanham, Maryland 20706
www.rowman.com

6 Tinworth Street, London SE11 5AL, United Kingdom

British Library Cataloguing in Publication Information Available

Library of Congress Cataloging-in-Publication Data

Names: Menard, Scott W., author. | Covey, Herbert C., author.
Title: Adolescent exposure to violence and adult outcomes : results from the National Youth Survey Family Study / Scott Menard and Herbert C. Covey.
Description: Lanham, Maryland : Lexington Books, an imprint of the Rowman & Littlefield Publishing Group, Inc., [2021] | Includes bibliographical references and index.
Identifiers: LCCN 2021014943 (print) | LCCN 2021014944 (ebook) | ISBN 9781793650504 (cloth) | ISBN 9781793650511 (epub)
Subjects: LCSH: Youth and violence.
Classification: LCC HQ799.2.V56 M397 2021 (print) | LCC HQ799.2.V56 (ebook) | DDC 303.60835—dc23
LC record available at https://lccn.loc.gov/2021014943
LC ebook record available at https://lccn.loc.gov/2021014944

Contents

Preface

This book is the culmination of a research project that the authors began over a decade ago on the long-term consequences of adolescent exposure to violence. We have previously published several journal articles, cited in this book, on different aspects of that research. This book gives us the opportunity to expand that research, and to offer a broader and more coherent view of the consequences of adolescent exposure to violence than is possible in one or two, or even a series of several, journal articles. We examine not only how adolescent exposure to violence leads to problem behaviors, but also its deleterious effects on positive, beneficial outcomes. We seek to provide a multifaceted examination of the impacts of exposure to violence during adolescence on longer term outcomes over the life course.

Violence in its various forms seems to be ubiquitous in our society. We may be exposed directly, as victims of violence, or indirectly, as witnesses to the victimization of others. Sometimes the consequences of violence are relatively short lived, but in other cases violence has lasting consequences and implications for the lives of those who experience it. There are numerous studies of the causes and consequences of violence over relatively short spans of time, but far fewer studies of the longer term outcomes of exposure to violence as they develop over the life course. Much of the information available to us comes from studies that focus on a single type of violence, rather than multiple dimensions of exposure to violence; studies that focus on causes, rather than consequences of exposure to violence; studies that focus on a very short time span, rather than examining results that span decades in the context of the life course; or studies that have limited generalizability because they are based on small, local, or clinical samples, rather than nationally representative samples that encompass both those who have and those who have not experienced different types of exposure to violence. There has been a particular dearth of studies that focus specifically on exposure to violence during the adolescent years, as opposed to early or middle childhood, and that trace the consequences of exposure to violence beyond adolescence or young adulthood.

This book seeks to unravel some of the challenging questions regarding the long-term consequences of adolescent exposure to violence. It relies on highly sensitive personal information collected from a nationally representative sample of respondents over a span of nearly 30 years, at ages ranging from early adolescence to middle adulthood. Our research considers both simple bivariate relationships, involving only a single form of exposure to violence and a single outcome, which are common in much of the literature on the consequences of exposure to violence; and also more intricate relationships involving multiple forms of adolescent exposure to violence and their impact on multiple outcomes, with statistical controls for other potential influences on those outcomes. It considers the impacts of different types of exposure to violence on not only problematic adult outcomes such as intimate partner violence and problem substance use but also more desirable or beneficial outcomes such as educational attainment and life satisfaction. It also pays close attention to how the responses to adolescent exposure to violence may be different for female and male respondents. In all of this, we seek to advance our understanding of the breadth and complexity of the impacts of adolescent exposure to violence on adult outcomes.

Dedication and Acknowledgments

First and foremost, we would like to acknowledge the respondents of the National Youth Survey (NYS) and later renamed National Youth Survey Family Study (NYSFS) who, for nearly three decades, were so generous with their time and candid with their responses, and also their parents, spouses, and children, who provided additional information that enriched this study. Their participation, given under a guarantee of confidentiality, gave us a wealth of data that helped us better understand the development of behavior over the life course, the multiple sources of problem behavior, and, in the present volume, the important impact of exposure to violence during adolescence. It is to them that this book is dedicated.

Delbert S. Elliott was the first principal investigator on the NYS, and it was he who provided the conceptualization and theoretical basis that carried through the 27 years of the study. David H. Huizinga, the second principal investigator of the study, was there from the beginning, a guiding force in the implementation of the study design and the analysis of the data. Both remained with the study from beginning to end. The senior author, Menard, would like to express his appreciation to both for their bringing him into the study at the beginning of its second decade, for all he learned from working for them and collaborating with them on the research for the study, and for eventually giving him the opportunity to take on the role of being the third principal investigator of the renamed (because of the expanded inclusion of parents, spouses, and children) NYSFS.

There were many others who made important contributions to the success of the study, and here we would like to single out two in particular. Bertha Thomas was an absolute bulldog when it came to the integrity of the data, and is in large measure responsible for the confidence we can have in its quality and accuracy. Linda K. Kuhn was in charge of the field effort for several years, including the most recent and most challenging years which started with a nearly 10-year gap between the last wave of the NYS format (1992–1993) and the first wave of the new NYSFS format (2001–2002). It is a credit to her diligence, persistence, and creativity in tracking respondents and securing their participation that led to the high response rates that further bolster our confidence in the quality of the data. There too many others to list all of them individually, but we would like to acknowledge all of the dedicated staff of the NYS and NYSFS for their valuable contributions to the success of the study.

We would be remiss if we did not also acknowledge the diverse funding agencies who made the study possible financially. They include (alphabetically) the Law Enforcement Assistance Administration, the National Institute of Justice, National Institute of Mental Health, the National Institute on Alcohol Abuse and Alcoholism, the National Institute on Drug Abuse, and the Office of Juvenile Justice and Delinquency Prevention.

Specific to the study of adolescent exposure to violence, Dr. Donald Bross of the C. Henry Kempe National Center for the Prevention and Treatment of Child Abuse and Neglect in Denver, Colorado, provided valuable encouragement and useful suggestions when the authors first embarked on the project of examining the impacts of adolescent exposure to violence. The authors benefited substantially from his expertise and the insights he shared with us as we pursued this research.

We also benefited from our collaboration with the coauthors on earlier papers published on this research: Leah McCoy Grubb, Abigail S. Tucker, Andrea J. Weiss, and especially our long-time friend, colleague, and coauthor, Robert J. Franzese.

Laura, Jessica, and Valery Menard (yes, there is a relationship there, but also academic backgrounds in education, English composition, history, literature, and political science) proofread all of the chapters, most of them more than once, and not only checked grammar, punctuation, and spelling, but also made valuable suggestions for improving the clarity and accessibility of the presentation, particularly in the results chapters. Marty Covey also provided valuable comments and support during the process.

Finally, we would like to thank Lexington Books, particularly acquisitions editor Courtney Morales, for their support for this project, and for their valuable feedback in guiding the book forward to publication.

Chapter 1

Adolescent Exposure to Violence

Today's adolescents seem to live in a violent world. Reports of mass shootings, some directed at schoolchildren and youth, random acts of violence, the carnage of foreign civil wars, domestic terrorism, hate crimes, law-enforcement-involved shootings, coupled with popular culture depictions of violent events, have surrounded many of America's youth in an apparent culture of violence. Media coverage of these events brings them into households throughout the country. It is within this macro-level context that American children and adolescents experience violence. This macro-level context occurs at a time when national data show that some rates of violent crime in America have declined notably over the past two decades. But these declines are not universal. Some American youth, such as those living in impoverished neighborhoods and those belonging to racial minorities, continue to experience high levels of crime and violence.

Other violence occurs at the individual or micro level, as children and youth are direct victims of crime, physical abuse, sex abuse, cyberbullying, and general bullying. They may also be exposed to family and neighborhood violence. These forms of violence, when coupled with macro-level violence, clearly help shape not only childhood and adolescence but also the entire lifespan. Years of research on Adverse Childhood Experiences (ACEs), which include violent events, have found lasting influences on problematic and antisocial behaviors. The preponderance of evidence indicates that, regardless of type of violence, macrosocial or microsocial, direct or indirect exposure to violence matters to children and adolescents. It makes a difference regarding their mental health, substance abuse, socioeconomic status, employment, marital status, involvement in criminal activities, stress, and in other important dimensions of health and behavior. In general, a frequent research conclusion is that exposure to violence places youth at significant

1

risk for social, psychological, academic, and physical harm and increases the chances of them being more likely to commit violence themselves (Buka et al. 2010). Multiple studies show a history of exposure to violence leads to less favorable socioeconomic outcomes and negative impacts on employment status (Metzler et al. 2017; Schurer and Trajkovski 2018; Topitzes et al. 2016) and lower incomes (Covey et al. 2013; Currie and Widom 2010; Zielinski 2009).

This book examines three basic forms of adolescent exposure to violence (AEV): direct physical abuse, exposure to neighborhood violence, and exposure to intimate partner (more specifically, parental) violence. In considering the nature of these forms of AEV, we begin with a basic introduction to exposure to intimate partner violence (IPV), often occurring within the homes of adolescents between parents or other significant adults, to provide a broader context for our concern with exposure to parental violence. Much of the literature conceptualizes exposure to violence into either direct (primary) or indirect (secondary) exposure. Throughout this book, direct exposure to violence includes both parental abuse and more general violent victimization, while indirect exposure includes witnessing parental violence and exposure to neighborhood violence.

INTIMATE PARTNER VIOLENCE

The Centers for Disease and Control and Prevention (CDC) reported that IPV is common as it affects millions of Americans every year. According to the CDC's database, the National Intimate Partner and Sexual Violence Survey (Centers for Disease Control and Prevention 2019a, 1):

- About 1 in 4 women and nearly 1 in 10 men have experienced contact sexual violence, physical violence, and/or stalking by an intimate partner during their lifetime and reported some form of IPV-related impact.
- Over 43 million women and 38 million men experienced psychological aggression by an intimate partner in their lifetime.

The CDC further reports that IPV often begins early and continues throughout the lifespan. The number of victims is significant. The CDC reports:

Among victims, about 11 million women and 5 million men who reported experiencing contact sexual violence, physical violence, or stalking by an intimate partner in their lifetime also indicated that they first experienced these or other forms of violence by that partner before the age of 18. A nationally representative survey of U.S. high school students also indicates high levels of teen dating violence, a risk factor for IPV in adulthood. Among students who reported dating, 9% of girls and 7% of boys had experienced physical dating violence and 11% of girls and 3% of boys had experienced sexual dating violence in the past 12 months. (Centers for Disease Control and Prevention 2019a, 1)

The costs and consequences of IPV are significant at the individual and societal levels on several dimensions. For example, the CDC data reveal that about 41% of female IPV and 14% of male IPV survivors experience some form of physical injury. The U.S. crime reports suggest that 16% of homicide victims are killed by an intimate partner, and that almost half of female homicide victims in the United States are killed by a current or former male intimate partner. Regarding health, a variety of negative health outcomes such as a range of cardiovascular, gastrointestinal, reproductive, musculoskeletal, and nervous system conditions may result from IPV. Survivors often experience mental health problems, including depression and post-traumatic stress disorder (PTSD). Survivors are also at greater risk of engaging in health risk behaviors such as smoking, binge drinking, and sexually transmitted diseases. In addition, individuals exposed to violence at any age are more likely to perpetrate and/or be victims of subsequent IPV (Beyer et al. 2013; Raghavan et al. 2006).

The CDC identified estimated lifetime and societal costs associated with IPV, many related to health care. It reported,

The lifetime economic cost associated with medical services for IPV-related injuries, lost productivity from paid work, criminal justice and other costs, such as victim property loss or damage was $3.6 trillion (2014 US dollars). The lifetime per-victim cost was $103,767 for women and $23,414 for men. (Centers for Disease Control and Prevention 2019a, 1)

Some research has found that women exposed to IPV have an increased risk of physical health issues such as injuries and mental health disorders such as disordered eating, depression, and suicidal ideation (Stockman et al. 2015).

NEIGHBORHOOD VIOLENCE

There is a substantial body of evidence that exposure to community violence has negative outcomes for youth. Exposure to violence in a community may occur in different forms and levels, such as personal victimization, directly witnessing violent acts, seeing property damage, or becoming aware of violent events from other community members (Buka et al. 2010). There is evidence that youth exposure to community (neighborhood) violence has negative impacts on adolescents, such as substance abuse, delinquency, and mental health issues (Lynch 2003; Margolin and Gordis 2000). In addition, the cumulative exposure to violence, such as bullying, gun threats, and witnessing violence, has been linked to lower self-ratings of adolescent health (Boynton-Jarrett et al. 2008).

While the association between childhood and youth exposure to violence has been studied at length, the complex relationships between exposure to violence and later outcomes remain relatively uncharted and not well-understood. Central questions such as whether exposure to violence matters more at some ages than others, has lasting effects, differs based on group characteristics, and others remain unanswered. Over the lifespan, most child welfare practice has focused on children ages 0–5 years, as they are viewed as very vulnerable and relatively defenseless. According to Children's Bureau statistics, 70.6% of child fatalities in the FY 2018 involved children younger than 3 years, and children younger than 1 year accounted for 46.6% of all fatalities (U.S. Department of Health and Human Services 2020, 20). Consequently, scholars have paid less attention to adolescents and their exposure to violence. While there is general agreement that adolescence is important on several dimensions as individuals move from childhood to adulthood, except for delinquency and antisocial behaviors, comparatively little research has been conducted. Given the significance of adolescence to the overall lifespan and the relative neglect of it in relationship to exposure to the various forms of violence, it is imperative that longitudinal studies be conducted to better understand and inform our programs and services. The focus here is on the relationships of exposure to violence occurring during adolescence to immediate and long-term outcomes. Consideration will be given to how the exposure to violence interfaces with the child protection system.

CHILD MALTREATMENT AND ADOLESCENT EXPOSURE TO VIOLENCE

According to the federal *Child Maltreatment 2018 Report* (U.S. Department of Health and Human Services 2020, 18), the estimated number of children who were investigated or had an alternative response for child maltreatment nationally increased from 3,261,000 in 2014 to 3,534,000 in 2018. This represents an 8.4% increase in responses to reported maltreatment. The number of confirmed child victims increased over this same span from 675,000 to an estimated 678,000, an increase of 0.4% (p. 19). Approximately, 60.8% of these confirmed cases were for neglect only, 10.7% for physical abuse only, and 7% for sexual abuse only. In 2018, approximately 1,770 children died from maltreatment, a rate of 2.39 per 100,000 children in the national population (U.S. Department of Health and Human Services 2020, 46).

Using different measures, the CDC calculated the extent of maltreatment in the United States:

> In fiscal year 2008, U.S. state and local child protective services (CPS) received more than 3 million reports of children being abused or neglected—or about 6 complaints per minute, every day. An estimated 772,000 children were classified by CPS authorities as being maltreated and 1,740 children aged 0 to 17 died from abuse and neglect in 2008. (Centers for Disease Control and Prevention 2014, 1)

More recently, the CDC (2019b, 1) reported:

- Child abuse and neglect are common. At least 1 in 7 children have experienced child abuse and/or neglect in the past year, and this is likely an underestimate.
- Children living in poverty experience more abuse and neglect. Rates of child abuse and neglect are 5 times higher for children in families with low socio-economic status compared to children in families with higher socio-economic status.
- Child maltreatment is costly. This economic burden rivals the cost of other high-profile public health problems, such as stroke and type 2 diabetes.

Notice that the CDC reports on incidents occurring to individuals up to age 17. The inclusion of both adolescent and preadolescent childhood in definitions of and statistics regarding child maltreatment is commonplace, but it is useful in our view to distinguish between maltreatment occurring in the first and second decades of life.

The financial costs of child maltreatment are significant. Fang et al. (2012) in a CDC study estimated the annual financial costs of confirmed maltreatment. Regardless of the type of child abuse, be it physical, sexual, or emotional, there are implications for public health, with the average lifetime health care costs per survivor being estimated to be $32,648 and the average adult medical costs for survivors averaging $10,530 (Fang et al. 2012). They also calculated that for the 579,000 confirmed maltreatment cases, the total estimated cost was $124 billion per year in 2008. A single child fatality resulting from abuse or neglect equated to a lifetime cost of $1.3 million per child, based on the money the child would have earned over a lifetime, had he or she lived. In addition to these financial costs, child maltreatment has been linked to a variety of harmful adult outcomes, including partner and non-partner violence victimization and perpetration, illicit substance use, mental health problems, low educational attainment, unemployment, and low income and net worth (Cicchetti and Rogosch 1997; Widom 2014). In a similar vein, the costs of ACEs over the life course are substantial. Bellis et al. (2019, 525) indicated that for Europe and North America, an estimated $1.3 trillion are used to address the impacts of ACEs. The same study estimated that a 10% reduction in ACEs would result in a $105 billion savings (p. 517).

The research presented in this book focuses on the long-term impact of a specific form of child maltreatment, exposure to violence, on such adult outcomes as violence, drug abuse, mental health problems, and socioeconomic status (SES) attainment. In this chapter, we continue with a brief overview of how child protection has evolved in the United States and the corresponding development of our definitions of child maltreatment and related phenomena. We then consider the importance of timing of exposure to violence in the early life course and the distinction between childhood and AEV. We next consider theoretical perspectives that help us understand the links between AEV and adult outcomes, focusing on perspectives that have been particularly helpful in framing the present study. We end this chapter with an outline of subsequent chapters in this book.

LEGAL CONTEXT

It was during the 1960s that child maltreatment became viewed as a national issue. Research by Dr. C. Henry Kempe and his associates (Kempe et al. 1962; see also Helfer and Kempe 1968) on child maltreatment gained attention and led to the concept of the "battered child syndrome." It was during this decade that the War on Poverty would be initiated, and a wide variety of federal programs were established to increase the opportunities for children and the impoverished. In 1974, Congress passed the Child Abuse Prevention and Treatment Act (CAPTA). CAPTA (Public Law 93-247) established national child protection norms comprised of laws, reporting requirements for suspected cases of maltreatment, agencies that investigated reports, and central registries of perpetrators and victims. This was accomplished by giving federal funds to states that met federal minimal requirements. In the 1990s, secretary of U.S. Department of Health and Human Services Louis W. Sullivan initiated new efforts to organize national support for the prevention and treatment of child maltreatment. In 1993, President Clinton signed the Family Preservation and Support Services Program Act (Public Law 103-66) into law which assisted communities in building systems to support families and vulnerable children to prevent maltreatment. In 1996, Congress reauthorized the CAPTA (Public Law 104-235) and added new requirements, including safeguards against false reports of child abuse and neglect, delays in termination of parental rights, and a lack of public oversight of child protection. There has always been a concern with family preservation and with making reasonable efforts to keep families together, but there was evidence that caseworkers and judges left children in dangerous homes. In 1997, Congress responded by passing the Adoption and Safe Families Act (Public Law 105-89). It made child safety the top priority for child protection programs. In 2000, increased attention was paid to the consequences of children being exposed to traumatic events. Numerous studies reported that negative childhood experiences had significant impacts on developing brains. The acknowledgment of the impact of trauma on developing children would represent a major paradigm shift for child protection in America.

In the beginning of the twenty-first century, there was renewed emphasis on helping families. Illustrative of this was Congress's enactment of the Promoting Safe and Stable Families amendments in 2001 (Public Law 107-133). The act promoted the expansion of services to strengthen families. In 2003, Congress reauthorized CAPTA under the Keeping Children and Families Safe Act (Public Law 108-36) which called for child protection agencies to coordinate services with other agencies, including public health and mental health. Seven years later, the CAPTA Reauthorization Act of 2010 (Public Law 111-32) further improved child protection service systems, in part recognizing the relationship between child maltreatment and substance abuse. In 2018, Congress passed the Family First Prevention Services Act (Public Law 115-123), which made basic changes to child-protection and child-welfare system. The Act provides services to at-risk families, such as substance abuse and/or mental health treatment, to prevent child maltreatment. A goal is to keep families together and out of the system. The basis of the Act was the perspective that children do better when they remain with their families rather than being placed in foster care. The Act promoted services that strengthen families. The Act also limits and reduces funding for residential placements of children in congregate care settings.

DEFINITIONS: MALTREATMENT, NEGLECT, ABUSE, ACE, AND EXPOSURE TO VIOLENCE

CAPTA was significant in helping to promote common definitions of the terms "child abuse" and "child neglect" but at present there is still no single consensus definition of what constitutes child maltreatment. Every state has its own definitions of child and abuse that must be consistent with federal standards. The CAPTA, as amended by the CAPTA Reauthorization of 2010 (Public Law 111-32), retained an earlier definition of child abuse and neglect as, at a minimum:

> Any recent act or failure to act on the part of a parent or caretaker which results in death, serious physical harm, sexual abuse or exploitation; or an act or failure to act, which presents imminent risk of serious harm. Most states recognize four

major types of maltreatment: neglect, physical abuse, psychological maltreatment, and sexual abuse. Although any of the forms of child maltreatment may be found separately, they can occur in combination. (U.S. Department of Health and Human Services 2019, viii)

Based on the criteria published by the Office of Juvenile Justice and Delinquency Prevention and summarized in Lemmon and Verrecchia (2009, 135, emphasis in original; see also Sickmund and Puzzanchera 2014), child maltreatment includes both abuse and neglect, and may be divided into six categories:

Physical abuse includes physical acts that caused or could have caused physical injury to the child. *Sexual abuse* is involvement of the child in sexual activity to provide sexual gratification or financial benefit to the perpetrator, including contacts for sexual purposes, prostitution, pornography, or other sexually exploitative activities. *Emotional abuse* is defined as acts or omissions that caused or could have caused conduct, cognitive, affective, or other mental disorders. *Physical neglect* includes abandonment, expulsion from the home, failure to seek remedial health care or delay in seeking care, inadequate supervision, disregard for hazards in the home, or inadequate food, clothing, or shelter. *Emotional neglect* includes inadequate nurturance or affection, permitting maladaptive behavior, and other inattention to emotional/developmental needs. *Educational neglect* [includes] permitting chronic truancy or other inattention to educational needs.

As noted by Lemmon and Verrecchia (p. 134), "While the definitions of physical and sexual abuse have been generally accepted among professionals and the public, there has been substantially less consensus over how psychological abuse and neglect should be defined." They continue (p. 135), "Neglect is the most common and most ambiguously defined form of child maltreatment, and clearly reflects the normative nature of child welfare services." As reported by Lemmon and Verrecchia, approximately 60% of all child maltreatment cases involve neglect, with the remainder, less than 40%, involving abuse.

Related to child maltreatment, neglect, and abuse is the term *adverse childhood experiences* or ACEs, as introduced by Felitti et al. (1998). Felitti et al. defined ACEs as potentially traumatic childhood events that can have negative, lasting effects on health and well-being. They present two broad categories of ACEs, abuse and household dysfunction. Under abuse, they include physical abuse (physical violence directed toward the child), sexual abuse (physical sexual contact with the child), and psychological abuse (threats and disparagement toward the child). Under household dysfunction, they include substance abuse (alcohol and street drugs) by others in the household, mental illness (including depression and attempted suicide) by a household member, violence toward the mother, and criminal behavior by anyone in the household. Like child maltreatment, there is variation in the proposed definitions of ACE. Monnat and Chandler (2015) add experiencing parental divorce to the list provided by Felitti et al. (1998), and Baglivio et al. (2017, 168) include ten ACEs, which include, in addition to those described in Felitti et al. (1998) and Monnat and Chandler (2015), emotional neglect and physical neglect. The list by Baglivio et al. encompasses all of the forms of child maltreatment listed by Lemmon and Verrecchia (2009) except for educational neglect, and also includes exposure to parental violence (specifically maternal violence victimization) plus exposure to marital dissolution, mental illness, substance abuse, and incarceration in the household. National estimates of the prevalence of ACEs based on retrospective survey data for adults 18–64 years old (Monnat and Chandler 2015) indicated that 58% reported at least one ACE. For separate types of ACE, this ranged from about one in four experiencing parental divorce or verbal abuse to less than one in ten living with someone who was incarcerated. A little over 10% reported either physical abuse, sexual abuse, parental domestic violence, or substance abuse in the household.

In studying children's exposure to violence, researchers using the National Survey of Children's Exposure to Violence (NatSCEV) (Finkelhor et al. 2009) included prospective (short-term recall of past year behaviors) and long-term retrospective (longer term recall of behavior more than a year, and typically several years, prior to questioning) measures of physical assault victimization, sexual victimization, bullying, child maltreatment (including physical abuse other than sexual assault, psychological abuse, emotional abuse, child neglect, and abduction by a parent or caregiver), witnessing violence in the family or community, indirect exposure to violence in the family or community, and also property victimization. Like ACE, the NatSCEV conceptualization includes most of the forms of child maltreatment listed by Lemmon and Verrecchia (2009), again excepting educational neglect, and in this respect includes items that clearly constitute maltreatment but go beyond what most would describe as violence. A narrower focus on exposure specifically to violence, but excluding items other than physical violence, would exclude psychological abuse, emotional abuse, child neglect, property victimization, and probably abduction by a parent or caregiver who neither intends nor inflicts harm on the child. Also of interest is the age range for "childhood" exposure to violence in the NatSCEV, which spans infancy to age 17, thus including adolescent as well as preadolescent childhood exposure to violence.

Prospective national data on past year exposure to violence for 14–17-year-olds from the first (2008) and second (2011) NatSCEV surveys (Finkelhor et al. 2009, 2015) indicate that, under the broad definition of exposure to violence used by NatSCEV, 60.6% in 2008 and 57.7% in 2011 had been exposed to violence in the past year. This number is similar to the prevalence of ACEs reported by Monnat and Chandler (2015). Lifetime prevalence was reported to be one-third to one-half higher than past year prevalence, with larger discrepancies for less frequent and more serious forms of victimization. For selected specific types of exposure, 50.2% of males and 42.1% of females in 2008, and 45.2% and 37.1% respectively in 2011, reported any physical assault, with or without a weapon or injury. Focusing on child abuse, witnessing violence, and indirect exposure to violence, for the 2008 survey physical abuse by an adult was reported by 4.3% of males and 4.4% of females for the past year (4.5% and 2.9% respectively in 2011), and by 9.8% of males and 8.3% of females (11.0% and 8.1% respectively in 2011) using retrospective lifetime estimates. Witnessing partner assault was reported by 5.7% of males and 6.8% of females for the past year in 2008 (6.0% and 17.6% respectively in 2011), and 15.6% of males and 17.0% of females (6.1% and 17.1% respectively in 2011) in lifetime retrospective data. Indirect exposure to community violence was reported by 9.3% of males and 10.2% of females for the past year in 2008 (2.9% and 2.1% respectively in 2011), and 20.0% of males and 21.2% of females (7.7% and 8.2% respectively in 2011) in lifetime retrospective data. Note that in the second NatSCEV survey (Finkelhor et al. 2015), similar results were reported for physical abuse by an adult, but prevalence of witnessing partner violence was both substantially lower for males and for past year, and more discrepant by gender, and prevalence of indirect exposure to neighborhood violence was substantially lower.

Research using the National Youth Survey Family Study (NYSFS) (Covey et al. 2013; Menard et al. 2015) to study AEV uses a narrower definition of exposure to violence for adolescents that includes three elements that overlap with the NatSCEV definition: being physically abused by parents (beaten up by parents), witnessing parental violence (including violence toward either parent), and neighborhood violence (problems of assaults or muggings in the neighborhood, which may reflect any one or more of being directly victimized, witnessing, or indirect awareness of such violence in their neighborhood). This is also consistent with the conception of exposure to violence suggested by Eitle and Turner (2002). The intent of the research from the NYSFS was to focus on the more serious forms of exposure to acts that were unquestionably violent in nature, to the exclusion of other forms of ACE such as neglect or property victimization. AEV thus conceived overlaps with, but is not the same as, child maltreatment, child abuse, or child neglect.

Strictly speaking, the term "adolescent exposure to violence," as used in the present study, includes physical abuse. In principle, it also includes sexual abuse, but there were too few cases of sexual abuse in the data to analyze separately, and sexual abuse in the sample always occurred in conjunction with, never independent of, physical abuse. Also noteworthy regarding the NYSFS studies is that the age range extends two years beyond what is typically con-sidered adolescence at both the lower and upper bounds, with "adolescent" exposure to violence including exposure for ages 11–15 for the youngest of the seven annual birth cohorts and 17–21 for the oldest cohort. The NYSFS provides retrospective data on witnessing parental violence and prospective longitudinal data on experiencing parental physical abuse and exposure to neighborhood violence, the latter two accumulated over a 5-year span from 1976 to 1980. It also includes a prospective measure of more general violent victimization besides parental physical abuse which includes attempted or completed robbery, sexual assault, attack with a weapon, or battery. This more general measure of adolescent violence victimization has been shown to be predictive of young adult and middle adult outcomes, including but not limited to subsequent violence victimization and perpetration (Franzese et al. 2017; Menard 2002; Menard et al. 2015).

The NYSFS data (Menard et al. 2015) indicate that 10.5% of males and 7.7% of females experienced physical abuse, while approximately 15% of both females and males were aware of neighborhood violence, during that 5-year time span. Retrospective data on witnessing parental violence indicated that when reports were consistent over time, 16.8% of males and 12.6% of females reported witnessing parental violence. Comparing NYSFS 5 year and retrospective estimates to NatSCEV lifetime estimates, NYSFS and NatSCEV are within one percentage point for physical abuse by parents; NYSFS is similar to NatSCEV for males but lower for females for witness-ing parental violence; and NYSFS 5-year estimates lie between NatSCEV past year and lifetime estimates for exposure to neighborhood violence. Such differences as there are may reflect differences in age range (primarily 11–21 for NYSFS, 0–17 for NatSCEV), time of measurement (primarily 1976–1980 vs. 2008 and 2011 for NatSCEV, but both including retrospective data), and specific elements of survey design such as question wording. Differences in time, and possibly in survey administration, may also explain differences in the results for the 2008 and 2011 NatSCEV surveys. To the extent that the cross-sectional NatSCEV and the longitudinal NYSFS surveys look at comparable offenses, they do appear to produce similar results, with NYSFS 5 year and retrospective estimates lying within the range of past year and lifetime estimates provided by the two NatSCEV surveys.

TIMING OF ABUSE/NEGLECT/ACE/EXPOSURE TO VIOLENCE AND SUBSEQUENT OUTCOMES

Past work on the study of childhood abuse and neglect has commonly found that maltreated children are more likely than their non-maltreated peers to have negative concurrent and longitudinal outcomes, ranging from feelings of depression to engaging in delinquency and in serious violence. Specifically, Cicchetti and Rogosch (1997) note that abused children suffer from a variety of childhood developmental deficits including externalizing behaviors, disruptive behaviors, behavioral and academic problems at school, and depressive symptoms. Wasserman and Seracini (2001) report that though early case studies and anecdotal reports in the histories of criminal adolescents and adults yielded abuse rates ranging from 26 to 85%; retrospective studies that examined only documented abuse yielded abuse rates of 8 to 26%; and prospective studies suggest that 20% of abused children become delinquent or criminal by adulthood. More broadly, there is evidence that different types of maltreatment generally, and exposure to violence in particular, may be predictive of different types of outcomes (illegal behavior, mental health, social status), but more detailed discussion of this is reserved for the chapters that focus on those specific outcomes.

While much of the research on the impact of maltreatment has focused on the period from early childhood up to but not including adolescence, adolescence may be a critical, particularly vulnerable stage of the life course when it comes to the impacts of abuse, neglect, ACEs, and exposure to violence. Adolescence is an important transition period of the lifespan bridging childhood to adulthood. It is a time when hormonal, relational, physiological, biological, brain development, psychological, social, and other changes are occurring. Adolescence is a time of identity formation and boundary testing. As explained by Rosenblum and Lewis (2003, 269), "Hormone levels, cognitive ability, and social experiences all shift during adolescence from their childhood to adult forms. Once so transformed, these factors stabilize for much of adulthood." They also note that adolescence also possesses unique characteristics that are not expected to persist into adulthood.

Another important aspect of adolescence involves addressing developmental tasks that mark the transition from childhood to adulthood. Developmental tasks in adolescence include the development of autonomy (Bell et al. 1996; Graber et al. 1996), choosing an educational outcome, and often transitioning to adult occupational careers (Vondracek and Porfeli 2003). For many, the end of adolescence marks the time of entry into full-time employment (Graber et al. 1996). Approximately half of all adolescents enter the labor force directly after graduating high school, with the other half largely continuing formal education (Vondracek and Porfeli 2003). Adolescence is also the period in which the major transitions involving education (dropping out, completion, or continuation to college and, in young adulthood, graduate education) are completed (Graber et al. 1996). Bell et al. (1996) characterize educational attainment and occupational prestige as two markers of the success of the transition from adolescence to early adulthood, and work and school are areas most frequently mentioned as being important by adolescents (Vondracek and Porfeli 2003). In addition to work and school, adolescence is a period marked by increased rates of transition into marriage or nonmarital intimate partnerships, and into parenthood (Graber et al. 1996).

There is evidence that maltreatment suffered during adolescence, whether initiated in adolescence or continued from earlier in childhood may have a greater impact than maltreatment that only occurs prior to adolescence (Kerig and Becker 2015). Some have concluded that exposure to violence during adolescence may be more impactful than during childhood (e.g., Ireland et al. 2002). Heinze et al. (2017, 31) wrote:

ETV [Exposure to Violence] during adolescent years may be particularly salient given that adolescents experience numerous physiological changes, in addition to forming their identity, developing and strengthening peer and significant other relationships, and increasing their independence from parents and caregivers. Violence exposure that disrupts or delays these critical tasks during adolescence may have a negative influence on later development.

This has been most extensively studied with respect to illegal behavior in adolescence as an outcome. Ryan et al. (2013) examined official records of apprehension and official records of neglect for high-risk juvenile offenders in Washington State to determine whether child neglect had an impact on recidivism. As control variables, they included measures of family relationships, parental supervision, parental substance use, household income, school involvement and commitment, peer associations, and individual attitudes. They found that adolescents with official records of ongoing neglect were more likely than individuals with no official history of neglect to be recidivists, as opposed to discontinuing their offending. Stewart et al. (2008) examined a birth cohort of children born in Queensland, Australia, in 1983 or 1984, and who had at least one contact with child protective services. They found that children whose maltreatment started in adolescence, or continued from earlier childhood into adolescence, had higher rates of offending than individuals whose maltreatment occurred only prior to, not during, adolescence.

Using data from the Rochester Youth Development Survey, Ireland et al. (2002) did an extensive examination of the impact of maltreatment in childhood only, adolescence only, and continuous maltreatment in both childhood and adolescence, on arrests, drug use, street crimes, violent crimes, and delinquency, separately in early and late adolescence. They found that childhood-only maltreatment was associated with increased risk of violent crime in early but not late adolescence, but had no other significant effects. Adolescent-only maltreatment was associated with arrest, drug use, street crimes, violent crimes, and delinquency in early adolescence, and with arrest, street crimes, and delinquency in later adolescence. Maltreatment that spanned both child-hood and adolescence was associated with arrest, drug use, and street crimes in early adolescence, and with arrest, drug use, street crimes, violent crimes, and delinquency in later adolescence. The authors discuss several reasons that childhood-limited maltreatment may not have been significant, including that abuse that began to occur in childhood may not have been substanti-ated until adolescence, resulting in a misclassification as adolescent-limited maltreatment.

Thornberry et al. (2001) incorporated measures related to mental health in addition to illegal behavior, including depressive symptoms and parent-reported internalizing and externalizing problems, and also school dropout and teen pregnancy, and for part of their analysis, split childhood into earlier and later childhood. For earlier adolescence outcomes, they found that both earlier and later childhood maltreatment were related to internalizing prob-lems, and later childhood maltreatment was related to externalizing prob-lems and delinquency; and for later adolescence outcomes, early childhood maltreatment had no apparent effects, but later childhood maltreatment was related to externalizing problems and school dropout. By comparison, ado-lescent maltreatment was predictive of all of the outcomes they considered (delinquency, drug use, alcohol problems, depressive symptoms, internal-izing problems, externalizing problems, teen pregnancy, and school dropout) in early adolescence, and delinquency and externalizing problems in later adolescence. Continuous maltreatment in both childhood and adolescence was predictive of most of the outcomes in early adolescence, and of delin-quency, drug use, and teen pregnancy in later adolescence. The broad pattern is that childhood-only maltreatment appears to be predictive of minor illegal behavior (delinquency) and of internalizing and externalizing problems, while adolescent-only maltreatment and maltreatment that is continuous from childhood to adolescence are predictive of a wider range of problems, includ-ing illegal behavior and substance use as well as mental health. The authors speculate that contributing factors may include fewer available programs for adolescent victims of maltreatment than are available for maltreated children, and that more autonomous adolescents may have greater access to illegiti-mate coping strategies.

In their review of studies suggesting that adolescent maltreatment may be more predictive of problematic outcomes than childhood-only maltreatment, Kerig and Becker (2015) draw four possible explanations from those studies. One is the possibility that children may be more "developmentally resilient" and that the short-term negative effects of maltreatment may dissipate once the maltreatment stops (in or by adolescence). Second, when the maltreat-ment continues into adolescence, both the duration of the maltreatment (if it is continued from childhood) and the co-occurring developmental changes that are taking place during adolescence may result in more enduring consequences. Third, it is possible that interventions from child protective services or other public agencies may be less available for and less effective with adolescents than with younger children. Fourth, the type of maltreatment experienced in adolescence may be qualitatively different from, and possibly more severe, than maltreatment that occurs in earlier childhood (e.g., physical abuse by parents might be more violent when directed toward an adolescent than toward a younger child), particularly with respect to maltreatment that would likely come to the attention of child protective services. In considering these explanations, note that in the studies reviewed here and in Kerig and Becker (2015), outcomes were measured at earlier stages of the life course, up to late adolescence and early adulthood, but not into later stages, in particular middle adulthood. This leaves open the question whether adolescent maltreatment, particularly AEV, should be expected to have impacts reaching into later stages of the life course.

EXPLANATIONS FOR THE LINKS
BETWEEN ADOLESCENT EXPOSURE TO
VIOLENCE AND ADULT OUTCOMES

In describing the theoretical framework that informs the present research, it is important to be clear that we are not using a theoretical perspective about a single outcome with multiple causes. Instead, we are focusing on the impact of a single (albeit multifaceted) predictor on multiple outcomes. AEV, with its three dimensions of direct experience of abuse, witnessing parental violence, and exposure to violence in the neighborhood, is the single influence on the multiple outcomes of violent behavior, illicit substance use, mental health, and SES. Our expectations for the impacts of AEV on adult outcomes are shaped largely by the strain theories of Merton (1938) and Agnew (1985), supplemented by the social learning theory of Akers (1985), and other theoretical perspectives that may be more relevant to some but not other specific outcomes.

Merton's (1938; updated in Merton 1968) anomie theory shares the theoretical structure of the present study as a theory of multiple outcomes of a single cause. Merton's theory focused on the impact of normlessness at both the social structural level (anomie) and the individual level (anomia). According to anomie theory, culturally universal success goals, coupled with differential access to or blockage of those goals, produce strain at both the social structural and the individual level. At the individual level, people resolve the strain in a variety of ways, including acceptance of both the cultural goals and the societal restrictions on the means to achieve those goals (which Merton termed "conformity"); continued acceptance of the goals, but rejection of the societal constraints on the means to achieve the goals ("innovation"); rejection of the goals but continued acceptance of the societal constraints on the means ("ritualism"); rejection of both the goals and the societal constraints on the means ("retreatism"); and, moving a step beyond retreatism, rejection of both goals and constraints on means, coupled with an attempt to institute new goals and new societally approved means ("rebellion").

Merton called conformity, innovation, ritualism, retreatism, and rebellion *modes of adaptation*, and these modes of adaptation highlight the possibility that the same stimulus may elicit different responses in different individuals. Merton further suggested that the different modes of adaptation would be associated with different types of outcomes. Conformity, initially the most common adaptation, should not be associated with any problematic outcomes. Innovation, still seeking success but rejecting the constraints on the legitimate means of achieving it, should, according to Merton, be associated with criminal behavior, particularly but not exclusively property crime. Ritualism, not striving for success but avoiding violating the norms, might not be associated with overtly problematic behavior, but might, according to Merton, be associated with neuroses or, by extension, other mental health problems. Retreatism was the mode of adaptation Merton thought would be most likely associated with licit and illicit substance use problems, and perhaps with more severe forms of mental health problems. Both ritualism and retreatism, with their abandonment of success goals, might be expected to be associated with lower levels of success in achieving higher SES, for example with respect to occupational status, income, and education.

While not explicitly suggested by Merton, later work on the expansion and application of Merton's theory to delinquent subcultures (Cloward and Ohlin 1960) seems consistent with the suggestion that perhaps the rebellion mode of adaptation may, at least in certain contexts, be associated with violent behavior. The theory thus predicts multiple outcomes, distinct from but not necessarily uncorrelated with one another, depending on one's response to the stimulus of strain, and does so for behaviors in which we are particularly interested in the present study. Research by Menard (1995, 1997) supported both Merton's original formulation of anomie theory and the extension by Cloward and Ohlin, including the relationship of strain via innovation to crime and retreatism to illicit drug use.

Merton focused on economic strains rather than experiences of victimization and exposure to violence as sources of strain, but the broader principle regarding different responses to the same stimulus still applies. Agnew (1985; see also Agnew 1992, 2002, 2012), in what he called his general strain theory, proposed that there are three types of strains: strains that result from the inability to achieve positively valued goals, strain that occurs when positively valued stimuli are removed, and, most relevant to the present study, strains that result from the introduction of negative or noxious stimuli, including but not limited to witnessing or being a victim of violence. In the context of general strain theory, violence, in particular, may occur to gain revenge, to express frustration, to try to exercise or regain a sense of control over one's circumstances, or by projecting an image of toughness, to deter further victimization (Baron 2009; Hay and Evans 2006; Rebellon and Van Gundy 2005). Not clear from the theory is whether we should expect only short-term effects, or whether the effects should persist in later life; and whether exposure to violence of a particular form in the home or community should result in the same forms of violence in the same specific contexts, or, as suggested by anomie theory, might result in a broader variety of outcome behaviors in a broader range of contexts. General strain theory does suggest that there will be gender differences in response to strain, with males more likely than females to engage in externalizing behaviors (e.g., violence) and females more likely than males to engage in internalizing behaviors (e.g., anxiety or depression) in response to strain (Broidy and Agnew 1997; Watts and McNulty 2013).

While general strain theory is primarily a theory of delinquency and crime, and more focused on predictions about crime perpetration in response to exposure to violence, social learning theory (Akers 1985; see also Akers and Sellers 2012; Bandura 1977; Mihalic and Elliott 1997a) predicts that exposure to violence will affect both perpetration and victimization, a prediction consistent with the intergenerational cycle of violence perspective and research pioneered by Straus et al. (1980) and Widom (1989b; see also Widom and Maxfield 1996). According to social learning theory, violent behavior is learned like any other behavior through a process of imitation, modeling, and differential reinforcement. Children who witness violence may interpret aggressive behavior (or submission to violence) as an appropriate response to conflict, leading them to more readily take on the roles of either or both victim or perpetrator (Edleson 1999; Egeland 1993; Egeland et al. 1988). Thus, where general strain theory would regard exposure to violence in the family and community as a noxious stimulus, social learning theory would regard it as a source of modeling and imitation. Note that both general strain theory and social learning theory are most applicable to violence perpetration and victimization. To understand the relationship of AEV to other outcomes, we must revert instead to anomie theory.

Also useful in understanding the role of AEV in influencing adult outcomes, but not something we are able to directly examine in the present study, is the neurobiological approach proposed by Perry (2001; see also Anda et al. 2006; Teicher et al. 2003; Teicher and Samson 2016). The neurobiological approach suggests that the impact of traumatic events and experiences, such as exposure to violence, on brain functioning leads to increased risk for mental health problems, including but not limited to anxiety, depression, and PTSD, and also to antisocial behaviors, victimization, and other negative life consequences. Changes in the brain that appear to result from abuse and neglect include changes to the visual, auditory, and somatosensory cortex, anterior cingulate, dorsal lateral prefrontal and orbitofrontal cortex; reduced size of portions of the corpus callosum; attenuated development of the left neocortex, hippocampus, and amygdala; and reduced functional activity of the cerebellar vermis (Teicher et al. 2003; Teicher and Samson 2016).

According to the neurobiological perspective, some of these responses are acute and others are long term. Responses to traumatic events vary across individuals and often are acute, but recollections of some traumatic events, such as physical abuse, are stored deep in the memory and may surface with environmental cues that remind the individual of the previous trauma. Thus, we might expect individuals exposed to violence during adolescence to have recurrent episodes of symptoms such as mental health problems, substance abuse, violence, and other problems. Elder et al. (1996) similarly indicate that exposure to psychological stress in childhood does not have uniform results in adulthood. As with general strain theory, we would expect to find gender differences in responses. Perry (2001) suggested that females are more likely than males to retreat and dissociate, and males more likely to become more aroused and active, in response to trauma, and Teicher et al. (2003) found gender differences in vulnerability and functional consequences of stress and maltreatment in childhood.

Other explanations have also been suggested for the relationship of AEV with adult outcomes, particularly to the development of criminal and anti-social behavior. These include, but are not limited to, social control theory, developmental theories, intergenerational theories, and other combinations of criminological theories such as social developmental theory (Bensley et al. 2003; Catalano and Hawkins 1996; Crittenden 1992; Herrenkohl et al. 2003; Hirschi 1969; Kerig and Becker 2015; Lansford et al. 2007; Lemmon 2006). While these theoretical perspectives may provide additional insights into the relationship of AEV and adult outcomes, and this may be worth pursuing in other research, it is strain theory, particularly anomie theory, first and foremost, that has guided our examination of the relationship of AEV and adult outcomes. In particular, the emphasis on the multiple possible responses to strain in general and to exposure to violence in particular is particularly well-suited to the examination of the single predictor or cause, AEV, on the multiple effects or outcomes in adulthood. However, we do find it useful to supplement strain theory with social learning theory, with particular reference to the intergenerational transmission of violence, and with insights from the neurobiological approach, particularly with reference to mental health issues and the diversity of responses to exposure to violence.

ISSUES IN PRIOR RESEARCH ON IMPACTS
OF ADOLESCENT MALTREATMENT
OR EXPOSURE TO VIOLENCE

While there is a very substantial literature on the consequences of childhood maltreatment and exposure to violence, some of which includes adolescents in the samples, there have been far fewer studies of specifically adolescent maltreatment, abuse, or exposure to violence, particularly with nationally representative samples in the United States. The NatSCEV study described earlier is one such study as is previous research using the NYSFS. Kitzmann et al. (2003) conducted a meta-analysis of 118 studies of childhood and adolescent exposure to interparental violence and found that only 10 utilized adolescent samples. In addition to its relative neglect of adolescence, the existing research on the relationship of AEV with adult outcomes has had several other issues.

First, sample sizes are frequently small and often limited to clinical samples of individuals with certain types of exposure to violence, or to predominantly urban, minority ethnicity, lower SES samples without comparison samples that would allow examination of differences between exposed and nonexposed individuals, rather than nationally representative general population samples (Gewirtz and Edleson 2007; Heyman and Slep 2002; Lynch 2003; Margolin and Gordis 2000; Rebellon and Van Gundy 2005). Note that the NatSCEV and NYSFS studies both employ national probability samples and are exceptions to this pattern.

Second, some studies have failed to distinguish between directly experiencing violence as a victim or perpetrator from broader exposure to violence such as witnessing violence in the family or awareness of violence in the neighborhood, or have incorporated exposure to violence as part of a larger measure that also includes less violent forms of neglect (Acosta et al. 2001; Gewirtz and Edleson 2007; Rebellon and Van Gundy 2005).

Third, the need for longitudinal studies in this area, to clearly establish causal order, has been noted (Kitzmann et al. 2003), and even in existing longitudinal studies, individuals are often followed only into adolescence (e.g., Ehrensaft et al. 2003) or young adulthood (e.g., Menard 2002; Mihalic and Elliott 1997a).

Fourth, there are issues with which variables are included in the analysis. Analyzing predictors one at a time, instead of examining their effects controlling for one another (and for other possible confounding influences) may lead to overestimation of the effects of a single type of violence on the outcome; and there is evidence that different types of AEV may affect different outcomes (Covey et al. 2013; Fitzpatrick 1993; Rebellon and Van Gundy 2005).

Fifth, studies of the impact of exposure to violence in the family or neighborhood context typically do not control for more general prior victimization or offending as risk factors which may have their own impact on adult violent offending and victimization, and which may, if included in the analysis, attenuate the relationship of adolescent or childhood exposure to violence in the family or neighborhood contexts with later adult violence perpetration and victimization (Finkelhor et al. 2007; Lynch 2003; Rebellon and Van Gundy 2005). This is particularly important given evidence that general violent victimization and offending in adolescence are predictive of violent victimization and offending in adulthood (Menard 2002).

The present research addresses the above weaknesses in past research, first by examining a national probability sample (as opposed to a local or clinical sample). Second, we distinguish among direct victimization (physical abuse by parents and more general violence victimization) and other forms of exposure to violence (witnessing parental violence and exposure to neighborhood violence). Third, we measure exposure to violence in adolescence and then outcomes in middle adulthood, thus adding to our knowledge of both of these otherwise underrepresented age ranges in this area of research. Fourth, we analyze the impacts of the different types of exposure to violence in the same analysis, controlling for one another. Fifth, we control for prior behaviors and outcomes in adolescence, as well as other potential confounding influences, including gender (by analyzing the data separately for females and males), ethnicity/race, urban-suburban-rural residence, and SES.

The separate analysis by gender is necessary because not only theory but also past research clearly suggests that females and males may respond differently to exposure to violence (Broidy and Agnew 1997; Gewirtz and Edleson 2007; Herrenkohl et al. 2008; Kendall-Tackett 2013; Kerig and Becker 2015; Widom 1989b), with females more likely to engage in internalizing behaviors and males more likely to engage in externalizing behaviors. Prior research indicates that the effects of AEV in the home and neighborhood are different for females and males (Cummings et al. 1999; Fang and Corso 2007; Gewirtz and Edleson 2007; Herrenkohl et al. 2008; Herrera and McCloskey 2001; Mihalic and Elliott 1997a; Sousa et al. 2011; Widom 1989b; Wolfe et al. 2001), but there is disagreement on whether the impact of abuse is greater for males (Watts and McNulty 2013) or females (Kerig and Becker 2015; Widom and White 1997). Widom et al. (2006) indicate that childhood maltreatment had direct associations with adult violent offending for men, but indirect influence, mediated by problematic alcohol use, for women. One could also justify separate analysis by gender based on some variants of feminist theories of illegal behavior; for example, what feminist scholars (Daly 1998; Irwin and Chesney-Lind 2008; Miller and Mullins 2006) would characterize as the generalizability problem or the issue of gendered pathways to crime, whether different processes explain female and male violence. In conclusion, there are both theoretical and empirical reasons for separate analysis by gender, with the latter in particular providing consistent support for this approach.

PLAN OF THIS BOOK

This chapter has reviewed the broad issue of the relationship between AEV and adult outcomes, and the relationship of AEV to similar concepts including child maltreatment, child abuse, and adverse childhood experiences. It has also presented the theoretical basis for our expectations regarding the relationship between AEV and various adult outcomes, including adult violence, substance use, mental health problems, and SES. The theoretical focus in the present research is a combination of two varieties of strain theory (anomie and general strain), social learning theory, and life course developmental theory.

Chapter 2 describes the design of the study, including a description of the sample, the NYSFS, used in this research. It also presents descriptions and univariate statistics for the measures used in the present research, including a consideration of their reliability and validity.

Chapter 3 examines the sociodemographic distribution of both AEV and the adult outcomes considered in the present research. It focuses primarily on bivariate relationships of sociodemographic characteristics with the predictors and outcomes used in the study, and secondarily on bivariate relationships among selected adult problem behavior outcomes.

Chapter 4 examines the relationship of AEV with adult SES, including marital status, educational attainment, employment, occupational status, and net worth.

Chapter 5 examines the relationship of AEV with adult mental health problems and briefly considers the relationship of AEV with adult physical health problems.

Chapter 6 examines the relationship of AEV with the frequency of adult illicit substance use and with problem substance use in adulthood.

Chapter 7 examines the relationship of AEV with adult general violence victimization and perpetration and with being arrested in adulthood.

Chapter 8 examines the relationship of AEV with adult IPV victimization and perpetration, a separate issue, often not adequately captured by questions about general violence perpetration and victimization.

Chapters 4–8 move from a focus on univariate (chapter 2) and bivariate (chapter 3) analysis to multivariate analysis, and to a more detailed consideration of gender differences in the relationship of AEV with the adult outcomes. Each of chapters 4–8 begins with a description of how we would expect AEV to be related to the adult outcomes, based on the theories reviewed here in chapter 1, followed by a review of past research on the relationships of the different forms of AEV on those outcomes, and then a statement of hypotheses based on the theory and past research. We begin the bivariate analysis with a description of the overall pattern of relationships between the adult outcomes and AEV, separately by gender, comparing individuals who have and those who have not experienced AEV. In these first sections of each chapter, there is sufficient overlap or repetition of key theoretical points and explanation of how to interpret the results to allow chapters 4–8 to be read in any order, not requiring earlier chapters as prerequisite to subsequent chapters.

Next in chapters 4–8, we move on to a brief examination of bivariate correlations of the adult outcomes with AEV, prior behavior, and sociodemographic characteristics, presenting in detail only those correlations that are statistically significant (or very nearly so) at $p \leq .05$. The purpose of this brief presentation of only statistically significant bivariate relationships is twofold. First, it allows the reader to compare the bivariate results of the present study with results from other past or future studies that limit themselves to bivariate relationships. Second, it allows us to describe the important differences between the bivariate and the multivariate results, with particular attention to the propensity of predictors that appear to be statistically significant in bivariate analysis to lose their statistical significance when other predictors are controlled.

The main part of each of chapters 4–8, the Multivariate Analysis section, focuses on the detailed results of the multivariate analysis, separately for females and males. For some readers, it may be useful at this point to read the extended discussion of the interpretation of the tables in chapters 4–8 that is presented only in the first two paragraphs of the Multivariate Analysis section in chapter 4. Following this are Discussion and Conclusions sections. The Discussion section in each chapter summarizes the results for each of the predictors, compares those results with results from previous studies utilizing the NYSFS sample, and also presents the results of formal tests for gender differences in the effects of AEV on the adult outcomes covered in each chapter. Finally, the Conclusions section summarizes the most pertinent findings in each of chapters 4–8 regarding the relationship between AEV and adult outcomes. For chapters 4–8, readers who want the full details regarding evidence for the conclusions at the end of each chapter can read the full chapter. The fully detailed description of each of the multivariate models is necessarily dense, examining results of each of the predictors separately for females and males. Readers who would prefer to skip the quantitative detail and get to the substantive conclusions specific to each of the predictors can do so by skipping to the end and reading the Discussion and Conclusions sections.

Chapter 9 synthesizes the results from the previous chapters, noting both similarities and differences in the impact of AEV on various adult outcomes, and seeking to explain the similarities and especially the differences in those patterns, including gender differences in the relationship of AEV and adult outcomes. The chapter also identifies some evidence-based approaches to prevention and intervention that focus on adolescents who have been or are at risk of being exposed to violence. We conclude chapter 9 with a discussion of the implications of the results of the present study for theory and for future research.

Chapter 2

Study Design and Sample Characteristics

This chapter presents information about the sample used in the present research, the National Youth Survey Family Study (NYSFS), and about the variables and measures used in this study. This study relies on self-report survey data for several conceptual domains: sociodemographic characteristics, mental health, substance use and problem use, intimate partner violence (IPV) victimization and perpetration, more general violence victimization and perpetration arrest, and adolescent exposure to violence (AEV). The chapter begins with a description of the source of data for the present study, the NYSFS, a longitudinal survey begun with a national probability sample of adolescents who were 11–17 years old at the beginning of the study in 1976, and 38–44 when last interviewed in 2003. Next, the conceptual variables used in the study and their operational measures are presented. For each of the conceptual domains, we present the operational definitions of the variables used in this study, a discussion of what we know about the reliability and validity (for a good general discussion of which see Zeller and Carmines 1980) of self-report measures in that domain, both in general and specific to the NYSFS, and univariate descriptive statistics for the variables used in this study.

THE SAMPLE: THE NATIONAL YOUTH SURVEY FAMILY STUDY

The NYSFS is an extension of the National Youth Survey (NYS) begun by Delbert S. Elliott and his colleagues in the mid-1970s. As described in Elliott et al. (1983, 1985, 1989) and Menard et al. (2011), the original NYS and subsequent NYSFS study design involves a multiple cohort sequential design

(Baltes et al. 1979) with twelve waves of data over a 27-year period. The survey sample is based on a probability sample of households in the continental United States selected using a multistage, cluster sampling design. The sample was drawn in late 1976 and contained 2,360 eligible youth respondents aged 11–17 at the time of the initial interview. Of these, 1,725 (73%) agreed to participate in the study, signed informed consents, and completed interviews in the initial survey. One parent (usually the mother) of each of these youth respondents was also interviewed in this first wave. An age, sex, and race/ethnicity comparison between nonparticipating eligible youth and participating youth indicates that the loss rate from any particular age, sex, or racial/ethnic group appeared to be proportional to that group's representation in the population. Further, with respect to these characteristics, NYSFS respondents appear to be representative of the total 11- through 17-year-old youth population in the United States as established by the U.S. Census Bureau for 1976 (Elliott et al. 1989).

Attempts were made to recontact and interview each of the original 1,725 respondents in each of the first four (annual) follow-up surveys. Overall completion rates over waves 2–4 were above 94%, and 87% for wave 5. At wave 5, attempts were also made to identify, contact, and interview the youth who had refused at the time of the initial interview. This was done because most of these initial refusals were "parent refusals" and it was hoped that as the youth themselves reached the age of majority or became older teenagers, the youth would be willing to participate in the survey. This effort resulted in identifying all original "refusal households," documenting whether the same family lived in the household continuously since 1976, and then obtaining consents and interviews with the eligible youth in such households. The identified households contained 193 youth who would have been eligible in 1976 of which 131 (67%) agreed to participate in the survey and completed wave 5 interview schedules. This "initial loss sample" was also interviewed in waves 6 and 8. Although not a probability sample of refusals, this sample provides information about survey effects and is, in fact, part of the originally selected sample. A comparison of participants and nonparticipants in each survey after wave 1 revealed some wave-specific selective loss by sex (W4), race/ethnicity (W2 and W3), social class (W2 and W3), age (W5), and residence (W2 and W3). There did not appear to be any selective loss relative to self-reported levels of delinquency. In fact, the direction of the observed differences indicates that those lost tended to be slightly less delinquent than those participating each year. While the comparison of participants and nonparticipants revealed some small but significant differences, a comparison of those participating in each survey with the total sample on the first survey has revealed no significant differences by age, sex, race/ethnicity, social class, place of residence, or level of delinquency. The selective loss was thus very small and has not had a major influence on the underlying distribution on these variables (as established on the first survey). It appears that the representativeness of the sample with respect to these variables has not been affected in any serious way by respondent loss. Completion rates were 87% for wave 6, 80% for wave 7, 83% for wave 8, and 78% for wave 9, and again at wave 9 there appeared to be no systematic loss based on demographic characteristics (Menard et al. 2001).

In addition to the original NYS respondents, data collection for waves 11 and 12 of the NYSFS included interviews with the current "marital partners" (either married or living together in an intimate relationship), the children of the original respondents age 11 and older as of 2003, and the parents of the original respondents (hence the change in designation from NYS to NYSFS). Data for waves 10, 11, and 12 were collected in 2002–2004. In wave 10, the original respondents were again interviewed, and family data were collected to help locate and interview their surviving parents, current spouses or partners, and adolescent and adult children for subsequent waves 11 and 12. Additional deaths among the respondents were identified during the wave 10–12 data collection, reducing the total eligible sample (including hard refusals, respondents who asked not to be contacted again) to 1,677. Of these 1,677, 1,266 or 75% were interviewed in wave 10 and 1,173 or 70% in wave 11. During wave 10, attempts were made to identify eligible (living and in sufficient physical and mental health to complete an interview) spouses and partners, parents, and children of the original respondents to be interviewed in waves 11 and 12. Of the known eligible parents, spouses, and children, in wave 11, 881 or 71% of the parents, 679 or 71% of current spouses or partners of the original respondents, 802 or 77% of their adolescent (age 11–17) children, and 464 or 66% of their 707 adult (age 18 and over) children were interviewed. In wave 12, only the children of the original respondents were interviewed; of the known eligible respondents, 815 or 78% of the adolescent children and 491 or 70% of the adult children were interviewed. For purposes of the present study, only the original respondents have the long-term longitudinal data needed for the analysis of the impact of adolescent exposure to violence on adult outcomes.

Compared to other major longitudinal studies, NYSFS participation and attrition rates are reasonable. With regard to participation rates, de Leeuw and van der Zouwen (1988) indicate that average participation rates are approximately 75% for face-to-face and 69% for telephone surveys, and de Leeuw and de Heer (2002) and Groves et al. (2004) offer evidence that there have been substantial increases over time in rates of nonresponse and refusal to participate in surveys, both in the United States and internationally. With regard to attrition, there is evidence that the departure from randomness of the attrition in the NYSFS is minimal, and analyses of its effects suggest that the attrition in the NYSFS has little or no impact on substantive findings (Bosick 2009; Brame and Paternoster 2003; Elliott et al. 1989; Jang 1999; Lackey 2003; Menard and Elliott 1993). Bosick (2009), in particular, found evidence *against* (a) the presence of testing effects or panel fatigue and (b) selective attrition, as explanations of declining crime rates in NYS data, and Brame and Paternoster (2003) found that attrition appears to have little impact on the substantive conclusions reached using NYS data.

NYSFS SOCIODEMOGRAPHIC CHARACTERISTICS IN ADOLESCENCE AND ADULTHOOD

Tables 2.1 and 2.2 present the distribution of the sociodemographic variables used in the present study for NYSFS in adolescence and middle adulthood, respectively. Sex/gender is coded as 0 = female, 1 = male. Race/ethnicity is coded as 0 = white/majority, 1 = nonwhite/minority, the latter including individuals who identify themselves as Latino or Hispanic. Consistent with U.S. Census Bureau classifications when the study began in 1976, Latino/Hispanic is not treated as a category separate from race. From this point onward, we

Table 2.1   Descriptive Statistics for Sociodemographic Characteristics in Adolescence

Variable Categories	Valid N	Minimum	Maximum	Proportion	Standard Deviation
Gender:	1,725	NA	NA		.499
Female	807			.468	
Male	918			.532	
Ethnicity:	1,725	NA	NA		.408
Majority	1,361			.789	
Minority	364			.211	
Place of Residence (Wave 1):	1,722	NA	NA		
Urban	446			.259	.438
Suburban (reference category)	773			.449	.498
Rural	503			.292	.455
Two-Parent Family Structure in Adolescence:	1,683	NA	NA		.403
No (reference category)	342			.203	
Yes	1,341			.797	
Parental SES:	1,623	NA	NA		
Upper/Middle Class	392			.241	.428
Working Class (reference category)	509			.314	.464
Lower Class	722			.445	.497

Note: NA = Not applicable. Standard deviations for categorical variables with more than two categories are presented separately for each categorical dummy variable.

Table 2.2 Descriptive Statistics for Sociodemographic Characteristics in Middle Adulthood

Variable Categories	N	Minimum	Maximum	Median/ Proportion	Standard Deviation
Gender:	1,111	NA	NA	Proportion	.500
Female (reference category)	574			.516	
Male	537			.483	
Ethnicity:	1,110	NA	NA	Proportion:	.399
Majority (reference category)	890			.802	
Minority	220			.198	
Place of Residence:	1,529	NA	NA	Proportion:	
Urban	331			.216	.412
Suburban (reference category)	944			.617	.486
Rural	254			.167	.372
Adult Educational Attainment (Highest Grade Completed)	1,295	6	17	Median: 13 (1 year beyond high school graduation)	2.22
Adult Employment:	1,293	NA	NA	Proportion:	.273
Unemployed (reference category)	105			.081	
Employed	1,188			.919	
Adult Income	1,262	1 (under $5,000)	10 (over $100,000)	Median: 6 ($25,000 to $34,999)	2.53
Adult Net Worth	1,237	1 (under $1,000)	8 (over $1 million)	Median: 5 ($50,000 to $100,000)	1.71
Adult Marital Status:	1,293	NA	NA	Proportion:	
Never Married (reference category)	206			.159	.366
Currently Married	836			.647	.478
Previously Married	251			.194	.396

Note: NA = Not applicable. Standard deviations for categorical variables with more than two categories are presented separately for each categorical dummy variable.

use the term "gender" in preference to the term "sex" as the former is less ambiguous and emphasizes social over biological identity, and we also use the term "ethnicity" with its implications more of geographic origin in preference to the term "race" with its historically biological connotations. Both gender and ethnicity were measured in the first wave of the NYSFS, and the original measures were carried forward in subsequent waves of the study.

For both adolescence and middle adulthood, place of residence is classified as urban, suburban, or rural, based on U.S. Census Bureau classifications of

places, and dummy variables for urban and rural residence in middle adulthood, with suburban as the reference category, are used in the prediction of
adult outcomes. As described in Elliott et al. (1983), urban residence consists
of central cities in Standardized Metropolitan Statistical Areas (SMSAs) with
populations of 100,000 or more; suburban areas are other parts of SMSAs or
central cities with populations less than 100,000; and rural areas are cities or
places that are not part of SMSAs or part of a central city in an urbanized
area, with a population of less than 25,000. For waves 10 and 11, census classifications had changed, but classification as urban, suburban, and rural were
based on criteria that paralleled those at wave 1. Family structure at wave 1 is
coded as 0 = other than a two-parent family and 1 = two-parent family, based
on the parent report of who was living in the same household as the adolescent respondent. Parental socioeconomic status (SES) refers to the SES of the
principal wage earner in the household at wave 1 based on the Hollingshead
index of social position (Bonjean et al. 1967), an index that combines parental
education and occupational prestige. For this index, as described in Elliott
et al. (1983), the upper/middle class consists primarily of individuals with
professional and managerial occupations and college educations; the working class consists primarily of owners of small businesses, clerical workers,
salespeople, and skilled manual workers who have completed high school
and possibly some college; and the lower class consists of semiskilled or
unskilled laborers with high school or less education. Parental SES is coded
into two dummy variables: upper/middle class and lower class, with working
class as the reference category.

For middle adulthood, marital status is coded as (a) never married, (b)
currently married, or (c) formerly married but currently not married (mostly
divorced, but also including widowhood and annulment). Employment is a
dichotomy, coded 0 for employed in neither wave 10 nor wave 11 and 1 for
employed at either wave 10 or wave 11. Educational attainment is measured
as the highest grade completed in waves 10 and 11. If different responses
were given in waves 10 and 11, the responses were averaged and rounded
up to the nearest year. Responses could in principle range from 0 (no school-
ing completed) to 17 (at least some education beyond college graduation),
but there was no one with less than a sixth-grade education. Self-reported
past year income was measured on a ten-point ordinal scale with categories
(1) under $5,000; (2) $5,000 to $9,999; (3) $10,000 to $14,999; (4) $15,000
to $19,999; (5) $20,000 to $24,999; (6) $25,000 to $34,999; (7) $35,000 to
$49,000; (8) $50,000 to $74,999; (9) $75,000 to $99,999; and (10) $100,000
or more. If there was a difference in reported income between waves 10 and
11, the average (mean rank) of the two was taken and rounded up to the next
highest rank. Self-reported net worth, available at wave 10 but not wave
11, was measured on an eight-point scale: (1) less than $1,000; (2) $1,000

to $5,000; (3) $5,000 to $10,000; (4) $10,000 to $50,000; (5) $50,000 to $100,000; (6) $100,000 to $500,000; (7) $500,000 to $1,000,000; and (8) more than $1,000,000.

There is relatively little available information on long-term reliability and validity for sociodemographic variables, some of which may be expected to remain stable for most individuals across the life course, and others of which may change within as well as between years. Comparing data from different waves, however, we may draw some conclusions about the reliability of self-reported sociodemographic characteristics in the present study. For gender, the correlation (Pearson's r) between wave 1 and wave 11 gender is .998, reflecting a single case reporting a different gender at the two waves. With the presently available data, we are not able to ascertain whether this represents a genuine change or a coding error, but the wave 1 reported gender is used in the present analysis, and should not materially affect the analysis. For ethnicity, the correlation (Pearson's r) between wave 1 and wave 11 is .948. Changes in reported ethnicity may represent coding errors or actual changes in self-perceived ethnicity (e.g., as a result of learning more about one's ancestry), or changes in self-defined ethnicity. Changes in self-defined ethnicity may or may not be related to changes in the use of the terms "race" and "ethnicity" by the Census Bureau spreading into more common usage, leading to a choice between ethnicity or race as the dominant concept (do I define myself as white race or Hispanic ethnicity?).

The reliability of self-reports on education may be assessed by comparing wave 10 and wave 11 reports of highest grade completed. Education may increase, but should not decrease, over time, and reports of lower education may be taken as indicative of unreliability, which may stem from coding errors, recall errors by the respondents at wave 10, or cognitive redefinition of one's educational experience. In the present study, education at wave 10 was correlated (Kendall's τ_b) .934 with education at wave 11, with 91% reporting the same or higher education in wave 11 as in wave 10, and 9% reporting lower education in wave 11 than in wave 10, suggesting that 91% is a reasonable upper estimate of reliability for educational attainment. Similar assessments of reliability are not available for the wave 1 assessment of whether the respondent lived in an intact two-parent family; for net worth, which may change from year to year, and for which data were in any case only collected at wave 10; and for marital status, employment, and income, all measured at both waves 10 and 11, but which like net worth may change from year to year. To the extent that reliability can be assessed, it appears that the self-reported sociodemographic characteristics in the present study have an acceptably high level of reliability.

As indicated in tables 2.1 and 2.2, in adolescence (age 11–17) in wave 1 (1976–1977), there were more males than females in the sample, but in middle adulthood (age 37–44) in waves 10 and 11 (2001–2002 and 2002–2003) higher attrition among males resulted in a sample with more nearly equal numbers of females and males, and slightly more females than males in total. In both adolescence and middle adulthood, approximately 80% of the sample is majority and 20% minority ethnicity. From adolescence, the sample became increasingly suburbanized, with 45% suburban in adolescence and 62% in adulthood, with corresponding losses in urban and especially rural residence, reflecting population trends more generally. Approximately 80% of the respondents were in two-parent families in wave 1 of the NYSFS, with approximately 24% of the families being classified as upper or middle class, 31% as working class, and 45% as lower class according to the Hollingshead index. In middle adulthood, the median education level was one year of education beyond high school; 92% of respondents were employed and 8% not employed. Median income in middle adulthood was $25,000 to $35,000, and median net worth was $50,000 to $100,000. In middle adulthood, approximately 65% were currently married, 19% were not currently married but had been previously married (mostly divorced), and 16% reported never having been married.

MENTAL HEALTH MEASURES IN THE NYSFS

In the present study, we consider combined prevalence of selected mental health problems for which measures are available in the NYSFS; frequency of mental health service use; and, as an indicator more of positive mental health than of mental illness, a measure of life satisfaction. Anxiety, depression, and post-traumatic stress disorder (PTSD) are diagnoses based on the National Institute of Mental Health (NIMH) Diagnostic Interview Schedule or DIS (Robins et al. 1981). The NIMH developed the DIS based on several then-current diagnostic systems, including the third edition of the American Psychiatric Association's *Diagnostic and Statistical Manual of Mental Disorders* or DSM-III (American Psychiatric Association 1980), the Research Diagnostic Criteria (Spitzer et al. 1978), and the Feighner criteria (Feighner et al. 1972). For prevalence of selected mental health problems, questions were asked at wave 11 (2003) which indicated whether the individual ever had clinical symptoms of chronic anxiety, depression, or PTSD, and also whether those symptoms occurred within the past year. The choice to focus on these three mental health problems in the NYSFS was based on earlier waves, in which it was found that other mental health problems lacked sufficient prevalence for separate analysis. In the present study, anxiety, depression, and PTSD are combined into a joint prevalence scale, coded 0 if none of the problems was present and coded 1 if the responses indicated clinical level symptoms of one or more of the three mental health problems at wave 11.

The measures of mental health service use are based on the NIMH Epidemiologic Catchment Area (ECA) program (Shapiro et al. 1984) and attempt to capture both narrowly professional and (inclusive of professional) more general mental health service seeking. The questions about mental health service use were asked in wave 11. Frequency of professional mental health service use refers to the number of times the individual has sought help for emotional or mental health problems from a psychologist or psychiatrist, physician, mental health clinic, hospital emergency room, or outpatient facility of a hospital or mental health clinic, in the past year. Frequency of general mental health service use refers to the number of times the respondent has sought professional mental health services, as described above, or help from anyone else including friends, clergy, social service agencies, spiritualists, herbalists, and so on in the past year.

The measure of life satisfaction is constructed from questions asked in both the tenth and the eleventh waves of the NYSFS. Respondents were asked, "Overall, how satisfied are you with your present standard of living and financial situation?" The response set consisted of the categories 1 = completely satisfied, 2 = almost completely satisfied, 3 = moderately satisfied, 4 = slightly satisfied, and 5 = not at all satisfied. These categories were reverse coded, then summed across the two waves to produce a single index ranging from 2 to 10 (equivalent to taking the mean and multiplying by 2 to eliminate decimal fractions), with higher numbers indicating higher satisfaction. This measure could arguably be included as a measure of SES but is instead included here because, in contrast to the more objective measures of sociodemographic characteristics (marital status, employment, education, income, net worth), life satisfaction is an attitudinal measure. Although we would expect a positive relationship between life satisfaction and objective SES, it is also the case that high SES may influence, but does not determine, one's level of life satisfaction.

As controls for mental health in adolescence, we use two measures of adolescent mental health that have been used in past research using the NYSFS. An emotional problems scale based on parent reports was available at wave 1, indicating the extent to which one of the parents (usually the mother) described the individual as being upset or having a lot of emotional problems. This scale, as described in greater detail in Elliott et al. (1989), has been shown to be predictive of mental health problems later in adolescence and in adulthood (Elliott et al. 1989; Menard 2002), and has a reliability of .70 to .80. Also described in greater detail in Elliott et al. (1989) is a mental health problem scale based on self-reports of the respondents' perceptions of whether friends and parents see them as having emotional problems, plus self-reports of social isolation and emotional isolation from parents and friends, the latter having scale reliabilities from .65 to .82 over time. These have been combined in prior research to produce a dichotomous indicator of absence (coded 0) or presence (coded 1) of mental health problems in adolescence. This scale is predictive of mental health service usage and specific mental health problems including depression, anxiety, and PTSD in adulthood (Elliott et al. 1989, 17–22; Menard 2002). Along with the parent report of emotional problems, this scale is used as a control in examining the impact of physical abuse, witnessing parental violence, and exposure to neighborhood violence on adult mental health.

Studies of the reliability and validity of the DIS (Hesselbrock et al. 1982; Robins et al. 1982) and, of its successor instrument, the Composite International Diagnostic Interview or CIDI (Wittchen 1994) have generally indicated that both reliability and validity were good. Several of the diagnoses in the DIS and the CIDI depend on whether the respondent reports *ever* having engaged in a particular behavior or *ever* experiencing a certain event or psychological state. To date, for the CIDI, the time span between measurements for reliability can be characterized as short term (a matter of 1–3 weeks or months) or moderate term (1–3 years), despite the fact that the recall period in many of the questions in these surveys requires long-term (1–3 decades) recall. To the best of our knowledge, the long-term reliability of these instruments has never been assessed. NYSFS estimates of mental health service usage were comparable to estimates from the Epidemiologic Catchment Area (ECA) studies at about the same time (Elliott et al. 1989, 18–19), indicating convergent validity in the different studies. The NYSFS measure of life satisfaction has not been previously tested for validity or test-retest reliability, but the two measures of life satisfaction (wave 10 and wave 11) are correlated (using an interval/ratio measure of association, Pearson's r = .589, p = .000; using a more appropriate ordinal measure of association, Kendall's τ_b = .525, p = .000) strongly enough to be reasonable for two measures of the same phenomenon which may change over the 1-year measurement interval. For the purposes of analysis, the summation of the two ordinal measures is treated as an interval scale, but we test the sensitivity of this assumption by examining results that assume instead that the resulting index is an ordinal rather than an interval scale.

Table 2.3 presents the univariate descriptive statistics for the mental health measures used in the present study. For parent reports of mental health in adolescence, the mean scale value is approximately 9, a bit lower than the midpoint of the scale, and, more informatively, the self-report of mental health problems indicates that just over 20% of adolescents appear to experience some form of mental health problems in adolescence. For middle adulthood, 13% appear to experience at least one of anxiety, depression, or PTSD to a degree that is clinically significant. Frequency of mental health service use in middle adulthood ranges from 0 to 12 times in the past year, with a

Table 2.3 Descriptive Statistics for Mental Health Measures

Variable Categories	N	Minimum	Maximum	Mean/ Proportion	Standard Deviation
Adolescent Mental Health Problems Scale Score (Parent Report)	1,683	4	20	Mean: 9.088	2.880
Prevalence of Adolescent Mental Health Problems (Self Report)	1,725	0	1	Proportion:	.409
No (reference category)				.788	
Yes				.212	
Combined Prevalence of Anxiety, Depression, and PTSD in Middle Adulthood:	1,107	0	1	Proportion:	.337
No (reference category)				.870	
Yes				.130	
General Mental Health Service Use in Middle Adulthood	1,170	0	12	Mean: .621	1.178
Professional Mental Health Service Use in Middle Adulthood	1,170	0	8	Mean: .297	.755
Life Satisfaction in Middle Adulthood	1,125	2	10	Mean: 6.880	1.829

mean of .621, for general mental health service use, and from 0 to 8 times in the past year, with a mean of .297, for professional mental health service use, indicating that use of professional mental health services is about half as frequent as seeking more general assistance with mental health problems. For the life satisfaction scale, the mean is a little less than 7, which represents a value about midway between "moderately satisfied" and "almost completely satisfied" on the modified (reverse-coded) scales.

FREQUENCY OF SUBSTANCE USE AND PROBLEM SUBSTANCE USE IN THE NYSFS

Five measures of middle adult self-reported substance use and problem use are considered in the present study, all from wave 11 (but not wave 10, in which the format of questions about illicit and problem substance use was about past-month days of use rather than annual frequency of use, different from the format at all other waves of the NYSFS): frequency of "hard" drug use, frequency of marijuana use, a scale score for problem hard drug use, a scale score for problem marijuana use, and a scale score for problem alcohol use. The frequency of hard drug use is an index used in previous research with this data set (Elliott et al. 1989; Menard 2002) taken from five questions which ask how many times in the past year the respondent has used amphetamines or other stimulants, barbiturates or other depressants, cocaine, hallucinogens, and heroin. In earlier waves, an attempt was made to specify nonprescription use of the "pills" (amphetamine and barbiturate use), but that restriction was not maintained in waves 10 and 11. Marijuana use (actually marijuana or hashish use) is represented by a single item asking how many times in the past year the respondent has used marijuana or hashish. Problem hard drug use, problem marijuana use, and problem alcohol use are scales involving eight items, reflecting negative social consequences of use of the respective substances. The general form of the items was: "How many times in the past year have you had problems with" (your family, your friends, your spouse/girlfriend/boyfriend, missing work, accidents, physical fights, physical health, arrests by the police) "as a result of your use of" (alcohol; marijuana or hashish; other drugs). If no more than one or two items were missing from the scale, their values were imputed based on the mean of the other items in the scale for the respondent for whom the items were missing.

These problem substance use measures were patterned after the problem alcohol use measures initially developed by Cahalan (1970), modified by Jessor and Jessor (1977), and subsequently used in other studies involving the NYS, including Elliott et al. (1989). Elliott et al. (1989) indicate that the internal consistency reliability for the problem substance use scales ranges from .70 to .73. We include problem use of alcohol, but not frequency of alcohol use, as an adult outcome measure because simple alcohol use is, unlike hard drug or marijuana use, not illegal, and even high frequencies of alcohol use may reflect nonproblematic lifestyle choices (e.g., a glass of wine with lunch and supper) rather than problematic use, which may occur even at relatively lower frequencies of alcohol use. As controls for adult frequency of hard drug use and adult frequency of marijuana use, we use cumulative frequency of adolescent hard drug use and cumulative frequency of adolescent marijuana and hashish use, summed across waves 1–5, and identical (with respect to the drugs about which questions were asked) to the adult measures of hard drug use and marijuana use at wave 11. For adult problem hard drug, marijuana, and alcohol use, we use adolescent problem drug use and adolescent problem alcohol use as controls. These measures were first taken for the full sample at waves 4 and 5 (ages 14–21). For each of the two adolescent problem substance use measures, we use the sum of the two measures across waves 4 and 5. The measure of adolescent problem alcohol use directly parallels the measure for adult problem alcohol use. Separate measures for problem marijuana use and problem hard drug use are available for adults, but the adolescent problem drug use scale includes both hard drugs and marijuana; there is no separate problem marijuana use measure available at waves 4 and 5. In selecting the adolescent controls for the adult outcomes, we chose those measures which most closely paralleled the adult outcomes (adolescent frequencies as controls for adult frequencies, adolescent problem use as controls for adult problem use).

Self-reports of illicit drug use in studies of general population samples (Barnea et al. 1987; Harrison 1995) as well as known addict samples (Ball 1967) have generally been found to be reliable and consistent. Self-reports of illicit drug use have also been compared with radioimmunoassay of hair (RIAH) and urinalysis (such as the enzyme multiplied immune test or EMIT) for incarcerated samples, with mixed results (Harrison 1995). Generally, comparison of the results of self-report and EMIT testing indicated that they were highly concordant with correlations in the range that one would expect for two measures of the same phenomenon (Mieczkowski 1990), but EMIT finds more heroin and cocaine use, about the same amount of amphetamine and PCP use (more if the self-reports refer to the past 72 hours, less if the self-reports refer to the past 30 days; see Fendrich and Xu 1994), and about the same or less marijuana use (for which false negative rates are highest for EMIT; see Visher and McFadden 1991), compared to self-reports (Fendrich and Xu 1994; Harrison 1995; Miczkowski 1990; Mieczkowski et al. 1993). RIAH finds more illicit substance use than either self-reports or EMIT (Mieczkowski et al. 1993), except for marijuana use, for which estimates are typically higher in self-reports (Ledgerwood et al. 2008; Miczkowski et al. 1993). Although it may be tempting to regard the differences between self-reports and urinalysis or RIAH as "errors" in the self-report data, Harrison et al. (2007) caution against this, noting the problems in both RIAH (external contamination and treatment of hair, sensitivity to hair color and type, and dosage and timing of substance use) and urinalysis (primarily the short period for which it is valid, typically less than a week, but longer, about 30 days, for frequent marijuana use). Menard et al. (2016) also indicate that reliability of and validity of self-reported substance use data involving long-term (more than 1 year) recall are problematic, but that is not an issue in the present study, which uses prospective (1-year recall) data. As suggested by Menard and Mihalic (2001), self-reports appear to be an appropriate option for obtaining data on substance use, both because of their generally high levels of validity and because of the practical issues involved in administering urinalysis or RIAH to a national general population sample.

Table 2.4 presents the descriptive statistics on the frequency of hard drug use and marijuana use in adolescence and middle adulthood, and the problem substance use scale scores in adolescence and middle adulthood. In waves 1–5, the substance use frequencies were restricted to 3 columns on a Hollerith card,

Table 2.4   Descriptive Statistics for Illicit and Problem Substance Use

Variable	N	Minimum	Maximum	Mean	Standard Deviation
Cumulative Frequency of Hard Drug Use in Adolescence	1,725	0	1,545	14.918	75.175
Cumulative Frequency of Marijuana Use in Adolescence	1,725	0	3,512	91.456	256.087
Problem Drug Use in Adolescence	1,460	10	32	10.847	2.421
Problem Alcohol Use in Adolescence	1,450	10	39	11.864	3.538
Past-Year Frequency of Hard Drug Use in Middle Adulthood	1,170	0	1,095	10.844	63.007
Past-Year Frequency of Marijuana Use in Middle Adulthood	1,168	0	3,650	18.895	154.143
Problem Hard Drug Use Scale Score in Middle Adulthood	1,156	5	23.75	5.101	.846
Problem Marijuana Use Scale Score in Middle Adulthood	1,158	5	11.25	5.049	.405
Problem Alcohol Use Scale Score in Middle Adulthood	1,121	5	17.50	5.335	1.167

so frequencies were truncated with 999 as the maximum possible value, but by waves 10 and 11, this restriction was no longer necessary or applied, and the frequencies were unbounded. In adolescence, therefore, the mean frequency of hard drug use and marijuana use is slightly underestimated, but this should not affect the utility of those measures as controls for adult substance use and problem use. For adolescents, the mean frequency of hard drug use was just under 15, or, dividing by 5 for the number of waves over which the data were collected, about three times per year. The mean frequency of marijuana use was just over 90, or about eighteen times per year. In middle adulthood, the mean frequency for the single year for which the data were collected for hard drug use was a little over 10, and the mean frequency of marijuana use was just under 19. The higher annual mean frequencies in middle adulthood compared to adolescence probably reflect a combination of lower substance use at the earliest ages (particularly ages 11–13) in waves 1–5, the elimination of the truncation at 999 for frequency of use, and the elimination of the restriction to nonprescription use in the later waves of the NYSFS for hard drug use.

The means of all three types of problem substance use in adulthood are a little over 5, close to the minimum for the scale, but lowest for problem marijuana use and highest for problem alcohol use. For adolescent problem hard drug and alcohol use, because the measures are summed over two years, the 2-year minimum of 10 corresponds to a 1-year minimum of 5, the same as for adult problem substance use. In adolescence, the 2-year maximum of 32 for problem drug use and 39 for problem alcohol use corresponds to single-year maximum values of 16 for problem drug use (lower than the adult maximum for adult problem hard drug use but higher than the adult maximum for adult problem marijuana use) and 20 (higher than the adult maximum) for problem alcohol use. The 2-year means of 10.847 and 11.864 translate to single-year means of 5.424 for adolescent problem drug use and 5.932 for adolescent problem drug use and adolescent problem alcohol use, respectively, both higher than the means for adult problem hard drug, marijuana, or alcohol use.

GENERAL VIOLENCE VICTIMIZATION, GENERAL VIOLENCE PERPETRATION, AND ARREST

To examine the impact of AEV on adult general violence victimization and perpetration and on adult arrest, we use frequency of serious violence victimization, frequency of serious violence perpetration, and frequency of arrest in adulthood. For all three measures, frequency was measured both at wave 10 and at wave 11, and we use the cumulative frequency (the sum of the frequencies at wave 10 and wave 11) as our dependent variables. For cases with data missing at either wave 10 or wave 11, data from the wave for which data were nonmissing were used, with the likely result that the frequencies are underestimated for those cases. Because the modal frequencies of all three variables were 0 or low (nearly all less than 10), we concluded that the small underestimation (quite possibly 0, the modal response, for most respondents) for the cases with missing data in only one wave was less problematic than the omission of those cases from the analysis. This is further reinforced by past research indicating that both victimization and perpetration of crime in general, including but not limited to violence, tends to be intermittent in nature, with victimization or perpetration often occurring in 1 year but not in the next (Menard 2000; Menard et al. 2016).

For frequency of violence victimization and offending, we focus on behaviors that are sufficiently serious to potentially warrant attention from the criminal or juvenile justice system to the exclusion of less severe behaviors. Frequency of violence victimization measures how many times in the past year the respondent has been a victim of sexual assault, robbery, attack with a weapon (including gun, knife, bottle, or chair), or battery, including attempts. Frequency of violence perpetration is measured as how many times in the past year the respondent has committed sexual assault, robbery, aggravated assault, or battery, including attempts. Frequency of arrest measures how many times in the past year the respondent has been arrested by the police for anything other than a minor traffic offense. For adult violence victimization and perpetration, to control for past offending and victimization, as suggested by Rebellon and Van Gundy (2005), and because Menard (2002) indicates that adolescent violent offending and victimization are predictive of later adult violent offending and victimization, two variables were constructed, paralleling the dependent variables, and summed across waves 1–5. Frequency of adolescent violence victimization includes the same items as adult victimization, and excludes being beaten up by parents (since being beaten up by parents is used as a separate predictor, and is one of the predictors on which we focus in the present study).

Adolescent violence perpetration consists of the same measures as adult violent offending except that while, in the present data set, adolescents were asked about gang fighting, adults were asked about battery. This minor difference, reflecting age differences in behavior, should not adversely affect the utility of the general measure of adolescent violence perpetration as a control for adult violence perpetration. For arrest, adolescent violence victimization is retained in the model as a more general measure of AEV, but three different control variables are employed, all summed across waves 1–5: frequency of general crime perpetration, frequency of adolescent marijuana use, and frequency of adolescent hard drug use. These variables are used in place of the narrower measure of adolescent violence perpetration because arrest may be affected not only by violence but by a broader range of illegal behaviors. Frequency of hard drug and marijuana use were discussed in the previous section. General offending includes the offenses used in constructing the index for violence perpetration in adolescence, plus minor assaults (hit teachers, parents, or students), burglary, various levels of larceny (less than $5, $5 to $50, over $50), theft of an automobile, joyriding, bought stolen goods, sold marijuana or hard drugs, prostitution, disorderly conduct, and carrying a hidden weapon.

Research on the reliability and validity of self-reported victimization has been limited, consisting primarily of comparison with officially recorded crime. In this regard, Schneider (1981), reporting on a comparison of victimization self-reports with police-recorded victimizations for the same individuals, found that victimization self-reports failed to detect some of the crimes reported to the police, even though victimization data still produced substantially higher estimates of the total amount of criminal behavior, on average about three times as much as official data on crimes known to the police (Skogan 1976). Skogan (1981) reported that there may be systematic bias against self-reporting victimizations in which the perpetrator is known to the offender. Mihalic and Elliott (1997b) indicated that questions about violent victimization fail to capture much of the domestic violence that is reported when questions specifically about domestic violence are asked. Specificity of the question also played a role in the self-reporting of rape victimization, with general questions about assault failing to capture a large proportion of the incidents of rape (Eigenberg 1980), a finding that led to the subsequent redesign of the National Crime Victimization Survey (NCVS) questions about rape victimization. The measure of victimization used in the NYSFS was designed to be similar to the NCVS measure, and Menard (2000) found that the distribution of self-reported victimization in the NYSFS was generally consistent with the distribution found in the NCVS and also in the British Crime Survey.

There is a long history of research (for a general review see Elliott et al. 1989, 4–9; Menard et al. 2016) indicating that self-report data on illegal behavior have high reliability, typically in the range of 85–90% (Dentler and Monroe 1961; Farrington 1973; Moffitt and Silva 1988) and validity, typically around 80% according to several criteria, including third-party reports (Gold 1966, 1970), the use of a polygraph test (as a threat of uncovering deception, not for actual verification; Clark and Tifft 1966), and comparison of self-reported and officially recorded arrests (Daylor et al. 2019; Dembo et al. 2002; Hardt and Peterson-Hardt 1977). Reliability and validity estimates tend to be higher when broad categories of offenses, rather than specific offense items, are used as the criterion (Gold 1966; Huizinga and Elliott 1986), and when shorter rather than longer recall periods, with lower risk of memory decay, are used (Elliott and Huizinga 1989; Huizinga and Elliott 1986; Menard and Elliott 1990; Menard et al. 2016; Zhang et al. 2000; see also Rutter et al. 1998). Results have been inconsistent regarding their accuracy for specific sociodemographic groups, with various studies indicating greater underreporting for females (Morris 1965) or males (Hindelang et al. 1981); greater underreporting for African American respondents (Hindelang et al. 1981; Huizinga and Elliott 1986) or no difference (Farrington et al. 1996; Knight et al. 2004; Maxfield et al. 2000; see also Thornberry and Krohn 2003); or underreporting related less to gender, ethnicity, or social class than to the seriousness of the offense (Gold 1966).

Reliability and validity specifically of NYSFS self-report data have been repeatedly tested. Huizinga and Elliott (1986) found that test-retest reliability over a 4-week interval for scales or indexes (relatively broad categories of offenses rather than more specific offense items) involving serious crime was high: .81 for prevalence of felony assault (the index of interest in the present study), .97 for robbery, and .99 for felony theft, but lower for less serious offenses. Reliability is better for low-frequency offenders than high-frequency offenders (and high frequency is correlated with seriousness; see Elliott et al. 1989). The pattern of the difference suggests that high-frequency offenders simply do not remember each of their many separate offenses with the same accuracy that low-frequency offenders remember each of their few offenses.

For self-reported victimization, self-reported perpetration, and self-reported arrest, in retrospective data with relatively long recall periods, respondents will deny ever engaging in behaviors that they previously admitted in prospective (1-year recall) data. Menard and Elliott (1990) and Menard et al. (2016) found that prospective data captured over 80%, often over 90%, of all the offenses reported by both methods combined, but retrospective data captured only about half to one-third of the total, except for illicit substance use. Similar patterns appear for self-reported arrest and victimization, most likely reflecting memory decay (Menard and Elliott 1990; Menard et al. 2016; Rutter et al. 1998). This is of interest in the present study not so much for self-reported violence victimization and perpetration, for which prospective data are used, but primarily to the extent that it affects the measurement of PTSD which, as described above, uses a screening question that asks whether the respondent has "ever" experienced certain traumatic events, including but not limited to criminal violence victimization. Another similar pattern appears when comparing official data on criminal behavior and arrests, with official arrest data (and also data on crimes known to the police) producing much lower estimates of total criminal behavior than victimization or self-report data for comparable offenses (Elliott 1995; Jackson 1990; Skogan 1976). Comparing official and self-reported data on arrests indicates a high level of agreement, around 80%, mostly reflecting consistent reports of *not* having been arrested; but the correlation between official and self-reported arrest in the NYSFS is only modest, with more total arrests being self-reported than officially recorded (Pollock et al. 2015), and evidence that the discrepancy often reflects errors in the official rather than the self-report data (Elliott 1995).

As shown in table 2.5, cumulative frequency over the first five waves of the NYSFS had a mean of almost 8 for violence victimization, and a little over 3 for violence perpetration, corresponding to approximately 1.58 per year for victimization and 0.46 per year for perpetration. In middle adulthood, the mean is 0.46 for violence victimization and 0.12 for violence perpetration, both about a third of the averages for adolescence, and consistent with the commonly observed decline in victimization with age. Note in particular the reduction in range for frequency of violence perpetration in middle adulthood, with a maximum of only 12. Also in table 2.5 is the cumulative frequency of general offending in adolescence, with a mean cumulative frequency of a little over 69, or just under fourteen offenses per year. Frequency of arrest ranges from 0 to 10, with a mean of .077, indicating the rarity of arrest in middle adulthood.

Table 2.5   Descriptive Statistics for General Violence and Arrest

Variable	N	Minimum	Maximum	Mean	Standard Deviation
Cumulative Frequency of General Violence Victimization in Adolescence (repeated in Table 2.6)	1,725	0	538	7.917	23.125
Cumulative Frequency of General Violence Perpetration in Adolescence (repeated in Table 2.6)	1,725	0	354	2.289	13.027
Cumulative Frequency of General Offending in Adolescence	1,725	0	4,320	69.314	245.868
Frequency of General Violence Victimization in Middle Adulthood	1,294	0	200	.460	6.056
Frequency of General Violence Perpetration in Middle Adulthood	1,138	0	12	.120	.567
Frequency of Arrest in Middle Adulthood	1,111	0	10	.077	.473

INTIMATE PARTNER VIOLENCE: VICTIMIZATION AND PERPETRATION

In the present study, general and serious partner violence perpetration and victimization are measured using physical aggression items taken from the Conflict Tactics Scale (CTS; Straus and Gelles 1990). Serious violence perpetration includes questions about kicking, biting, or hitting one's spouse or intimate partner with one's fist; hitting or trying to hit one's spouse or partner with something; beating up one's spouse or partner; threatening one's spouse or partner with a knife or gun; or using a knife on, or firing a gun at, one's spouse or partner in the past year. General violence perpetration includes these questions plus questions about less serious forms of violence including slapping, throwing something at, threatening to hit or throw something at, or insulting or swearing at your spouse or partner in the past year. Parallel items are used for serious and general partner victimization. Past research using these scales in the NYSFS (Mihalic and Elliott 1997a; Menard et al. 2014; Morse 1995; Simmons et al. 2015, 2018) suggests that results using the more serious scale of physical aggression may produce different substantive results than those produced using the more general scale. For all of the

CTS measures, the standard CTS coding of 0 = never, 1 = once, 2 = twice, 3 = 3–5 times, 4 = 6–10 times, 5 = 11–20 times, and 6 = more than 20 times is used, and the scale is constructed by summing the items for waves 10 and 11. Where data are missing for one wave, the data from the single wave with available data are used, reducing respondent loss at the expense of possibly underestimating the level of IPV for some respondents. As controls for adolescent behaviors, we include adolescent violence victimization and adolescent violence perpetration, the same controls used for adult general violence victimization and perpetration, as described in the previous section. In adolescence, more so than in adulthood, many respondents are not in intimate relationships, so a direct control for specifically intimate partner, as opposed to more general, violence perpetration and victimization is simply not available.

The CTS and its successor the Revised Conflict Tactics Scale (CTS2) have been extensively used in the United States and internationally in the study of IPV (Chapman and Gillespie 2019), and the reliability and validity of the CTS and CTS2 have been extensively studied. The CTS2 was formulated in response to critiques of the original CTS, with the changes including clarifying the wording of items, more clearly distinguishing minor and severe acts, changing question ordering, replacing some items, and increasing the number of items and scales (Chapman and Gillespie 2019; Straus et al. 1996). In a review of longitudinal studies of the impact of childhood or adolescent developmental risk factors on IPV (excluding studies limited to adolescent dating), all of the twenty-five studies that met the criteria for review used the CTS, CTS2, or individual items from the CTS or CTS2 scales (Costa et al. 2015). Tests of the overall internal consistency reliability of the CTS as a whole, and of the minor and serious physical aggression scales that are used in the present study, have produced reliabilities generally averaging close to .80, in the range from .70 to .90 and sometimes higher (Chapman and Gillespie 2019; Straus et al. 1996; Straus and Mickey 2012). Test-retest reliabilities for physical aggression using a subset of items from the CTS ranged from .66 and .47 for serious aggression victimization and perpetration to .74 and .62 for minor aggression victimization and perpetration in Simmons et al. (2015), and .76 for a variety score using CTS2 items for physical aggression (Vega and O'Leary 2007), with some evidence of higher test-retest reliability for women than for men (Goodman et al. 1999).

Table 2.6 presents the summary statistics for adult marital status, here coded as simply not married (the reference category) or married, plus the cumulative frequency of violence victimization and perpetration in adolescence, plus the four adult outcome measures (CTS scores for general and serious assault victimization and perpetration in middle adulthood). A word of explanation may

be in order here. In order for IPV to occur, one must have an intimate partner, and that is indicated by the adult marital status variable (which includes
cohabitation as well as legal marriage). The NYSFS does not provide data on
the degree of contact or intimacy in non-cohabiting (e.g., dating) relationships,
so the use of marriage/cohabitation provides the best screener available in the
data for the presence of an intimate relationship. This is the reason why there
is such a discrepancy between the number of valid cases for the CTS scores
compared to other measures. As noted earlier, we also lack indicators of violence directed specifically at intimate partners in waves 1–5 of the NYSFS, so
the general measures of adolescent violence victimization and perpetration are
the best available controls for precursors to IPV in middle adulthood.

**Table 2.6   Descriptive Statistics for Intimate Partner Violence Victimization and
Perpetration**

Variable *Categories*	N	Minimum	Maximum	Mean/ Proportion	Standard Deviation
Adult Marital Status:	1,293	0	1	Proportion:	.478
Currently Not Married *(reference category)*	457			.353	
Currently Married	836			.647	
Cumulative Frequency of General Violence Victimization in Adolescence (repeated in Table 2.5)	1,725	0	538	Mean: 7.917	23.125
Cumulative Frequency of General Violence Perpetration in Adolescence (repeated in Table 2.5)	1,725	0	354	Mean: 2.289	13.027
Conflict Tactics Scale Serious IPV Victimization in Middle Adulthood	822	0	24	Mean: .321	1.651
Conflict Tactics Scale Serious IPV Perpetration in Middle Adulthood	822	0	14	Mean: .122	.786
Conflict Tactics Scale General IPV Victimization in Middle Adulthood	822	0	63	Mean: 1.381	5.170
Conflict Tactics Scale General IPV Perpetration in Middle Adulthood	822	0	38	Mean: .825	3.112

Note: IPV = intimate partner violence.

Table 2.6 indicates that approximately two-thirds of the respondents are married or cohabiting in middle adulthood. In adolescence, the mean frequency of violence victimization was about eight times per year, close to four times as much as the mean frequency (approximately 2) of serious violence perpetration in adolescence. In middle adulthood, the CTS general assault victimization score with a mean of nearly 1.4 is over four times the scale score for serious assault victimization, with a mean of approximately 0.3. Similarly, the mean for general assault perpetration at .825 is almost seven times as large as the mean of .122 for serious assault perpetration. Notice that the mean levels of self-reported perpetration for both general and serious assault are substantially lower than the mean levels of self-reported victimization, suggesting that respondents may be more likely to interpret the behavior of others than their own behavior as constituting aggression or assault.

MEASURES OF ADOLESCENT EXPOSURE
TO VIOLENCE IN THE NYSFS

There are three core measures of adolescent AEV in the neighborhood and family contexts used in the present study. For the focal predictors in this study, we use multiple waves of a single measure for each of being physically abused by parents, witnessing parental violence, and exposure to neighborhood violence. In selecting these variables, we seek both to broadly cover and to compare different aspects of adolescent AEV: direct victimization, direct witnessing, and general awareness of or AEV, respectively, all within the immediate environments of the family and neighborhood, where it may be most difficult to escape. To the extent that past research serves as a guide, we may expect that all three types of AEV may independently affect adult outcomes.

For cumulative frequency of being physically abused by parents, we use a single item asking how many times the respondent was beaten up by a parent in the previous year, measured at waves 1–5 (ages 11–17 to 15–21). For respondents who did not have all five waves of data, individuals who did not report being beaten up by a parent in any of the waves for which they had valid data were coded as not having been beaten up by a parent, as were individuals who had all five waves of valid data and did not report having been beaten up by a parent. Individuals who reported being beaten up by a parent one or more times were coded as having been beaten up by a parent, regardless of whether they had missing data for one or more waves. This gives us a conservative measure of cumulative frequency of being beaten up by a parent for waves 1–5. Separately, as described earlier, we use a measure of adolescent violence victimization as a control for adult violence victimization and offending. We also use it as a broader, more general form of adolescent AEV which involves direct victimization and which may have an impact on adult outcomes separately from, or in addition to, AEV specifically in the home. This allows us to test whether physical abuse, violent victimization more generally, or both, are related to adult outcomes, recognizing that much of the literature considers not only parental physical abuse but also violent victimization more generally (e.g., Kendall-Tackett 2013; Menard 2002; Ruback and Thompson 2001).

For witnessing parental violence, respondents were asked whether they had ever witnessed either of their parents hurting the other parent during a fight or an argument. These are retrospective questions asked at waves 8, 9, 10, and 11 (ages 24–30 through 37–43). It would have been desirable to have shorter term retrospective data, but such data are not available to us in the present study. Respondents who had one or more waves of data missing, and who did not report having witnessed parental violence in any of the waves for which they had nonmissing data, were coded as not having witnessed parental violence, as were individuals who had all four waves of valid data and did not report ever having witnessed parental violence. Individuals who reported having witnessed parental violence in at least one wave, but who then reported *not* having witnessed parental violence in at least one *subsequent* wave, were coded as having inconsistent reports of parental violence. Individuals who reported having witnessed parental violence in at least one wave, and who did not subsequently report *not* having witnessed parental violence (and who therefore may either have subsequently remembered, or subsequently witnessed, parental violence) were coded as having a consistent report of parental violence. As will be seen in the results, this distinction is an important one. This three-point scale was recoded into two dummy variables, with no parental violence as the reference category, and (a) inconsistent reporting of parental violence and (b) consistent reporting of parental violence as the two dummy variables. Strictly speaking, this variable measures exposure to parental violence which may have occurred during adolescence, but may also have occurred either before or after the adolescent period. Given the typical pattern of moving out of the parental home at or shortly after the end of adolescence, it seems most likely to us that the violence witnessed would have been during adolescence rather than at a later period, but this not entirely certain. Note that for physical abuse and exposure to neighborhood violence, both measured prospectively, the issue of potential inconsistency in reporting (a concern with the long-term retrospective measurement of witnessing parental violence) does not arise.

For exposure to neighborhood violence, we have only parental reports at wave 1, and respondent reports at waves 5 and subsequently. In each case, the response set included three categories indicating whether assaults and muggings were (1) not a problem, (2) somewhat of a problem, and (2) a serious problem in the neighborhood. For individuals with either only parental reports or only self-reports of whether assaults and muggings were a problem in the neighborhood, the available scale was used and multiplied by two. For individuals with both parental and self-reports (the vast majority of the cases), the sum of the parental and self-reports was used. In both cases, this resulted in a scale ranging from 2 to 6 numerically. We thought it preferable to use a measure based, to the extent possible, on both parent and child reports; but separate analysis, not detailed here, indicates that the use of parental reports produces the same substantive results regarding the impact of adolescent AEV on the adult outcomes (but with forty-three fewer cases because of missing data for some respondents on the parent measure, but not the self-report measure, of neighborhood AEV).

Widom and her associates (Widom and Shepard 1996; Widom and Morris 1997; Widom et al. 1999) have compared prospective and retrospective data on self-reports of abuse and neglect, including separate comparisons for females and males. Compared to prospective data on officially substantiated instances of abuse and neglect (with a recall period of a year or less), long-term retrospective self-reports of abuse and neglect (with a recall period of more than a year) showed substantial underreporting for physical and sexual abuse. Other studies have produced similar findings. Everson et al. (2008) reported poor agreement between retrospective self-reports of abuse and documented child protection services (CPS) determinations of abuse. Most of the discrepancy was attributable to higher rates of abuse in the self-report than the official data, with prevalence rates in the self-report data being four to six times as high as in the official data (see also Shaffer et al. 2008; Swahn et al. 2006). It is important to note that most instances of alleged child maltreatment reported to the authorities and investigated are found to be unsubstantiated, that is, insufficient evidence is available to conclude that maltreatment has occurred. According to the U.S. Department of Health and Human Services (2020, 19), there was strong enough evidence to conclude that maltreatment had occurred in approximately 17% (16.1% substantiated and 0.7% maltreatment indicated) of reports investigated.

Also of concern, however, was that in the retrospective data, nearly half of the CPS-documented cases, which did include probable as well as firmly substantiated abuse, were not reported. Hardt and Rutter (2004) found that longer term recall data on adverse childhood experiences (ACEs) showed evidence of substantial underreporting and measurement error compared to shorter term recall data, but concluded that false positive reports were relatively rare. They urged caution in the use of long-term retrospective data in investigating ACEs.

For retrospective data on witnessing parental violence, in a longitudinal series of four retrospective measurements of varying length taken over a span of 13 years, prior research using the NYSFS (Covey et al. 2013) found that while 15% of the NYSFS sample consistently reported having witnessed parental violence, another 10% provided inconsistent reports, first reporting having witnessed parental violence in an earlier wave of the data, then indicating that they had not previously witnessed parental violence in a later wave of the data.

Based on these studies, four conclusions seem warranted. First, as with self-report criminal victimization and crime perpetration data, self-report data on maltreatment and AEV reveal much more than is found in official sources like CPS reports. The difference, moreover, appears to reflect not overreporting in the self-report data but serious underreporting (perhaps more specifically, under-detection) in the official data. Second, again paralleling self-report victimization and crime data, retrospective data involving long recall periods (in some of the aforementioned studies 10–20 years) appear to produce substantial underreporting and, when repeated retrospective measures are available (as in Covey et al. 2013), an uncomfortably high proportion of inconsistent reporting of AEV. Third, there is some evidence that there may be gender differences in the reliability and validity of self-reports. Fourth, these discrepancies may lead to different conclusions regarding the impacts of childhood maltreatment or adolescent AEV on subsequent behaviors or other outcomes.

In table 2.7, the cumulative frequency of parental physical abuse ranges from 0 to 412, the maximum representing an average of over eighty assaults per year over the 5-year period, but the mean is less than 1, indicating an average of .17 assaults per year. Just under 75% of the respondents report never having witnessed parental violence, with about 10% providing inconsistent reports (first reporting, then later denying having ever witnessed parental violence), and 15% providing consistent reports of parental violence. It is this latter figure that is probably the more reliable estimate of the prevalence of witnessing parental violence. It is similar in magnitude to the 17% who report AEV in the neighborhood. Finally, in table 2.7, the number of different types of AEV experienced by the respondents is presented. Just about two-thirds report no exposure to the types of violence captured in our three measures of AEV; about one-fourth report exposure to only one of the three; about 6% report exposure to two; and just under 1% report exposure to all three types of AEV measured in the present study. Except to briefly illustrate the broad pattern of association between AEV and the adult outcomes at the beginning of chapters 4–8, where we combine it with the prevalence of adolescent general violence victimization, we do not use this summary prevalence measure as a predictor (or as an outcome) in the present study, because past research with this sample has indicated that it provides no additional information, and may actually obscure the specific source (parental abuse, witnessing,

Table 2.7 Descriptive Statistics for Adolescent Exposure to Violence

Variable Categories	N	Minimum	Maximum	Mean/ Proportion	Standard Deviation
Cumulative Frequency of Parental Physical Abuse in Adolescence	1,725	0	412	Mean: .848	13.505
Retrospective Prevalence of Witnessing Parental Violence:	1,488	NA	NA	Proportion:	
None (reference category)				.747	.435
Inconsistent				.103	.304
Consistent				.150	.358
Prevalence of Neighborhood Violence in Adolescence:	1,470	0	1	Proportion:	.376
No (reference category)				.830	
Yes				.170	
Number of Types of Adolescent Exposure to Violence in Adolescence:	1,371	0	3	Mean: .408 Proportion:	.651
0	923			.673	
1	349			.255	
2	86			.063	
3	13			.009	

Note: NA = Not applicable. Standard deviations for categorical variables with more than two categories are presented separately for each categorical dummy variable.

neighborhood violence) of the impact of AEV on adult outcomes (Menard et al. 2014). It does, however, serve here to illustrate the extent of polyvictimization (Finkelhor et al. 2007) in the NYSFS sample.

SUMMARY

In the present chapter, we have provided details on the NYSFS, the source of the data used in the present study. The NYSFS is a nationally representative longitudinal sample of individuals who were 11–17 years old in 1976–1977, from whom data were collected on a variety of domains including sociodemographic characteristics, attitudes, and both prosocial and illegal behaviors. The focal respondents were last interviewed in 2002–2003. The NYSFS has been used extensively in past research, particularly on illicit substance use and other forms of illegal behavior. We also presented the measures for our variables in the domains of sociodemographic characteristics, mental health, substance use, IPV, general violence, and our focal predictors, measures of adolescent AEV, including the available evidence regarding their reliability and validity. Finally, we presented the univariate distributions of the variables representing adult outcomes, adolescent precursors to adult outcomes, and adolescent AEV. In the next chapter, we examine the joint distribution of the measures of adolescent AEV, plus the sociodemographic distribution of adolescent AEV, adult outcomes, and their adolescent precursors.

Chapter 3

Distribution of Adolescent Exposure to Violence and Adult Outcomes

Thirty years before the present study, Elliott et al. (1989) described the distribution of delinquency, substance use, and mental health problems in the National Youth Survey, including their joint distribution and their sociodemographic distribution in adolescence and young adulthood, ages 11–24. The present chapter parallels chapters 2 and 3 in Elliott et al. (1989) with three important distinctions. First, the data presented here cover a broader age range, 11–44, beginning as did Elliott et al. (1989) in early adolescence, but here extending into middle adulthood. Second, where Elliott et al. (1989) described the distributions of a broad range of illegal behaviors, licit and illicit substance use, and mental health problems in adolescence and early adulthood, the present chapter focuses on (1) adult outcomes, including socioeconomic status (SES), mental health, substance use (which includes alcohol use as well as illicit drug use), and both intimate partner and general violence at ages 37–44; as predicted by (2) three measures of adolescent exposure to violence (AEV) (parental physical abuse, witnessing parental violence, exposure to neighborhood violence), plus adolescent general violence victimization, at ages 11–21; and as control variables (3) adolescent versions or precursors of the adult outcomes, which like the focal predictors are measured at ages 11–21. Third, the adolescent measures are cumulative, combining up to five years of data (1975–1976 to 1979–1980) in a single measure, rather than separate single-year measures as used in Elliott et al. (1989).

In examining the relationship of urban, suburban, and rural residence to the adult outcomes, we have used adult rather than adolescent residence. Our expectation is that it is current rather than past residence that will matter most in predicting the adult outcomes. In contrast, we would expect parental SES and two-parent family structure to matter more if measured during adolescence than adulthood (i.e., whether one's parents are living together at age 15 is likely to matter more to one's adult outcomes than whether one's parents are living together when one is age 35). While the domains covered in Elliott et al. (1989) and the present study overlap extensively, the measures themselves are different, and insofar as we present data on the distributions of the variables in middle adulthood, this chapter updates the information provided in Elliott et al. (1989). Given the additional measures included here, the present chapter should also be regarded as an expansion of that study.

A word is in order about the interpretation of statistical significance as opposed to substantive or practical significance in the results to be presented in the present and following chapters. Statistical significance is the likelihood of obtaining a relationship as strong as the observed relationship in repeated studies or trials if the true strength of the relationship is zero, that is, if there is no relationship. It is technically incorrect but heuristically useful to think of statistical significance as the probability (p) that there really is no relationship between the variables for which a correlation, regression coefficient, or other measure of the strength of the relationship has been calculated. A commonly applied criterion for statistical significance in the social sciences is the $p = .05$ (often to only two decimal places) cutoff. If there is only a .05 (5%) chance that the relationship is really zero, then we accept the relationship as being statistically significant. This cutoff, however, is arbitrary. Substantive significance, in contrast, refers to whether the relationship is strong enough to be interesting. Practical or clinical significance, closely related to substantive significance, refers to whether the relationship is strong enough that, if we change one variable, we should see enough of a change in the other variable to be useful in a practical or clinical sense (whether there will be enough of an improvement to matter). Substantive significance does not depend on the size of the sample, but statistical significance does. For a relationship of any given strength (substantive significance), larger sample size will result in improved (lower p) statistical significance.

In many studies in the social sciences, samples are relatively small, less than 100, but in the National Youth Survey Family Study (NYSFS), the sample size, even when we examine results separately by gender, is several hundred. Thus, even relatively weak relationships (a correlation or standardized regression coefficient less than .100) will be statistically significant ($p \leq .05$). In a more technical sense, the NYSFS sample has sufficient statistical power to detect relationships that are even weaker than the minimum strength relationship in which we would typically be interested. In the present sample, therefore, it is substantive rather than statistical significance that provides the more stringent criterion for whether a relationship is strong enough to be of concern. As a loose guideline, correlations or, in subsequent chapters, standardized coefficients less than .100 can be regarded as sufficiently weak to be of questionable substantive significance, while those greater than .100 (or one might reasonably want an even higher threshold; .100 is as arbitrary for substantive significance as .05 is for statistical significance) can be regarded as at least meeting a reasonable minimum threshold for substantive significance.

In the tables that follow, most of the correlations presented involve Pearson's r, a proportional reduction in error measure of association appropriate for correlations involving interval or ratio scaled variables, or dichotomous variables, or a combination of the two. Three variables, each having three categories, two of which are ordinal (parental SES and urban/suburban/rural residence) and one of which is nominal (adult marital status), are broken up into their constituent categories, each of which is a dichotomy, and Pearson's r is used for them as well. Adult income and adult net worth are ordinal categorical variables with more than three categories, and for these two variables, the correlations presented use Kendall's τ_b, an ordinal measure of association which, like Pearson's r, has a proportional reduction in error interpretation. For general discussions of measures of association, see Liebtrau (1983) and Chen and Popovich (2002); and specific to Kendall's τ_b as a proportional reduction in error measure of association, Menard (2010, Appendix C).

ADOLESCENT AND ADULT
SOCIOECONOMIC STATUSES

We begin by examining the relationship between adolescent and adult SES. In adolescence, the socioeconomic characteristics used to predict adult outcomes are gender, ethnicity, parental SES, and whether the respondent lived in a two-parent household at the first wave of the survey, in 1976–1977. As noted above, we also include adult residence (urban, suburban, or rural) as a sociodemographic predictor. In adolescence, gender is unrelated to ethnicity, parental SES, residence, or being in a two-parent family (boys and girls alike are born into and have grown up in ethnic majority and minority, higher and lower SES, urban, suburban, and rural locations, and two-parent as well as other types of households). Ethnic minority respondents are significantly less likely than ethnic majority respondents to have parents who are upper or middle SES (Pearson's r = −.205, p = .000) or working class (r = −.052, p = .035), but more likely to have lower SES parents (Pearson's r = .225, p = .000). They are also more likely to reside in urban (r = .328, p = .000) and not suburban (r = −.188, p = .000) or rural (r = −.118, p = .000) areas, and less likely (r = −.295, p = .000) to be in two-parent households. Respondents with lower SES parents are slightly less likely to live in suburban areas (r = −.073, p = .006) and slightly more likely to live in rural areas (r = .086, p = .001), but parental SES and residence are not strongly related. Two-parent family structure is more prevalent among upper and middle SES parents (r = .112, p = .000) and less prevalent among working-class parents (r = −.064, p = .010). It is also less prevalent among urban residents (r = −.183, p = .000) and more prevalent among suburban (r = .102, p = .000) and rural (r = .067, p = .009) residents.

Table 3.1 presents the relationship between the measures of SES in adolescence and adulthood. Past studies have found that educational attainment for females has been lower than for males (Elman and O'Rand 2004), although the gap has been narrowing over time (Breen and Goldthorpe 1997), lower for ethnic minority than majority respondents (Elman and O'Rand 2004), higher for respondents with higher parental SES (Breen and Goldthorpe 1997; Dubow et al. 2009; Elman and O'Rand 2004; Solon 1992), and higher for individuals who grew up in two-parent households (Kuh and Maclean 1990). In the present sample, gender appears to be unrelated to adult educational attainment, but adult educational attainment is negatively related to ethnic minority status (r = −.177, p = .000), lower parental SES (r = −.344, p = .000), and rural residence in adulthood (r = −.099, p = .000). Adult educational attainment is positively related to upper or middle parental SES (r = .382, p = .000), suburban residence (r = .099, p = .000), and two-parent family structure in adolescence (r = .151, p = .000). For employment, past studies have found employment to be higher for males and lower for females, and lower for ethnic minority than majority group members (Altonji and Blank 2005), and higher for individuals from higher SES and two-parent families (Caspi et al. 1998). In the present study, employment in middle adulthood is higher for males (r = .119, p = .000) and slightly, perhaps negligibly, lower for respondents from lower parental SES backgrounds (r = −.057, p = .047), but not significantly different across ethnicity, adult residence, or two-parent family structure in adolescence.

Adult income is typically lower for females (Blau and Kahn 2017; Ruel and Hauser 2013) and African Americans (Elman and O'Rand 2004), and higher for individuals from higher parental SES backgrounds (Elman and O'Rand 2004). There are mixed results on the relationship of gender to adult net worth, with different studies indicating higher net worth for males (Ruel and Hauser 2013) or females (Altonji et al. 2000), possibly depending on how net worth was measured. There is more consistency in the finding that net worth tends to be lower for ethnic minority group members, particularly African Americans (Altonji et al. 2000; Blau and Graham 1990; Gittleman and Wolff 2004), and higher for respondents with higher SES parents (Gittleman and Wolff 2004) and two-parent family structures in adolescence (Christopher et al. 2002). As indicated in table 3.1, although income is higher for males (using the ordinal measure of association, Kendall's τ_b = .272, p = .000), net worth, which was

Table 3.1 Adolescent and Adult Socioeconomic Statuses

	Adult Educational Attainment — Mean — Pearson's r (p)	Adult Employment (Employed) — Proportion — Pearson's r (p)	Adult Income — Median category — Kendall's τ_b (p)	Adult Net Worth — Median category — Kendall's τ_b (p)	Adult Marital Status: Never Married — Proportion — Pearson's r (p)	Adult Marital Status: Married — Proportion — Pearson's r (p)	Adult Marital Status: Formerly Married — Proportion — Pearson's r (p)
Gender: Female	13.63	.87	$25,000–$34,999	$50,000–$99,999	.12	.67	.21
Male	13.61	.95	$35,000–$49,999	$50,000–$99,999	.19	.63	.18
	-.005 (.857)	.119 (.000)	.272 (.000)	-.036 (.150)	.093 (.001)	-.044 (.118)	-.033 (.236)
Ethnicity: Majority	13.81	.93	$35,000–$49,999	$50,000–$99,999	.13	.69	.18
Minority	12.82	.89	$15,000–$19,999	$10,000–$49,999	.30	.46	.24
	-.177 (.000)	-.053 (.059)	-.134 (.000)	-.175 (.000)	.189 (.000)	-.188 (.000)	.053 (.059)
Parental SES: Lower	12.82	.90	$25,000–$34,999	$50,000–$99,999	.16	.62	.23
	-.344 (.000)	-.057 (.047)	-.165 (.000)	-.162 (.000)	.009 (.757)	-.074 (.010)	.081 (.004)
Parental SES: Working	13.72	.93	$25,000–$34,999	$50,000–$99,999	.17	.67	.16
	.014 (.628)	.031 (.277)	-.005 (.841)	.024 (.267)	.027 (.351)	.023 (.411)	-.053 (.064)

(Continued)

Table 3.1 Adolescent and Adult Socioeconomic Statuses (Continued)

	Adult Educational Attainment	Adult Employment (Employed)	Adult Income	Adult Net Worth	Adult Marital Status: Never Married	Adult Marital Status: Married	Adult Marital Status: Formerly Married
	Mean Pearson's r (p)	Proportion Pearson's r (p)	Median category Kendall's τ_b (p)	Median category Kendall's τ_b (p)	Proportion Pearson's r (p)	Proportion Pearson's r (p)	Proportion Pearson's r (p)
Parental SES: Upper/Middle	15.15 .382 (.000)	.94 .032 (.259)	$35,000–$49,999 .195 (.000)	$100,000–$499,999 .155 (.000)	.13 –.039 (.174)	.70 .060 (.035)	.17 –.037 (.195)
Residence: Urban	13.50 –.025 (.366)	.93 .024 (.393)	$25,000–$34,999 –.048 (.044)	$10,000–$49,999 –.101 (.000)	.29 .183 (.000)	.48 –.178 (.000)	.23 .047 (.096)
Residence: Suburban	13.78 .099 (.000)	.92 –.008 (.787)	$35,000–$49,999 .070 (.003)	$50,000–$99,999 .086 (.000)	.14 –.080 (.004)	.67 .080 (.004)	.19 –.022 (.430)
Residence: Rural	13.13 –.099 (.000)	.91 –.061 (.571)	$25,000–$49,999 –.039 (.110)	$50,000–$99,999 –.002 (.936)	.09 –.093 (.001)	.74 .089 (.002)	.17 –.022 (.443)
Two-Parent Family: No	12.96	.90	$25,000–$49,999	$10,000–$49,999	.21	.52	.27
Yes	13.79 .151 (.000)	.92 .034 (.220)	$35,000–$49,999 .123 (.000)	$50,000–$99,999 .158 (.000)	.15 –.074 (.009)	.68 .134 (.000)	.17 –.094 (.001)

measured for households rather than individuals, is not significantly different by gender. Ethnic minority group members have lower income ($\tau_b = -.134$, p = .000) and net worth ($\tau_b = -.175$, p = .000). Income ($\tau_b = -.165$, p = .000) and net worth ($\tau_b = -.162$, p = .000) are lower for respondents with lower SES parents, and income ($\tau_b = .195$, p = .000) and net worth ($\tau_b = .155$, p = .000) are higher for respondents with upper or middle SES parents, reflecting a tendency toward intergenerational transmission of SES. Income in middle adulthood appears to be very weakly negatively related to urban residence ($\tau_b = -.048$, p = .044) and positively related to suburban residence ($\tau_b = .070$, p = .003), a relationship which may reflect the impact of income on residence rather than residence on income. Similarly, net worth is lower for urban residents ($\tau_b = -.101$, p = .000) and higher for suburban residents ($\tau_b = .086$, p = .000). It is worth emphasizing that all of these relationships are quite weak. Stronger are the relationships of income ($\tau_b = .123$, p = .000) and net worth ($\tau_b = .158$, p = .000) with having had a two-parent family structure in adolescence.

Research by Kuh and Maclean (1990) and Wolfinger (2000) suggests that individuals who experienced instability in their parents' marital situation in adolescence are more at risk of marital instability of their own in adulthood. This is borne out in the present study, with individuals who were not in two-parent family structures in adolescence more likely to be either never married (r = −.074, p = .009) or formerly married (divorced, separated, or widowed; r = −.094, p = .001) in middle adulthood, and individuals who were in two-parent families in adolescence more likely to be married in middle adulthood (r = .134, p = .000). In addition, males are more likely than females to have never been married (r = .093, p = .001), and ethnic minority status is associated with higher likelihood of having never been married (r = .189, p = .000) and lower likelihood of being currently married (r = −.188, p = .000) in middle adulthood. Respondents with lower SES parents are slightly more likely to be formerly married (r = .081, p = .004) and less likely to be currently married (r = −.074, p = .010), while respondents with upper or middle SES parents are slightly more likely to be married (r = .060, p = .035). Being formerly married is not significantly associated with residence, but being never married is positively associated with urban residence (r = .183, p = .000) and negatively associated with suburban (r = −.080, p = .004) and rural (r = −.093, p = .001) residence. Being currently married in middle adulthood is negatively associated with urban residence (r = −.178, p = .000) and positively associated with suburban (r = .080, p = .004) and rural (r = .089, p = .002) residence. To some extent, these findings may reflect the impact of marriage on residence, with married couples preferring to move out of urban areas if they are financially able to do so. With regard to marriage, the most informative finding is the tendency toward a pattern of intergenerational transmission of marital stability or instability.

MENTAL HEALTH

Elliott et al. (1989), in previous research on this sample in adolescence and early adulthood, found that general mental health problems, depression, and mental health service use were all higher among females than among males, a finding paralleled for anxiety, depression, post-traumatic stress disorder (PTSD), psychological stress, and mental health service use in other studies (Cohen and Janicki-Deverts 2012; Kessler et al. 2005, 2009; Silva et al. 2016). The association of mental health problems with ethnicity varies by the type of problem or outcome measure, with rates of general mental health problems in adolescence being higher for minority ethnic group members, particularly African Americans (Elliott et al. 1989), a relationship which may disappear controlling for other demographic characteristics such as SES (Cohen and Janicki-Deverts 2012). Rates of some specific mental health problems such as anxiety, depression, mood disorder, and mental health service use, however, tend to be lower for ethnic minority group members in adolescence and adulthood (Elliott et al. 1989; Kessler et al. 2009; Weaver et al. 2015), although Merikangas et al. (2010) report higher rates of mood disorders for ethnic minority group members. Mental health problems are higher among children of parents with lower SES (Cohen and Janicki-Deverts 2012; Elliott et al. 1989; Silva et al. 2016), but mental health service use is higher for individuals with higher parental SES (Elliott et al. 1989). Note the discrepancy for individuals from lower socioeconomic backgrounds between having higher rates of mental health problems in general, but lower rates of mental health service use (with the exception of depression, for which rates are lower for individuals with lower SES backgrounds), a discrepancy which seems to imply differential access based on SES to mental health services. Mental health problems also appear more prevalent among individuals in urban areas (Elliott et al. 1989) and slightly less prevalent in rural areas (Merikangas et al. 2010), and higher among individuals who have experienced parental divorce or separation (Kuh and Maclean 1990; Merikangas et al. 2010).

In the present study, the two adolescent mental health problem measures are significantly positively related to one another ($r = .283$, $p = .000$), and to adult mental health problems, measured here as the combined past year prevalence of depression, anxiety, and PTSD ($r = .114$, $p = .000$ for parent reports, $r = .194$, $p = .000$ for self-reports). Parent reports of adolescent mental health problems are very weakly or nonsignificantly associated with adult general ($r = .059$, $p = .046$) and professional ($r = .053$, $p = .074$) mental health service use, respectively, but self-reports of adolescent mental health problems are significantly associated with adult general ($r = .121$, $p = .000$) and professional ($r = .128$, $p = .000$) mental health service use. Both parent reports ($r = -.176$, $p = .000$) and self-reports ($r = -.170$, $p = .000$) of adolescent mental health problems are associated with lower adult life satisfaction. The combined prevalence of depression, anxiety, and PTSD in adulthood is strongly associated with the frequency of both general ($r = .527$, $p = .000$) and professional ($r = .506$, $p = .000$) mental health service use, and negatively ($r = -.249$, $p = .000$) associated with life satisfaction. The measure of professional mental health service use is a subset of the measure of general mental health service use, so the two are predictably highly correlated ($r = .884$, $p = .000$). Life satisfaction is negatively associated with general ($r = -.211$, $p = .000$) and professional ($r = -.195$, $p = .000$) mental health service use.

Table 3.2 indicates no significant difference between females and males for the cumulative prevalence of mental health problems in adolescence (and note that this cumulative measure is different from the annual measure used in Elliott et al. 1989), but males have lower rates for the adult combined prevalence of anxiety, depression, and PTSD ($r = -.110$, $p = .000$), general mental health service use ($r = -.158$, $p = .000$), and adult professional mental health service use ($r = -.133$, $p = .000$). Males also report having lower life satisfaction ($r = -.118$, $p = .000$). Adolescent mental health problems are higher according to both parent reports ($r = .096$, $p = .000$) and self-reports ($r = .159$, $p = .000$), and adult life satisfaction is lower ($r = -.123$, $p = .000$), for ethnic minority group members, but there are no significant differences by ethnicity in adult combined anxiety, depression, and PTSD, or in adult general or professional mental health service use. The cumulative prevalence of adolescent mental health problems is higher for respondents with lower SES parents according to both parental reports ($r = .138$, $p = .000$) and self-reports ($r = .165$, $p = .000$), and lower for respondents with working class ($r = -.073$, $p = .003$ for parent reports, $r = -.074$, $p = .003$ for self-reports) and upper or middle class ($r = -.081$, $p = .001$ for parent reports, $r = -.112$, $p = .000$ for self-reports) parents. There is a very weak negative relationship between lower parental SES and adult general mental health service use ($r = -.059$, $p = .051$), but parental SES is otherwise unrelated to adult mental health problems, mental health service use, and life satisfaction.

Rural residence in adulthood is not significantly related to any of the mental health problem measures, and neither urban nor suburban residence in adulthood is significantly related to adult mental health problems or adult mental health service use, but individuals who had mental health problems in adolescence are more likely to be urban residents ($r = .108$, $p = .000$ for parent reports, $r = .100$, $p = .000$ for self-reports) and less likely to be suburban residents ($r = -.093$, $p = .000$ for parent reports, $r = -.060$, $p = .019$) in adulthood; and urban residents are more likely to have lower levels of life satisfaction ($r = -.078$, $p = .005$). Finally, being in a two-parent family in adolescence is associated with lower cumulative prevalence of adolescent mental health problems according to both parent reports ($r = -.122$, $p = .000$)

Table 3.2 Adolescent and Adult Mental Health

	Adolescent Mental Health Problems (Parent Report) Scale	Adolescent Mental Health Problems (Self-Report) Prevalence	Adult Combined Anxiety, Depression, and PTSD Prevalence	Adult General Mental Health Service Use Frequency	Adult Professional Mental Health Service Use Frequency	Adult Life Satisfaction Scale
	Mean / Pearson's r (p)	Proportion / Pearson's r (p)	Proportion / Pearson's r (p)	Mean / Pearson's r (p)	Mean / Pearson's r (p)	Mean / Pearson's r (p)
Gender:						
Female	9.00	.23	.17	.80	.40	7.06
Male	9.16	.20	.09	.43	.19	6.62
	.028 (.244)	−.039 (.104)	−.110 (.000)	−.158 (.000)	−.133 (.000)	−.118 (.000)
Ethnicity:						
Majority	8.95	.18	.14	.63	.29	6.96
Minority	9.63	.34	.11	.59	.31	6.37
	.096 (.000)	.159 (.000)	−.034 (.259)	−.012 (.687)	.008 (.792)	−.123 (.000)
Parental SES: Lower	9.47	.28	.12	.55	.27	6.68
	.138 (.000)	.165 (.000)	−.032 (.300)	−.059 (.051)	−.038 (.209)	−.092 (.001)
Parental SES: Working	8.72	.16	.14	.68	.33	6.77
	−.073 (.003)	−.074 (.003)	.012 (.566)	.032 (.280)	.027 (.373)	−.036 (.205)
Parental SES: Upper/Middle	8.62	.13	.14	.69	.32	7.34
	−.081 (.001)	−.112 (.000)	.018 (.563)	.033 (.278)	.015 (.624)	.145 (.000)
Residence: Urban	9.63	.29	.13	.73	.37	6.56
	.108 (.000)	.100 (.000)	.002 (.955)	.049 (.095)	.051 (.083)	−.078 (.005)
Residence: Suburban	8.83	.19	.13	.61	.28	6.92
	−.093 (.000)	−.060 (.019)	.007 (.812)	−.012 (.682)	−.029 (.316)	.047 (.090)
Residence: Rural	9.05	.18	.12	.52	.27	6.94
	.002 (.933)	−.032 (.217)	−.011 (.717)	−.037 (.203)	−.017 (.561)	.023 (.417)
Two-Parent Family:						
No	9.78	.33	.17	.81	.41	6.28
Yes	8.91	.18	.12	.58	.27	6.98
	−.122 (.000)	−.146 (.000)	−.063 (.038)	−.079 (.007)	−.072 (.015)	.148 (.000)

and self-reports (r = −.146, p = .000). Two-parent family structure is weakly related to lower prevalence of adult mental health problems (combined anxiety, depression, and PTSD; r = −.063, p = .038); to lower frequency of both general (r = −.079, p = .007) and professional (r = −.072, p = .015) mental health service use; and to higher adult life satisfaction (r = .148, p = .000).

FREQUENCY OF SUBSTANCE USE AND PROBLEM SUBSTANCE USE

Past research on the sociodemographic distribution of substance use and problem use, based on both earlier analysis of the present sample (Elliott et al. 1989) and other studies (e.g., Merikangas et al. 2010) are fairly consistent in finding that adolescent substance use is higher among males, lower among ethnic minorities (including African Americans), higher in urban metropolitan areas, and lower for adolescents in two-parent families. Findings for parental SES are not quite as consistent, with Elliott et al. (1989) finding higher hard drug (there termed "polydrug") use and problem use among respondents with higher parental SES, but Merikangas et al. (2010) finding lower rates of problem substance use (substance use disorder) among respondents who had more educated parents.

In the present sample, cumulative frequencies of adolescent hard drug and marijuana use are strongly associated with one another (r = .437, p = .000). Adolescent measures of problem alcohol and drug use are very strongly correlated with each other (r = .610, p = .000), and also with adolescent frequency of hard drug use (r = .408, p = .000 for problem drug use; r = .286, p = .000 for problem alcohol use), and with adolescent frequency of marijuana use (r = .475, p = .000 for problem drug use; r = .355, p = .000 for problem alcohol use). Adolescent frequency of hard drug use is statistically significantly but not very strongly associated with adult frequency of hard drug use (r = .075, p = .010), and not significantly associated with adult problem drug use (r = .018, p = .553), but more strongly associated with adult frequency of marijuana use (r = .256, p = .000), problem marijuana use (r = .211, p = .000), and problem alcohol use (r = .149, p = .000). Adolescent frequency of marijuana use is significantly associated with all five of the adult substance use measures: fairly strongly with adult frequency of marijuana use (r = .316, p = .000) and more weakly with adult frequency of hard drug use (r = .093, p = .001), problem drug use (r = .100, p = .001), problem marijuana use (r = .098, p = .001), and weakest of all with adult problem alcohol use (r = .059, p = .050). Adolescent problem drug use is moderately strongly associated with adult frequency of marijuana use (r = .245, p = .000), more weakly associated with adult problem drug use (r = .133, p = .000), problem marijuana use (r = .155, p = .000), and problem alcohol use (r = .165, p = .000), and least strongly but still significantly with adult frequency of hard drug use (r = .078, p = .011). Adolescent problem alcohol use is not quite significantly associated with adult problem drug use (r = .059, p = .055), but is significantly associated with adult frequency of hard drug use (r = .097, p = .002), frequency of marijuana use (r = .166, p = .000), problem marijuana use (r = .117, p = .000), and problem alcohol use (r = .167, p = .000).

Table 3.3 shows the sociodemographic distribution of the substance use variables. Males are more likely than females to use hard drugs (r = .054, p = .025), marijuana (r = .132, p = .000), and to have problem drug use (r = .095, p =v.000) and problem alcohol use (r = .167, p = .000) in adolescence. Males also have a higher frequency of marijuana use (r = .072, p = .013) but not hard drug use (r = −.006, p = .835) in adulthood. Males are very weakly or nonsignificantly more likely than females to experience problems associated with hard drugs (r = .066, p = .025)), marijuana (r = .050, p = .091) and alcohol use (r = .082, p = .006) in adulthood. Ethnic minority group membership has a very weak to nonsignificant negative relationship with adolescent frequency of hard drug use (r = −.056, p = .021), frequency of marijuana use (r = −.046, p = .057), and adolescent problem alcohol use (r = −.066, p = .012). Ethnicity has no significant relationship with adult frequency of hard drug or marijuana use, or with adult problem use of hard drugs, marijuana, or alcohol. Parental SES is not significantly associated with hard drug use, marijuana use, or problem drug or alcohol use in adolescence, with the single exception of a very weak positive relationship between working-class SES parents and adolescent marijuana use (r = .051, p = .040). Parental SES is not significantly associated with hard drug or marijuana use, or with problem substance use, in middle adulthood. Suburban residence is positively (r = .072, p = .015) associated with adult hard drug use frequency and negatively (r = −.072, p = .015) associated with adult problem hard drug use, but except for these two weak relationships, residence is generally not significantly associated with substance use or problem use. Two-parent family structure is negatively (r = −.089, p = .000) associated with adolescent marijuana use, problem drug use (r = −.100, p = .000), and very weakly but still significantly with problem alcohol use (r = −.055, p = .039), but otherwise not significantly associated with adolescent or adult substance use or problem use.

GENERAL VIOLENCE VICTIMIZATION AND OFFENDING, GENERAL OFFENDING, AND ARREST

For the respondents in the present study when they were adolescents and young adults, Elliott et al. (1989) found that rates of more serious violent

Table 3.3　Adolescent and Adult Substance Use and Problem Use

	Adolescent Hard Drug Frequency	Adolescent Marijuana Use Frequency	Adolescent Problem Drug Use Scale Score	Adolescent Problem Alcohol Use Scale Score	Adult Hard Drug Use Frequency	Adult Marijuana Use Frequency	Adult Problem Hard Drug Use Scale	Adult Problem Marijuana Use Scale	Adult Problem Alcohol Use Scale
	Mean Pearson's r (p)	Mean Pearson's r (p)	Mean Pearson's r (p)	Mean Pearson's r (p)	Mean Pearson's r (p)	Mean Pearson's r (p)	Mean Pearson's r (p)	Mean Pearson's r (p)	Mean Pearson's r (p)
Gender:									
Female	10.59	55.42	10.61	11.25	11.13	8.62	5.05	5.03	5.24
Male	18.73	123.14	11.07	12.43	10.37	21.03	5.16	5.07	5.43
	.054 (.025)	.132 (.000)	.095 (.000)	.167 (.000)	-.006 (.835)	.072 (.013)	.066 (.025)	.050 (.091)	.082 (.006)
Ethnicity:									
Majority	17.08	97.51	10.85	11.98	10.70	15.97	5.12	5.05	5.34
Minority	6.84	68.80	10.85	11.41	11.01	9.10	5.03	5.06	5.33
	-.056 (.021)	-.046 (.057)	-.000 (.999)	-.066 (.012)	.002 (.947)	-.032 (.282)	-.041 (.160)	.009 (.765)	-.001 (.971)
Parental SES: Lower	16.06	86.63	10.83	11.88	12.17	19.36	5.10	5.04	5.35
	.005 (.849)	-.019 (.451)	-.009 (.740)	.003 (.920)	.027 (.365)	.048 (.111)	.007 (.829)	-.012 (.681)	.018 (.549)
Parental SES: Working	17.49	111.75	10.97	11.92	9.59	8.86	5.12	5.06	5.36
	.016 (.518)	.051 (.040)	.034 (.203)	.009 (.751)	-.008 (.790)	-.046 (.129)	.021 (.497)	.016 (.599)	.022 (.465)
Parental SES: Upper/Middle	12.51	76.57	10.74	11.79	7.89	13.76	5.05	5.05	5.23
	-.023 (.356)	-.034 (.176)	-.027 (.320)	-.012 (.647)	-.023 (.449)	-.006 (.836)	-.029 (.329)	-.003 (.928)	-.045 (.142)
Residence: Urban	11.88	100.15	10.86	11.73	6.58	17.40	5.18	5.04	5.27
	-.015 (.571)	.020 (.425)	.007 (.807)	-.015 (.586)	-.036 (.226)	.016 (.589)	.049 (.099)	-.012 (.697)	-.029 (.333)

(Continued)

Table 3.3 Adolescent and Adult Substance Use and Problem Use (Continued)

	Adolescent Hard Drug Use Frequency		Adolescent Marijuana Use Frequency		Adolescent Problem Drug Use Scale Score		Adolescent Problem Alcohol Use Scale Score		Adult Hard Drug Use Frequency		Adult Marijuana Use Frequency		Adult Problem Hard Drug Use Scale		Adult Problem Marijuana Use Scale		Adult Problem Alcohol Use Scale	
	Mean	Pearson's r (p)	Mean	Pearson's r (p)	Mean	Pearson's r (p)	Mean	Pearson's r (p)	Mean	Pearson's r (p)	Mean	Pearson's r (p)	Mean	Pearson's r (p)	Mean	Pearson's r (p)	Mean	Pearson's r (p)
Residence: Suburban	14.96	.019 (.453)	89.41	−.005 (.854)	10.83	−.000 (.988)	11.86	.010 (.712)	14.33	.072 (.015)	13.66	−.016 (.580)	5.05	−.072 (.015)	5.05	−.004 (.901)	5.38	.047 (.116)
Residence: Rural	12.41	−.009 (.724)	81.06	−.016 (.522)	10.79	−.007 (.804)	11.86	.003 (.906)	3.60	−.054 (.068)	15.47	.004 (.898)	5.17	.040 (.181)	5.06	.017 (.563)	5.26	−.029 (.332)
Two-Parent Family: No	19.63	−.031 (.211)	136.72	−.089 (.000)	11.32	−.100 (.000)	12.24	−.055 (.039)	12.51	−.017 (.571)	19.65	−.027 (.360)	5.09	.005 (.859)	5.06	−.006 (.828)	5.39	−.022 (.462)
Two-Parent Family: Yes	13.88		79.85		10.72		11.77		9.92		13.72		5.10		5.05		5.32	

offenses (their felony assault scale, similar in content to the measure of violent offending used in the present study) were higher for males, African Americans, respondents with lower SES parents, and urban residents, and lower for females, majority ethnic group members, and rural residents. These findings parallel the findings from other studies (Bastian 1993; Bishop and Leiber 2012; Farrington 2012; Leiber and Peck 2015; Pardini et al. 2015; Turner et al. 2006). Elliott et al. (1989) also found rates of general (violent plus property plus public order) offending to be higher for males and urban residents, but more mixed for ethnicity and SES, with some offenses having higher rates for nonminority respondents and respondents with higher parental SES.

Additionally, rates of both general and violent offending are higher for individuals from households with single parents, broken families, and caretaker transitions (Farrington 2012; Pardini et al. 2015; Simons et al. 2012; Turner et al. 2006). Rates of arrest are higher for males, although the difference between females and males has been decreasing over time (Snyder and Sickmund 2006; Steffensmeier et al. 2006), higher for ethnic minorities, particularly African Americans (Bishop and Leiber 2012; D'Alessio and Stolzenberg 2003; Leiber and Peck 2015; Snyder and Sickmund 2006), and based on official rather than self-report data, higher for individuals from lower SES households (Tapia 2010), rural residents (Federal Bureau of Investigation 2019), and divorced or single-parent households (Ellis et al. 2009).

The correlates of violent victimization are similar, with higher rates for males (Bastian 1993; Finkelhor et al. 2005; Snyder and Sickmund 2006), although differences in rates between females and males appear to have been decreasing, based on a comparison of data from the first and second revisions of the National Crime Victimization Survey (NCVS); compare Bureau of Justice Statistics (1988) and Bastian (1993) with Morgan and Truman (2018), and see also Sickmund and Puzzanchera (2014). Finkelhor et al. (2005) report mixed results with respect to ethnicity, and Menard (2012) reports that using the NYSFS and controlling for other predictors, the relationship of ethnicity with violent victimization is significant in adulthood but not earlier in the life course. Results from other studies (Bastian 1993; Bureau of Justice Statistics 1988; Morgan and Truman 2018; Snyder and Sickmund 2006; Turner et al. 2006), however, are consistent in reporting higher rates of violent victimization for ethnic minorities, particularly African Americans. Rates of violent victimization are also higher in low-income households (Bastian 1993; Bureau of Justice Statistics 1988; Morgan and Truman 2018; Turner et al. 2006), urban locations (Bastian 1993; Bureau of Justice Statistics 1988), and single or stepparent households (Turner et al. 2006).

In the present study, adolescent violence victimization is positively associated with adolescent violent offending (r = .412, p = .000), adolescent general offending (r = .527, p = .000), adult violent offending (r = .196, p = .000), and adult arrest frequency (r = .234, p = .000), but not significantly with adult violence victimization (r = .041, p = .141). Adolescent violence perpetration is similarly not significantly associated with adult violence victimization (r = .044, p = .115) but positively associated with adult violence perpetration (r = .116, p = .000) and adult arrest (r = .220, p = .000). Adolescent general offending is not significantly associated with adult violence victimization (r = .013, p = .645) but positively associated with adult violence perpetration (r = .270, p = .000) and arrest (r = .107, p = .000). Adult violence victimization is not significantly associated with adult violence perpetration (r = −.002, p = .939) but weakly positively associated with adult arrest (r = .063, p = .035), and adult violence perpetration is not significantly associated with adult arrest (r = .006, p = .838). The positive association between victimization and offending in adolescence, coupled with the decline in their association in adulthood, has previously been noted for the NYSFS sample by Menard (2012).

As indicated in table 3.4, being male is associated with higher frequencies of adolescent violence victimization (r = .170, p = .000), violence perpetration (r = .105, p = .000), general offending (r = .136, p = .000), and also with adult arrest (r = .134, p = .000). Being male is not, however, significantly associated with adult violence victimization or offending, the latter finding possibly reflecting the trend over time, as noted above, toward decreased differences in rates of female and male violence victimization and perpetration. Minority ethnicity is not significantly associated with adolescent or adult violence victimization or with adolescent general offending but weakly associated with adolescent (but not adult) violence perpetration (r = .062, p = .010) and adult arrest (r = .088, p = .003). Lower parental SES is not associated with any of the victimization or offending outcomes; working class parental SES is weakly positively associated with adolescent violence victimization (r = .089, p = .000) and adult violence perpetration (r = .071, p = .012), but not with the other victimization or offending outcomes; and upper/middle parental SES is weakly negatively associated with adolescent violence victimization (r = −.081, p = .001), violence perpetration (r = −.061, p = .015), and general offending (r = −.059, p = .018), plus adult arrest (r = −.086, p = .005), but not with adult violence victimization or perpetration. A similar pattern is found for two-parent family structure, which has a negative association with adolescent violence victimization (r = −.108, p = .000), violence perpetration (r = −.074, p = .002), and general offending (r = −.084, p = .001), plus adult arrest (r = −.113, p = .000), but not with adult violence victimization or perpetration. Urban/suburban/rural residence is not significantly associated with any of the adolescent victimization or offending outcomes.

Table 3.4 Adolescent Violence Plus General Illegal Behavior, and Adult Violence Plus Arrest

	Adolescent General Violence Victimization Frequency	Adolescent General Violence Perpetration Frequency	Adolescent General Offending Perpetration Frequency	Adult Violence Victimization Frequency	Adult Violence Perpetration Frequency	Adult Arrest Frequency
	Mean / Pearson's r (p)	Mean / Pearson's r (p)	Mean / Pearson's r (p)	Mean / Pearson's r (p)	Mean / Pearson's r (p)	Mean / Pearson's r (p)
Gender:						
Female	3.99	.84	33.69	.22	2.47	.02
Male	9.78	3.56	100.63	.70	2.13	.14
	.170 (.000)	.105 (.000)	.136 (.000)	.040 (.155)	−.005 (.847)	.134 (.000)
Ethnicity:						
Majority	6.96	1.87	67.79	.43	2.76	.06
Minority	7.48	3.85	75.01	.60	.41	.16
	.013 (.603)	.062 (.010)	.012 (.619)	.011 (.684)	−.029 (.299)	.088 (.003)
Parental SES: Lower	6.69	2.79	79.01	.56	.96	.08
	−.013 (.588)	.030 (.220)	.033 (.182)	.014 (.633)	−.040 (.166)	.048 (.122)
Parental SES: Working	9.09	2.79	76.72	.54	5.94	.08
	.089 (.000)	.023 (.348)	.019 (.448)	.007 (.803)	.071 (.012)	.030 (.335)
Parental SES: Upper/Middle	4.59	.89	43.55	.22	.61	.01
	−.081 (.001)	−.061 (.015)	−.059 (.018)	−.023 (.413)	−.031 (.276)	−.086 (.005)
Residence: Urban	7.90	2.66	74.65	.37	1.18	.10
	.022 (.383)	.015 (.559)	.018 (.480)	−.008 (.780)	−.018 (.517)	.024 (.432)
Residence: Suburban	7.24	2.11	68.36	.51	2.37	.07
	.005 (.846)	−.017 (.496)	.008 (.747)	.010 (.716)	.002 (.952)	−.006 (.852)
Residence: Rural	5.97	2.46	51.36	.40	3.55	.06
	−.031 (.223)	.006 (.810)	−.031 (.229)	−.005 (.868)	.017 (.538)	−.018 (.542)
Two-Parent Family:						
No	10.83	4.25	111.25	.53	4.28	.19
Yes	6.21	1.82	59.42	.45	1.86	.05
	−.108 (.000)	−.074 (.002)	−.084 (.001)	−.006 (.844)	−.030 (.289)	−.113 (.000)

ADULT INTIMATE PARTNER VIOLENCE

The concerns with the Conflict Tactics Scale (CTS) as a measure of intimate partner violence (IPV) were raised in the previous chapter, but it bears repeating here that the CTS focuses on measuring the behavior of perpetrators of IPV from the perspective of both victim and perpetrator, but not the physical or other consequences to the victim, in particular, not the degree of injury inflicted; and for the same physically aggressive behaviors by females and males, physical aggression by males, as measured in the CTS, tends to inflict greater physical damage than the same acts of physical aggression by females (Archer 2000; Morse 1995; Tjaden and Thoennes 2000). With that qualification in mind, the present study, like other studies using the CTS, focuses on the behavior not on its consequences, and that must be borne in mind when comparing female and male rates of IPV victimization and perpetration.

The general finding in past studies has been that females are more often the perpetrators and males more often the victims of IPV, but females are more likely than males to suffer serious injury as a result of IPV (Archer 2000; Field and Caetano 2005; Morse 1995; Tjaden and Thoennes 2000). IPV victimization is higher for ethnic minority group members, particularly African Americans, but that relationship is attenuated when controls for other predictors are introduced (Field and Caetano 2005; Tjaden and Thoennes 2000). IPV is also associated with lower education and income in adulthood (Tjaden and Thoennes 2000), lower SES in the family of origin (Costa et al. 2015), and rural residence (Edwards 2014; Rennison et al. 2013). IPV is negatively associated with being raised in a two-parent family (Costa et al. 2015).

In the present study, as shown in table 3.5, CTS serious violence victimization is highly correlated (r = .915, p = .000) with CTS general violence victimization, of which it is a subset, and CTS serious violence perpetration is likewise strongly correlated (r = .811, p = .000) with CTS general violence perpetration, of which it is similarly a subset. CTS general violence victimization is also associated with CTS general violence perpetration (r = .487, p = .000) and CTS serious violence perpetration (r = .474, p = .000). CTS serious violence victimization is associated with CTS general violence perpetration (r = .407, p = .000) and CTS serious violence perpetration (r = .476, p = .000). There are weak positive relationships between being male and experiencing serious (r = .070, p = .046) and general (r = .073, p = .026) CTS victimization, and somewhat stronger and negative relationships between being male and serious (r = −.106, p = .002) and general (r = −.110, p = .002) CTS perpetration. Ethnic minority group membership is associated with adult serious CTS perpetration (r = .096, p = .006) but not with the other three CTS measures. Parental SES and residence are not significantly related to adult IPV as measured by the CTS. Being in a two-parent family in adolescence is not significantly related

Table 3.5 **Adult CTS Violence Victimization and Perpetration**

	Adult CTS Serious Victimization Scale	Adult CTS General Victimization Scale	Adult CTS Serious Perpetration Scale	Adult CTS General Perpetration Scale
	Mean Pearson's r (p)	Mean Pearson's r (p)	Mean Pearson's r (p)	Mean Pearson's r (p)
Gender:				
Female	.21	1.00	.20	1.15
Male	.44	1.80	.03	.46
	.070 (.046)	.078 (.026)	−.106 (.002)	−.110 (.002)
Ethnicity:				
Majority	.29	1.33	.09	.76
Minority	.53	1.72	.31	1.25
	−050 (.156)	.026 (.451)	.096 (.006)	.054 (.119)
Parental SES:	.38	1.60	.13	.97
Lower	.044 (.215)	.048 (.178)	.041 (.249)	.055 (.120)
Parental SES:	.21	1.01	.06	.58
Working	−.037 (.296)	−.041 (.249)	−.041 (.247)	−.044 (.212)
Parental SES:	.27	1.23	.10	.70
Upper/Middle	−.010 (.776)	−.010 (.773)	−.003 (.944)	−.015 (.675)
Residence:	.33	1.55	.19	1.13
Urban	.002 (.954)	.014 (.695)	.041 (.240)	.043 (.216)
Residence:	.33	1.38	.13	.82
Suburban	.008 (.813)	−.002 (.946)	.005 (.889)	−.004 (.900)
Residence:	.28	1.28	.05	.60
Rural	−.012 (.732)	−.010 (.773)	−.045 (.199)	−.036 (.307)
Two-Parent Family:				
No	.55	1.78	.36	1.50
Yes	.28	1.32	.08	.70
	−.059 (.093)	−.032 (.356)	−.133 (.000)	−.094 (.008)

to either of the CTS victimization measures, but being in a two-parent family in adolescence is associated with lower CTS serious (r = −.133, p = .000) and general (r = −.094, p = .008) intimate partner aggression perpetration.

ADOLESCENT EXPOSURE TO VIOLENCE

Prior research, particularly from the National Survey of Children's Exposure to Violence (NatSCEV) and the NCVS, on the distribution of AEV, in the forms of physical abuse by parents, witnessing violence between parents, and exposure to violence in the neighborhood, indicates that AEV is more prevalent among ethnic minorities (Buka et al. 2001; Finkelhor et al. 2005, 2011; Sickmund and Puzzanchera 2014), households with lower income or lower SES parents (Finkelhor et al. 2005, 2007, 2011), urban residents (Buka et al. 2010; Finkelhor et al 2007, 2011; Sickmund and Puzzanchera 2014), and less prevalent for children in two-parent families (Finkelhor et al. 2007, 2011; Sickmund and Puzzanchera 2014). The distribution of AEV by gender, however, varies with females slightly more likely than males to be victims of physical abuse by parents (Hamby et al. 2011); either less (Buka et al. 2010) or slightly less (Hamby et al. 2011) likely to witness parental violence; and less likely to be victims of multiple forms of exposure to violence, including but not limited to exposure to neighborhood violence (Finkelhor et al. 2007, 2011).

Finkelhor et al. (2007, 2011) refer to exposure to multiple forms of exposure to violence as polyvictimization, and in their analysis of thirty-three different types of exposure, found that of the 71% who had experienced any one of the thirty-three different types of victimization, 69% had experienced at least one other type of victimization in the past year, with a mean of three different types of victimization. For the three different types of AEV considered in the present study with the NYSFS sample, 29% reported at least one of the three types of victimization, with 5% reporting two or more types of victimization. In the present study, inconsistent reports of witnessing of parental violence are (as might be expected) negatively associated with consistent reports of witnessing of parental violence ($r = -.143$, $p = .000$), but not significantly associated with frequency of physical abuse by parents ($r = -.000$, $p = .993$) or exposure to neighborhood violence ($r = .022$, $p = .426$). Consistent reports of witnessing parental violence are positively associated with physical abuse ($r = .089$, $p = .001$) but not significantly associated with exposure to neighborhood violence ($r = .009$, $p = .732$). Frequency of physical abuse is not significantly associated with exposure to neighborhood violence ($r = .004$, $p = .892$). Note that these results differ from results using prevalence (yes or no, *whether* it occurs) instead of frequency (number of times it occurs) of parental physical abuse (Covey et al. 2013), for which it was found that prevalence of physical abuse was positively associated with both consistent reports of witnessing interparental violence and with exposure to neighborhood violence.

One of our objectives in the present study is to compare results for frequency (how many times in the past year) of parental physical abuse with past results regarding prevalence of parental physical abuse, both cumulative over a 5-year span (1976–1977 to 1981–1982), to see whether the results are substantially different for frequency and prevalence of parental physical abuse. Table 3.6 presents the distribution of AEV, including both prevalence and frequency of physical abuse (physical assault victimization) by parents, the three categories (none, inconsistent, and consistent) of reported witnessing of violence between parents, and the prevalence of exposure to neighborhood violence. Going directly to the comparison of prevalence and frequency of parental physical abuse, it does appear that the results are different for prevalence and frequency. Prevalence of parental physical abuse is not significantly associated with gender, parental working-class SES, or suburban residence but weakly positively associated with minority ethnicity ($r = .063$, $p = .009$), lower parental SES ($r = .066$, $p = .008$), and urban residence ($r = .066$, $p = .010$), and negatively with upper/middle parental SES ($r = -.093$, $p = .000$), rural residence ($r = -.059$, $p = .021$), and two-parent family structure ($r = -.106$, $p = .000$). If we use a cutoff of $p \leq .050$, frequency of parental physical abuse is not significantly associated with any of gender, ethnicity, parental SES, residence, or two-parent family structure. At least with respect to bivariate relationships, it appears that sociodemographic characteristics are predictive of whether, but not how many times, parental physical abuse occurs.

Gender is not significantly associated with witnessing parental violence or with neighborhood exposure to violence, a result that makes sense when you consider that females and males are embedded within the same families and neighborhoods. Minority ethnicity is weakly negatively associated with reporting witnessing no parental violence ($r = -.084$, $p = .001$), weakly positively associated with inconsistent reports of witnessing parental violence ($r = .066$, $p = .010$), and more strongly positively associated with exposure to neighborhood violence ($r = .243$, $p = .000$). Broadly speaking, SES is negatively associated with witnessing parental violence. Respondents who report witnessing no parental violence are less likely to have lower SES parents ($r = -.104$, $p = .000$) and more likely to have upper or middle SES parents ($r = .114$, $p = .000$), and respondents who give consistent reports of having witnessed parental violence are less likely to have upper or middle SES parents ($r = -.104$, $p = .000$) and more likely to have lower SES parents ($r = .089$, $p = .001$), with no significant associations between working-class SES and witnessing, and no significant associations between inconsistent witnessing and SES. SES is not significantly associated with exposure to neighborhood violence. In something of a reverse of the relationships involving SES, residence is not significantly associated with witnessing parental violence, but exposure to neighborhood violence is higher for individuals who (in adulthood) are or become urban residents ($r = .185$, $p = .000$) and lower for suburban ($r = -.063$, $p = .020$) and rural ($r = -.120$, $p = .000$) residents. Two-parent family structure in adolescence is positively associated with witnessing no parental violence ($r = .183$, $p = .000$), and negatively associated with both consistent reports of witnessing parental violence ($r = -.185$, $p = .000$) and exposure to neighborhood violence ($r = -.187$, $p = .000$).

Table 3.6   Adolescent Exposure to Violence

	Adolescent Parental Physical Abuse Victimization Prevalence (Proportion)	Adolescent Parental Physical Abuse Victimization Frequency (Mean)	Retrospective Witnessing Parental Violence: None (Proportion)	Retrospective Witnessing Parental Violence: Inconsistent (Proportion)	Retrospective Witnessing Parental Violence: Inconsistent (Proportion)	Adolescent Neighborhood Violence Prevalence (Proportion)
Gender:						
Female	.10	1.47	.73	.10	.17	.17
Male	.09	.30	.77	.10	.13	.17
Pearson's r (p)	−.021 (.383)	−.043 (.071)	.045 (.082)	−.006 (.814)	−.050 (.055)	.006 (.831)
Ethnicity:						
Majority	.09	.96	.76	.09	.14	.12
Minority	.13	.41	.67	.14	.18	.35
Pearson's r (p)	.063 (.009)	−.017 (.491)	−.084 (.001)	.066 (.010)	.045 (.081)	.243 (.000)
Parental SES: Lower	.11	.97	.70	.12	.18	.16
Pearson's r (p)	.066 (.008)	.007 (.784)	−.104 (.000)	.044 (.098)	.089 (.001)	.002 (.734)
Parental SES: Working	.10	1.19	.75	.10	.15	.16
Pearson's r (p)	.015 (.541)	.016 (.524)	.005 (.850)	−.008 (.751)	.001 (.970)	−.009 (.734)
Parental SES: Upper/Middle	.05	.24	.83	.08	.09	.17
Pearson's r (p)	−.093 (.000)	−.025 (.312)	.114 (.000)	−.042 (.117)	−.104 (.000)	.007 (.796)
Residence: Urban	.13	.59	.74	.11	.15	.30
Pearson's r (p)	.066 (.010)	−.003 (.902)	−.011 (.678)	.016 (.537)	−.001 (.980)	.185 (.000)
Residence: Suburban	.09	.36	.75	.11	.14	.15
Pearson's r (p)	−.011 (.680)	−.035 (.176)	.008 (.751)	.002 (.930)	−.012 (.642)	−.063 (.020)
Residence: Rural	.06	1.83	.75	.09	.16	.07
Pearson's r (p)	−.059 (.021)	.049 (.057)	.001 (.967)	−.021 (.430)	.017 (.528)	−.120 (.000)
Two-Parent Family:						
No	.16	1.95	.59	.13	.28	.31
Yes	.08	.58	.79	.10	.11	.13
Pearson's r (p)	−.106 (.000)	−.040 (.100)	.183 (.000)	−.044 (.090)	−.185 (.000)	−.187 (.000)

To summarize briefly: (1) parental physical abuse victimization is not significantly related to gender, and nonsignificantly (frequency) to weakly (prevalence) positively related to ethnic minority status, lower parental SES, and urban as opposed to rural residence. (2) Witnessing parental violence is not significantly related to gender or residence, but is positively related to minority ethnicity and lower parental SES, and negatively related to two-parent family structure. (3) Exposure to neighborhood violence is not significantly related to gender or parental SES, but has a relatively strong positive relationship to ethnic minority status and urban residence, and a negative relationship to rural residence and two-parent family structure.

MULTIPLE PROBLEM ADULTS:
THE JOINT DISTRIBUTION OF PROBLEM
OUTCOMES IN ADULTHOOD

In *Multiple Problem Youth*, Elliott et al. (1989) described the joint distribution of substance use, other illegal behavior, and mental health problems in adolescence and young adulthood. Here, we extend that analysis to middle adulthood for the same sample. Partly to make the discussion manageable, and partly to focus on the behaviors that are of greatest concern, we limit the results in this section to the most seriously problematic outcomes in adulthood for all except substance use, and exclude adolescent problem behaviors (which are covered for these respondents in Elliott et al. 1989). For mental health, we include only the joint prevalence of anxiety, depression, and PTSD as a measure of adult mental health problems, plus professional mental health service use, to the exclusion of general mental health service use and life satisfaction. For substance use, we include all five of the adult measures: frequency of both marijuana and hard drug use, which for the historical period in question are as much measures of illegal behavior as of substance use, plus problem use of hard drugs, marijuana, and alcohol. For IPV, we include only serious and not general CTS aggression measures of victimization and perpetration. For more general victimization and offending, we include adult violence victimization and perpetration. Table 3.7 presents the correlations (Pearson's r) among these measures of adult problem outcomes.

Elliott et al. (1989) found a strong association between illicit substance use and other illegal behavior; a similarly strong association between illicit substance use and mental health problems; and a weaker, but still substantial, association between non-substance illegal behavior and mental health problems in adolescence and young adulthood. Turning first to the associations among measures for, broadly, the same concepts (mental health, substance use, violence victimization, and perpetration), table 3.7 indicates that for

Table 3.7 Problem Outcomes in Adulthood

	Mental Health Problems (Anxiety, Depression, PTSD)	Professional Mental Health Service Use	Hard Drug Use	Marijuana Use	Problem Hard Drug Use	Problem Marijuana Use	Problem Alcohol Use	General Violence Victimization	General Violence Perpetration	CTS Serious Victimization	CTS Serious Perpetration
Mental Health Problems	1.000										
Professional Mental Health Service Use	.507 (.000)	1.000									
Hard Drug Use	.139 (.000)	.143 (.000)	1.000								
Marijuana Use	.140 (.000)	.005 (.878)	.181 (.000)	1.000							
Problem Hard Drug Use	.071 (.019)	.083 (.005)	.249 (.000)	.063 (.032)	1.000						
Problem Marijuana Use	.034 (.244)	.031 (.293)	.058 (.047)	.263 (.000)	.232 (.000)	1.000					
Problem Alcohol Use	.134 (.000)	.116 (.000)	.019 (.535)	.153 (.000)	.134 (.000)	.451 (.000)	1.000				
General Violence Victimization	.017 (.552)	.015 (.611)	.001 (.978)	.066 (.024)	.006 (.827)	.036 (.228)	.016 (.592)	1.000			
General Violence Perpetration	-.008 (.767)	.078 (.008)	.402 (.000)	.260 (.000)	.026 (.379)	.079 (.007)	-.011 (.714)	-.002 (.939)	1.000		
CTS Serious Victimization	.148 (.000)	-.006 (.856)	.001 (.983)	.325 (.000)	.050 (.156)	.321 (.000)	.207 (.000)	.016 (.639)	-.010 (.779)	1.000	
CTS Serious Perpetration	.109 (.002)	.009 (.793)	-.014 (.692)	.093 (.008)	.063 (.071)	-.005 (.887)	.120 (.001)	.022 (.539)	-.004 (.910)	.476 (.000)	1.000

adults there is, not unexpectedly, a strong association between the two mental health problem measures: mental health problems (the combined prevalence of anxiety, depression, and PTSD) and professional mental health service use (r = .507, p = .000).

The frequencies of hard drug use and marijuana use are positively associated (r = .181, p = .000), but this association appears to be weaker than that observed in Elliott et al. (1989) for adolescence and young adulthood. Hard drug use frequency is associated with problem hard drug use (r = .249, p = .000) and, weakly, with problem marijuana use (r = .058, p = .047). Marijuana use frequency is associated with problem marijuana use (r = .263, p = .000) and, weakly, with problem hard drug use (r = .063, p = .032). Problem hard drug use is also associated with problem marijuana use (r = .321, p = .000). Adult problem alcohol use is not significantly associated with adult frequency of hard drug use (r = .019, p = .535), but it is significantly positively associated with frequency of marijuana use (r = .153, p = .000), with problem hard drug use (r = .134, p = .000), and particularly strongly with problem marijuana use (r = .451, p = .000) in adulthood.

CTS serious victimization is positively associated with CTS serious perpetration (r = .476, p = .000), suggesting a tendency for some individuals to be both victims and perpetrators in relationships characterized by IPV. Aside from this relationship, however, none of the measures of intimate partner or general violence victimization and perpetration are significantly related to one another. This is particularly notable with regard to the relationship between general violence victimization and perpetration, which tend to be fairly strongly positively associated in adolescence; but as Menard (2012) found, the association between general (non-IPV) victimization and offending diminishes over the life course, and has been largely attenuated by middle adulthood.

Mental health problems are positively associated with frequency of both hard drug use (r = .139, p = .000) and marijuana use (r = .140, p = .000), but these relationships appear to be weaker than those found in Elliott et al. (1989) for adolescence. Mental health problems are weakly associated with problem hard drug use (r = .071, p = .019), not significantly associated with problem marijuana use (r = .034, p = .244), and significantly positively associated with problem alcohol use (r = .134, p = .000). Professional mental health service use is positively associated with frequency of hard drug use (r = .143, p = .000), with problem hard drug use (r = .083, p = .005), and with problem alcohol use (r = .116, p = .000), but not with frequency of marijuana use or with problem marijuana use. Mental health problems are associated with serious IPV victimization (r = .148, p = .000) and perpetration (r = .109, p = .002), but not with general violence victimization or perpetration. Professional mental health service use is weakly associated with general violence perpetration (r = .078, p = .008), but not significantly associated with general violence victimization, or with IPV perpetration or victimization.

Neither hard drug use frequency nor problem hard drug use is significantly associated with serious IPV victimization or perpetration, or with general violence victimization. Serious general violence perpetration is associated with frequency of hard drug use (r = .402, p = .000), as was the case in adolescence (Elliott et al. 1989), but not with problem hard drug use or problem alcohol use. Serious CTS violence victimization is positively, and relatively strongly, associated with marijuana use frequency (r = .325, p = .000) and problem marijuana use (r = .321, p = .000), and not quite as strongly with problem alcohol use (r = .207, p = .000). Serious CTS violence perpetration is associated with marijuana use frequency (r = .093, p = .008), but not with problem marijuana use. Marijuana use frequency is weakly positively associated with general violence victimization (r = .066, p = .024), and more strongly associated with general violence perpetration (r = .260, p = .000), an association weaker than the aforementioned association of hard drug use frequency with general violence perpetration. Problem marijuana use is also weakly associated with general violence perpetration (r = .079, p = .007), but not significantly associated with general violence victimization. Problem alcohol use is significantly associated with neither general violence victimization nor general violence perpetration. To the extent that the present study is comparable with Elliott et al. (1989), the relationship of illicit substance use with non-substance offending appears to be weaker in middle adulthood, but otherwise similar between adolescence and young adulthood (Elliott et al. 1989) and middle adulthood (in the present study).

SUMMARY

The bivariate relationships presented in the present chapter were for the full sample, female and male combined. In the following chapters, we move to multivariate models and examine each set of adult outcomes in turn, this time separately by gender, to further examine the impacts of AEV on adult outcomes. On a technical note, observe that all of the relationships that satisfied the (admittedly arbitrary) criterion for substantive significance, a correlation greater or equal to .100 in magnitude, also satisfied the (equally arbitrary but generally accepted) criterion for statistical significance (p ≤ .05), and in fact were statistically significant at p ≤ .002.

Focusing on the findings that are most closely parallel between the present study and Elliott et al. (1989) indicates similarity in the joint distribution of problem behaviors in adolescence/early adulthood and middle adulthood. Differences in general violence perpetration (the felony assault index) were significant for prevalence but not frequency of felony assault in adolescence, and differences in general violence perpetration frequency are not significant in middle adulthood. Both prevalence and frequency of hard drug and marijuana use were significantly associated with prevalence of self-reported mental health problems in adolescence, and frequency of hard drug and marijuana use are significantly associated with the combined prevalence of anxiety, depression, and PTSD in middle adulthood. Both hard drug and marijuana users had significantly higher prevalence and frequency of violence perpetration in adolescence, and both hard drug use and marijuana use frequency are significantly associated with violence perpetration in adulthood. Even though the measures are not identical, the patterns in adolescence and adulthood are closely parallel.

Going beyond the findings in Elliott et al. (1989), the present study indicates that in middle adulthood, mental health problems are more closely associated with frequency than with problem use of hard drugs and marijuana (although they are associated with problem alcohol use), and more with IPV than with violence more generally. IPV does not appear to have a strong association with general violence for either victimization or perpetration, suggesting that the two are relatively distinct phenomena in middle adulthood. With the exception of a weak relationship with marijuana use frequency, general violence victimization appears to be largely unrelated to the other problem behavior outcomes in middle adulthood, but IPV victimization appears to be more strongly associated with marijuana use and problem use, with problem alcohol use, and with mental health problems, than does more general violent victimization.

More broadly, returning to the results for sociodemographic correlates of AEV and adult outcomes, the patterns of association vary, sometimes markedly, by outcome. Where differences are significant, adult SES outcomes are generally more favorable for males than for females, ethnic majority rather than ethnic minority group members, individuals who were in two-parent family structures in adolescence, suburban residents, and individuals with higher SES parents in adolescence. Adult mental health problems are more likely to be experienced by females and by individuals who had other than two-parent family structures in adolescence, while adolescent mental health problems are not significantly associated with gender, but are more prevalent for ethnic minority group members, respondents with lower SES parents, urban residents, and again individuals who had other than two-parent family structures in adolescence. Frequency of substance use in both adolescence and adulthood, and problem substance use in adulthood, is associated with being male and, in adolescence but not adulthood, with ethnic majority rather than minority group membership, and negatively associated with two-parent family structure for frequency of marijuana use, problem drug use, and problem alcohol use.

Here as in past studies, IPV victimization appears to be higher and IPV perpetration lower for males than for females, and perpetration is lower for individuals from two-parent family structures in adolescence. The qualifications concerning the use of the CTS to measure IPV have been noted earlier, but once again, the pattern appears to be that, in simple terms, females hit more often but males hit harder, resulting in higher rates of perpetration for females but, if we were able to assess the actual physical harm in each assault, a higher rate of more serious injury for female victims. Given the present data, we are not able to adequately assess the results (physical damage), only the behavior, across all incidents of IPV. General violence victimization and perpetration in adolescence, and arrest in adulthood, are higher for males and lower for individuals from two-parent family backgrounds, and arrest is higher for ethnic minorities and individuals from upper or middle parental SES backgrounds. Finally, AEV is not significantly associated with gender, but is associated with minority ethnicity, lower as opposed to upper or middle parental SES, urban residence for exposure to violence in the neighborhood, and negatively associated with two-parent family structure in adolescence. Comparing the different predictors with one another, a striking aspect of these findings is the apparent widespread beneficial effect of having a two-parent family structure in adolescence for many outcomes in both adolescence and adulthood.

Chapter 4

Adolescent Exposure to Violence and Adult Socioeconomic Statuses

Although there is no theory specifically formulated or proposed to explain the impact of adolescent exposure to violence (AEV) on adult socioeconomic status (SES), the combination of Agnew's (1985, 1992) general strain theory and Merton's (1938) anomie theory, as described in chapter 1, is particularly useful in understanding the link between AEV and adult SES outcomes. Agnew's general strain theory provides the overarching description of the type of strain posed by AEV: exposure to noxious stimuli, whether that be direct physical victimization, witnessing violence between parents, or exposure to violence in the neighborhood. Merton's modes of adaptation help us understand how this exposure to noxious stimuli might affect such outcomes as marriage, employment, education, income, and net worth.

Most often in discussions of anomie theory, the focus has been on the use of illegitimate means such as crime to achieve the desired goals (keeping the goals but rejecting the societal norms or proscriptions on illegal behavior, an adaptation Merton called innovation). Less attention has been paid to what Merton called retreatism, rejecting both the goals and the societal norms regarding the means of achieving those goals, an adaptation Merton suggested might be manifested in activities such as alcohol and drug abuse. Even less attention has been paid to the adaptation Merton called ritualism, in which individuals continue to abide by social norms regarding legitimate means, but lower their aspirations or ambitions and abandon the culturally approved goals for success. Both retreatism and ritualism suggest reduced effort to achieve success, which would result in lower SES in the form of lower income, education, and other positively valued social statuses.

Based on the combination of general strain and anomie theory, we would expect the strain of exposure to violence in the home or neighborhood to increase not only (and perhaps not even primarily) the likelihood of innovation, the mode of adaptation most associated with crime, but also the likelihood of modes of adaptation (retreatism and ritualism) involving rejection of conventional success goals and hence more likely to result in lower or less desirable SES outcomes (employment, marriage, education, income, wealth). Ritualists would abandon the conventional goals (income and wealth, possibly marriage). Retreatists would abandon those goals and also the means (education, employment) of achieving them. The strains of exposure to violence in the home and neighborhood (and exposure to violence more generally) should therefore result on average in lower or less desirable SES.

Research on the relationship between AEV and SES has most often focused on socioeconomic factors as determinants of neglect, maltreatment, and abuse, rather than on the effects of AEV on adult SES (Bowker et al. 1988; Garbarino and Crouter 1978; Kruttschnitt et al. 1994; Siegel and Williams 2003; Straus and Gelles 1990). Adverse childhood experiences (ACEs), including but not limited to AEV, have been linked to higher levels of unemployment and household poverty (Liu et al. 2013; Metzler et al. 2017). Schurer and Trajkovski (2018, 1–2) suggested that ACEs "capture the key risk factors that interfere with a child's lifetime economic potential, independent of a child's access to material or educational resources" and concluded that irrespective of parental SES, ACEs affect children's developmental pathways and adult socioeconomic outcomes.

More specific to AEV, research by Covey et al. (2013) on the present sample found that physical abuse by parents in adolescence was associated with higher odds in adulthood of being never married or formerly married as opposed to currently married, and of having lower educational attainment, lower income, and lower net worth. Adolescent exposure to neighborhood violence was negatively related to adult employment, and witnessing parental violence was negatively related to adult income and net worth. Currie and Widom (2010) found that adults with documented histories of childhood abuse or neglect were less likely to have graduated high school, and more likely to be unemployed or underemployed, to have lower earnings and assets, and to be divorced or separated. Several studies have found a higher risk for dropout, failure to complete high school, or declines in adult academic attainment for abused or neglected children (Currie and Widom 2010; Perez and Widom 1994; Reynolds et al. 2004), physically abused youth (Lansford et al. 2007), and children exposed to domestic violence (Herrenkohl et al. 2008).

In a systematic review of longitudinal research on the impact of child (including adolescent) maltreatment (including exposure to violence), Bunting et al. (2018) found that maltreatment was associated with a range of negative economic outcomes, including in particular a consistent negative relationship between experiencing physical abuse in childhood or adolescence and employment and income in adulthood. Zielinski (2009) reported that compared to non-victims of child maltreatment (physical abuse, sexual abuse, and severe neglect), victims of child maltreatment were twice as likely to be unemployed and twice as likely to have incomes below the poverty line. Menard (2002) found that violent victimization in adolescence led to a variety of negative outcomes in adulthood, including reduced odds of successful transition from adolescence to adulthood, defined in part in terms of employment or financial stability. Macmillan (2000) studied the relationship between adolescent criminal victimization and adult socioeconomic outcomes, and found that adolescent victimization from any type of violence resulted in a decrease of over 1 dollar per hour in adult wages, plus reduced educational and occupational attainment. Macmillan and Hagan (2004) reported that adolescent victimization led to lower adult occupational status and reduced the odds of employment in adulthood by 51%.

Common to many, but not all, of these studies is the focus on one type of violence experience (most often physical abuse or more general maltreatment) to the exclusion of other forms of exposure to violence (particularly exposure to neighborhood violence, but also witnessing parental violence), or one type of SES (particularly educational attainment) as opposed to multiple measures of SES. Correspondingly, there is a need to increase our understanding of how these three different aspects of AEV influence different measures of adult SES. The present chapter seeks to address this by examining the long-term impacts of AEV on marital status, educational attainment, employment, income, and wealth (more specifically, net worth), for respondents in middle adulthood. Here we expand on the results in Covey et al. (2013) by considering cumulative frequency (how many times) instead of prevalence (zero versus one or more times) of parental physical abuse over the first five waves of the study, by including adolescent violence victimization as an additional predictor, and by estimating separate models for females and males, as suggested from the literature on gender differences in responses to maltreatment and abuse reviewed in chapter 1.

Based on the theory and literature reviewed in chapter 1, we hypothesize that (a) being married as opposed to being never married or having experienced marital dissolution (being formerly married), (b) educational attainment, as measured by highest level of education completed, (c) being employed, (d) income, and (e) wealth, as measured by net worth, will all be negatively related to at least one of (1) physical abuse during adolescence, (2) witnessing parental violence, (3) being exposed to violence in the neighborhood during adolescence, and (4) adolescent general violence victimization. We have some idea from Covey et al. (2013) which types of AEV are predictive of which SES outcomes. However, those empirical results do not constitute a sufficient basis for expecting the same results with a change in two of the major predictors (in the present study, using frequency instead of

prevalence of parental abuse, and adding adolescent general violence victimization as a new predictor), plus the estimation in the present study, but not in
Covey et al. (2013), of separate models for females and males.

ANALYTICAL APPROACH

The analyses in this chapter parallel the analyses in Covey et al. (2013), but
to reiterate, given the literature suggesting that the impacts of exposure to
violence may be different for females and males, the present analyses are
performed separately by gender. As described in chapter 1, the analysis here
(and in chapters 5–8) begins with a selective examination of bivariate relationships of AEV to the adult outcomes, before moving to our main focus, the
multivariate models for the adult outcomes, presented separately by gender.

Educational attainment (highest grade completed) is a slightly truncated ratio
scale variable (all graduate education is given the same score, 17) for which
ordinary least squares multiple regression analysis (see, for example, Cohen
et al. 2003) should be appropriate. For the remaining outcome variables in this
chapter, three different types of logistic regression analysis (see, for example,
Menard 2010) are used. Employment is a dichotomous or binary variable, for
which binary logistic regression analysis is appropriate. Income and net worth
are categorical ordinal outcomes, for which ordinal logistic regression using
the cumulative logit model is used. Marital status is a nominal variable with
three categories, for which polytomous nominal logistic regression using the
reference category multinomial logit model is used. For controls for SES in
adolescence, measures specific to the adolescents themselves are either not
available or not meaningful, because so few adolescents have entered into
marriage or made more than preliminary choices about participation in the
labor force, and because there is a great deal of uniformity until middle adolescence, and a lack of finality even in late adolescence, regarding educational
attainment. For this reason, parental SES, one of the control variables used in
all of the analyses in the present study, is also the adolescent control variable
used in the analysis of adult SES. It is also reasonable to consider being in an
intact two-parent family in adolescence as a control variable in the analysis of
adult marital status, given the tendency of individuals to replicate their parents' patterns of marital stability or instability (Wolfinger 2000).

BIVARIATE RELATIONSHIPS

Figure 4.1 illustrates the relationships of AEV to the five SES outcome
variables. AEV is coded "no" for respondents who reported neither parental

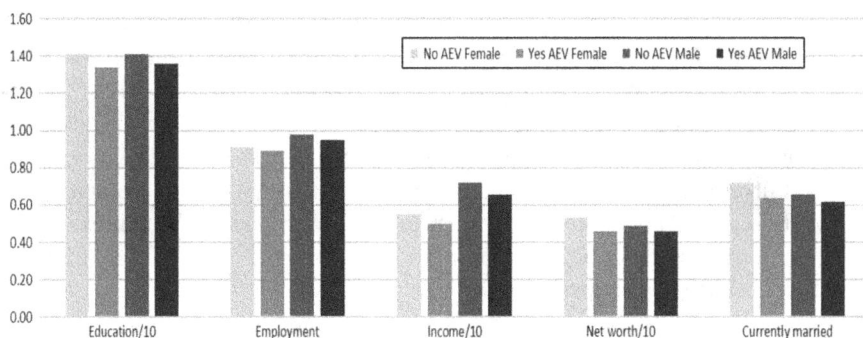

Figure 4.1   AEV and Adult Socioeconomic Statuses. *Source:* Created by the authors.

physical abuse nor witnessing parental violence nor exposure to neighborhood violence nor general violence victimization in adolescence, and "yes" for respondents who reported any one or more of those forms of AEV. The figure is split by gender, going (from left to right within each outcome) from females who reported no AEV to females who reported some (yes) AEV, to males who reported no AEV, and to males who reported some (yes) AEV. As noted above, employment and marital status are prevalence measures, coded zero or one, while the other three measures are ordinal or interval scales with a much wider range of values. To make the chart easier to read, given these different scales, the scores of education, income, and net worth have been divided by 10. The informal picture given by figure 4.1 is clear: for both females and males, education, employment, income, net worth, and the likelihood of being married are all lower for individuals who have experienced AEV than for those who have not.

Breaking down these relationships by specific types of AEV as well as gender, bivariate correlations indicate that adult educational attainment for females is significantly negatively related to parental physical abuse ($r = -.105$, $p = .007$), consistent witnessing of parental violence ($r = -.079$, $p = .046$), and general violence victimization ($r = -.134$, $p = .000$) in adolescence. Similarly, adult educational attainment for males is significantly negatively related to parental physical abuse ($r = -.112$, $p = .005$), consistent witnessing of parental violence (more strongly for males than for females, $r = -.119$, $p = .003$), and, not as strongly for males as for females, general violence victimization ($r = -.082$, $p = .039$) in adolescence. Also, minority ethnic group members have lower adult educational attainment than majority group members, and the difference is more pronounced for females ($r = -.246$, $p = .000$) than for males ($r = -.104$, $p = .008$). Gender differences are smaller for the impact of parental SES on adult educational attainment, with upper/middle parental SES having a positive relationship ($r = .388$, p = .000 for females; r = .376, p = .000 for males), and lower parental SES having a negative relationship (r = −.348, p = .000 for females; r = −.340, p = .000 for males), with adult educational attainment. Urban and rural residence do not appear to be significantly related to adult educational attainment for females, but rural residence is negatively associated (r = −.158, p = .000) with adult educational attainment for males. Finally, for both females and males, being in a two-parent family in adolescence appears to be positively associated with adult educational attainment (r = .160, p = .000 for females; r = .145, p = .000 for males).

Adult employment is significantly negatively associated only with parental physical abuse for females (r = −.101, p = .010) and with adolescent exposure to neighborhood violence for males (r = −.126, p = .002). For females, none of the sociodemographic predictors is significantly associated with adult employment. For males, adult employment is negatively associated with minority ethnicity (r = −.156, p = .000) and positively associated with upper/middle parental SES (r = .082, p = .042), suggesting that ethnicity and socioeconomic background are more important for males than for females as influences on adult employment status.

Adult income is significantly negatively related to parental physical abuse (r = −.107, p = .014 for females; r = −.112, p = .000 for males) and to consistent reports of having witnessed parental violence (r = −.092, p = .005 for females; r = −.066, p = .028 for males), and significantly but weakly (r = −.066, p = .028 for females) or not quite significantly (r = −.051, p = .089 for males) to adolescent general violence victimization. For males but not for females, adult income is significantly negatively related to minority ethnicity (r = −.238, p = .000), and positively related to having been in a two-parent family at the beginning of the study (r = .191, p = .000). For females it is weakly but significantly negatively related (r = −.077, p = .023) to rural residence, and for males it is significantly negatively related (r = −.133, p = .000) to urban residence (and we know from chapter 3 that income tends to be highest among suburban residents). For both females and males, income is higher for respondents from higher parental SES backgrounds (r = .145, p = .000 for females; r = .273, p = .000 for males) and lower for respondents from lower parental SES backgrounds (r = −.153, p = .000 for females; r = −.216, p = .000).

Adult net worth is significantly negatively related to parental physical abuse, more for females (r = −.172, p = .000) than for males (r = −.112, p = .000). It is also negatively related to consistent (but not inconsistent) reports of witnessing parental violence, again more so for females (r = −.138, p = .000) than for males (r = −.078, p = .021), to adolescent general violence victimization (r = −.120, p = .000 for females; r = −.100, p = .001 for males), and, for females but not for males, to exposure to neighborhood violence (r = −.123, p = .001). For both females and males, adult net worth is lower for ethnic minorities (r = −.188, p = .000 for females; r = −.161, p = .000 for males), urban residents (r = −.103, p = .008 for females; r = −.101, p = .006 for males), and respondents from lower parental SES backgrounds (r = −.204, p = .000 for females; r = −.118, p = .001 for males), and higher for respondents from higher parental SES backgrounds (r = .135, p = .000 for females; r = .174, p = .000 for males) and respondents who were in two-parent families (r = .197, p = .000 for females; r = .120, p = .001 for males) at the beginning of the study.

Being currently married is significantly negatively related to physical abuse (r = −.173, p = .000 for females; r = −.148, p = .000 for males) and to exposure to neighborhood violence (r = −.087, p = .033 for females; r = −.104, p = .011 for males). Being formerly married is significantly positively associated with parental physical abuse (r = .146, p = .000 for females; r = .129, p = .001 for males) and adolescent general violence victimization (r = .113, p = .004 for females; r = .095, p = .016 for males). Also, for both females and males, being never married is positively associated with exposure to neighborhood violence (r = .136, p = .001 for females; r = .137, p = .001 for males). Neither consistent nor inconsistent reports of witnessing parental violence, however, are significantly associated with marital status in middle adulthood for either females or males.

There is an extensive web of relationships between adolescent socioeconomic background and adult marital status. For both females and males, being currently married is negatively associated with minority ethnicity (r = −.200, p = .000 for females; r = −.176, p = .000 for males) and urban residence (r = −.223, p = .000 for females; r = −.135, p = .001 for males), and being never married is positively associated with minority ethnicity (r = .243, p = .000 for females; r = .144, p = .000 for males) and urban residence (r = .219, p = .000 for females; r = .159, p = .000 for males). Also, for both females (r = .091, p = .021) and males (r = .093, p = .020), being currently married is weakly significantly positively associated with rural residence. For females but not for males, urban residence is also positively associated with being formerly married (r = .081, p = .040), and rural residence is negatively associated with being never married (r = −.135, p = .001). For females, parental SES is not significantly associated with adult marital status, but for males, upper/middle parental SES is positively (r = .098, p = .016) and lower parental SES is negatively (r = −.116, p = .004) associated with being currently married, and lower parental SES is positively associated with being formerly married (r = .109, p = .007). For both females and males, having been in a two-parent family at the beginning of the study is significantly positively associated with being currently married (r = .155, p = .000 for females; r = .115, p = .004 for males), and negatively associated with being formerly married (r = −.085, p = .033 for females; r = −.105, p = .108 for males) in middle adulthood. Additionally, for females, having been in a two-parent family is negatively associated (r = −.118, p = .003) with being never married.

In general, the bivariate results indicate that AEV is negatively associated with the attainment of a variety of adult SES for both females and males. They also indicate that physical victimization has the most pervasive negative effects, followed by consistent witnessing of parental violence, then exposure to neighborhood violence. Reinforcing the importance of the distinction between consistent and inconsistent reports of parental violence, inconsistent reports of parental violence are not significantly related to any of the adult socioeconomic outcomes. The patterns of association appear to be very similar for females and males. If we were to rely solely on the bivariate relationships, we would conclude that the hypothesis that AEV has a negative impact on the attainment of adult SES is well-supported in the present study. It is important, however, to go beyond the bivariate relationships to see whether those associations persist when controlling for other variables, particularly the ascribed adolescent SES variables of parental SES, ethnicity, and (for marital status) single-parent family structure.

MULTIVARIATE ANALYSIS

For some readers, it may be useful here to explain the structure of the tables for the multivariate analysis results used in chapters 4–8. In each table, the first column presents the names of the predictors represented in each row. The second column presents the standardized coefficient, a measure of the strength of the *direct effect* of the predictor on the outcome (the relationship of the predictor with the outcome, controlling for the other predictors in the model). As noted in the previous chapter, for the standardized coefficients, a rough guideline is that a coefficient with an absolute value (ignoring plus or minus signs) of less than .100 is quite weak, while coefficients with larger absolute values (e.g., .278 or −.187, again ignoring the minus sign) indicate stronger relationships. The third column presents the unstandardized coefficient, which is used in calculating the predicted value of the outcome variable, and is also used in calculating the statistical significance of the relationship. In tables involving logistic regression (binary, ordinal, and polytomous nominal), the odds ratio, a different way of presenting an unstandardized coefficient that provides exactly the same statistical information but in a different format as the unstandardized coefficient (Menard 2010), is also presented. The standard error is used in calculating statistical significance, and is presented in the fourth column. The final column in each table presents the statistical significance of the relationship, which is assessed in the same way as statistical significance in chapter 3, with $p \leq .05$ as the traditional cutoff for a statistically significant relationship, and $p > .05$ typically being interpreted as nonsignificant. It is worth repeating the caution that this cutoff is arbitrary, and in discussing the results, we will sometimes consider p values that may almost, but not quite, meet the traditional criterion for statistical significance. For more detailed discussions of standardized coefficients, unstandardized coefficients, odds ratios, standard errors, and statistical significance, see, for example, Cohen et al. (2003) and Menard (2010).

In columns 2–5, results are presented for females/males, that is, results for females before the "/" and results for males after the "/." At the bottom of each table, either R^2 for OLS regression, R_L^2 for binary or polytomous nominal logistic regression, or Kendall's τ_b^2 for ordinal logistic regression is presented. The easiest way to think of R^2, R_L^2, and τ_b^2 is as a squared correlation (at the appropriate level of measurement) between the actual observed value and the predicted value (based on the unstandardized coefficients) of the outcome variable. This squared correlation gives the *explained variance*, or for logistic regression the *explained variation* (see Menard 2010 for the distinction) in the outcome variable. This is the proportion (or, if multiplied by 100, the percentage) by which some measure of the error of prediction, aggregated over all of the cases, is reduced by using, as opposed to not using, the information provided by the predictor variables when predicting the values of the outcome variable. Also presented at the end of each table are the statistical significance of R^2, R_L^2, or τ_b^2, plus the number of cases used in the analysis. All of the tables in chapters 4–8 follow this same format.

Table 4.1 presents the OLS regression results for adult educational attainment for females and males, respectively. For females, significant predictors of *lower* educational attainment (negative relationships) include adolescent general violence victimization, minority ethnicity, and lower parental SES. The one significant predictor of *higher* educational attainment (positive relationship) is upper/middle parental SES. Controlling for the other variables in the model for females, the relationships of educational attainment to parental physical abuse, consistent reports of witnessing of parental violence, and two-parent family, although significant in the bivariate analysis, are not statistically significant in the multivariate model, suggesting that their influence may be spurious with or mediated by other variables in the model. Based on the standardized coefficients in table 4.1, parental SES and minority ethnicity are the strongest predictors of adult educational attainment for females. For females, 21.4% of the variance ($R^2 = .214$, $p = .000$) in adult educational attainment is explained by the predictors in the model.

For males, significant predictors of *lower* educational attainment include parental physical abuse, lower parental SES, and rural residence, while the

Table 4.1 OLS Regression Results for Educational Attainment (Highest Grade Completed)

Predictors	Coefficients: Female/Male			
	Standardized Coefficient (b*)	Unstandardized Coefficient (b)	Standard Error of b	Statistical Significance (p)
Parental Physical Abuse	−.018/−.107	−.070/−.656	.165/.246	.671/.008
Witnessing Parental Violence (Inconsistent)	.006/−.049	.042/−.342	.253/.278	.868/.219
Witnessing Parental Violence (Consistent)	−.005/−.061	−.028/−.418	.232/.272	.905/.124
Neighborhood Violence	.069/.005	.405/.029	.228/.262	.077/.913
Adolescent General Violence Victimization	−.089/−.045	−.178/−.087	.083/.078	.033/.266
Minority Ethnicity	−.132/−.007	−.756/−.043	.241/.252	.002/.863
Upper/Middle Parental SES	.278/.244	1.364/1.291	.212/.243	.000/.000
Lower Parental SES	−.158/−.187	−.671/−.846	.186/.209	.000/.000
Urban	−.001/.039	−.005/.221	.215/.236	.983/.350
Rural	−.008/−.138	−.048/−.795	.220/.231	.828/.001
Two-Parent Family Structure	.047/.052	.254/.327	.225/.261	.258/.211
Constant	NA/NA	13.692/13.994	.274/.333	.000/.000

Note: R^2 = .214, p = .000, N = 573 for females; R^2 = .211, p = .000, N = 547 for males. NA = not applicable.

only significant predictor of *higher* educational attainment is upper/middle parental SES. Controlling for other variables in the model for males, the relationships of educational attainment to consistent reports of witnessing parental violence, adolescent general violence victimization, minority ethnicity, and two-parent family are not statistically significant in the multivariate model, suggesting that although they were significant in the bivariate analysis, the influence of those variables may be spurious with or mediated by other variables in the model. Based on the standardized coefficients in table 4.1, parental SES plus, in adulthood, rural residence are the strongest predictors of adult educational attainment, but in contrast to the results for females, parental physical abuse is also one of the stronger predictors, having a standardized coefficient greater than .100 in absolute magnitude, with b* = −.107. For males, similarly to females, 21.1% of the variance in adult educational attainment is explained by the predictors in the model. Direct physical victimization in adolescence is thus significantly predictive of lower adult educational attainment for both females and males. There is, however, a difference by gender, insofar as it is general violence victimization for females, and specifically parental physical abuse for males, that are predictive of lower adult educational attainment.

Table 4.2 presents the binary logistic regression results for adult employment. Significant predictors of *lower* adult employment for females include only parental physical abuse and exposure to neighborhood violence in adolescence, both with standardized coefficients close to .100. The bivariate relationship of adult employment with exposure to neighborhood violence was not significant, so it appears that there may be a suppressor effect (the significant impact of a predictor is evident only in the presence of controls for other variables) in the relationship of adult employment with adolescent exposure to neighborhood violence. Explained variation is assessed using R_L^2, a likelihood ratio measure of the accuracy of prediction of a logistic regression model, which indicates that the explained variation in adult employment using the predictors in the model is only 5%.

The only significant direct effect on adult employment for males is the negative effect of exposure to neighborhood violence, and that effect appears to be weak with a standardized coefficient (b*) of only −.074, but the overall explanatory power of the predictors for adult employment is a respectable 12.5%. The bivariate relationships of adult employment to minority ethnicity and upper/middle parental SES were significant, but in the multivariate model of table 4.2, those relationships are not statistically significant, suggesting that they are spurious with or mediated by other variables in the multivariate model. In contrast to the bivariate results, then, AEV does have a negative effect on adult employment, with exposure to neighborhood violence mattering for both females and males, but parental physical abuse mattering for females and not for males.

Table 4.3 presents the ordinal logistic regression results for adult income. Briefly, the constants (cutpoints) at the bottom of the table are used in calculating the model, but convey no substantive information about the relative importance of the predictors in the model. The only significant predictors of adult income for females are upper/middle and lower parental SES, both with coefficients close to .100 in absolute value, and in the expected direction that higher parental SES in adolescence is predictive of higher income in adulthood. Significant bivariate correlations were found for adult income with parental physical abuse, consistent reports of witnessing parental violence, and rural residence, but controlling for the other predictors in the model, these relationships are not significant in the multivariate model, suggesting that the relationships for females of adult income with parental physical abuse, consistent reports of witnessing parental violence, and rural residence are spurious with or mediated by other variables in the model in table 4.3.

Table 4.2   Binary Logistic Regression Results for Employment

Predictors	Coefficients: Female/Male			
	Standardized Coefficient (b*)	Unstandardized Coefficient (b) [Odds ratio]	Standard Error of b	Statistical Significance (p)
Parental Physical Abuse	−.108/−.015	−.553/−.214 [.575/.808]	.219/.481	.012/.656
Witnessing Parental Violence (Inconsistent)	.009/−.031	.074/−.487 [1.077/.615]	.474/.577	.876/.399
Witnessing Parental Violence (Consistent)	−.053/−.004	−.389/−.060 [.678/.942]	.388/.632	.316/.925
Neighborhood Violence	−.099/−.073	−.757/−1.055 [.469/.348]	.361/.518	.036/.042
Adolescent General Violence Victimization	.028/−.072	.074/−.202 [1.076/.817]	.152/.195	.627/.300
Minority Ethnicity	.024/−.074	.177/−.980 [1.194/.375]	.450/.526	.694/.063
Upper/middle Parental SES	−.032/.106	−.201/1.272 [.818/3.566]	.404/1.113	.618/.253
Lower Parental SES	−.084/−.056	−.462/−.578 [.630/.561]	.340/.522	.175/.268
Urban	.099/.041	.666/.534 [1.947/1.706]	.456/.585	.144/.361
Rural	−.035/.022	−.256/.291 [.774/1.337]	.359/.667	.475/.663
Two-Parent Family Structure	−.034/−.009	−.241/−.136 [.786/.873]	.409/.578	.556/.814
Constant	NA/NA	2.786/4.309 [16.210/74.382]	.516/.825	.000/.000

Note: R_L^2 = .050, p = .059, N = 573 for females; R_L^2 = .125, p = .014, N = 546 for males. NA = not applicable.

Following Menard (2010), explained variation is assessed using Kendall's τ_b^2, and explained variation in adult income for females is very weak, 2.9%, despite being statistically significant (p = .000).

In contrast to the model for females, the explained variation is higher at 9.4%, and more of the predictors have significant relationships with adult income, for males. Significant predictors of *lower* adult income include parental physical abuse, adolescent general violence victimization, minority ethnicity, lower parental SES, and rural residence. Upper/middle parental SES and urban residence are significantly predictive of *higher* adult income. Relative to the bivariate relationships, two that were significant (consistent reports of witnessing parental violence and two-parent family) are not significant in the

Table 4.3   Ordinal Logistic Regression Results for Income

Predictors	Coefficients: Female/Male			
	Standardized Coefficient (b*)	Unstandardized Coefficient (b) [Odds Ratio]	Standard Error of b	Statistical Significance (p)
Parental Physical Abuse	−.073/−.096	−.279/−.498 [.756/.608]	.169/.214	.098/.020
Witnessing Parental Violence (Inconsistent)	.023/−.039	.141/−.230 [1.152/.795]	.247/.258	.568/.372
Witnessing Parental Violence (Consistent)	−.067/−.034	−.348/−.198 [.706/.820]	.210/.240	.098/.410
Neighborhood Violence	.013/.030	.070/.161 [1.072/1.174]	.224/.234	.755/.493
Adolescent General Violence Victimization	−.017/−.087	−.032/−.138 [.969/.871]	.079/.070	.687/.047
Minority Ethnicity	.002/−.380	.012/−.723 [1.012/.485]	.225/.229	.958/.002
Upper/Middle Parental SES	.099/.175	.445/.777 [1.560/2.174]	.204/.231	.030/.000
Lower Parental SES	−.107/−.128	−.417/−.486 [.659/.615]	.173/.185	.016/.009
Urban	.036/−.100	.174/−.478 [1.190/.620]	.206/.209	.396/.022
Rural	−.058/−.090	−.299/−.433 [.741/.648]	.203/.202	.141/.032
Two-Parent Family Structure	.010/.082	.050/.437 [1.051/1.548]	.207/.232	.809/.059
Constants:	NA/NA		NA/NA	NA/NA
cutpoint 1		−2.480/−3.675		
cutpoint 2		−1.698/−3.153		
cutpoint 3		−1.235/−2.575		
cutpoint 4		−.774/−2.126		
cutpoint 5		−.298/−1.615		
cutpoint 6		.414/−.868		
cutpoint 7		1.386/.166		
cutpoint 8		2.662/1.104		
cutpoint 9		3.559/1.962		

Note: $\tau_b^2 = .029$, p = .000, N = 563 for females; $\tau_b^2 = .094$, p = .000, N = 536 for males. NA = not applicable.

multivariate model (although two-parent family comes close at p = .059), suggesting spurious or mediated effects; and one that was not significant (rural residence) emerges as significant in the multivariate model, suggesting a suppressor effect. For females, then, AEV is not significantly predictive of adult income. For males, direct experiences of physical violence in adolescence, both in the form of general violence victimization and more specifically parental physical abuse, are predictive of lower income in adulthood.

Table 4.4 presents the ordinal logistic regression results for adult net worth. For females, significant predictors, all of *lower* adult net worth, include parental physical abuse, consistent reports of having witnessed parental violence, and lower parental SES. For exposure to neighborhood violence and adolescent general violence victimization, both of which are significant

Table 4.4   Ordinal Logistic Regression Results for Net Worth

Predictors	Coefficients: Female/Male			
	Standardized Coefficient (b*)	Unstandardized Coefficient (b)/ Odds Ratio	Standard Error of b	Statistical Significance (p)
Parental Physical Abuse	−.116/−.045	−.409/−.231 [.664/.793]	.187/.211	.028/.272
Witnessing Parental Violence (Inconsistent)	.005/−.047	.028/−.272 [1.029/.761]	.247/.250	.909/.276
Witnessing Parental Violence (Consistent)	−.095/−.032	−.478/−.184 [.620/.831]	.230/.246	.038/.452
Neighborhood Violence	−.073/.006	−.392/.034 [.675/1.035]	.229/.247	.087/.890
Adolescent General Violence Victimization	−.086/−.093	−.155/−.149 [.856/.862]	.083/.070	.062/.033
Minority Ethnicity	−.060/−.101	−.308/−.500 [.735/.607]	.242/.236	.203/.034
Upper/Middle Parental SES	.029/.113	.127/.500 [1.136/1.648]	.209/.223	.542/.025
Lower Parental SES	−.151/−.071	−.581/−.271 [.560/.752]	.182/.189	.001/.150
Urban	−.071/−.101	−.332/−.480 [.717/.619]	.220/.217	.130/.027
Rural	−.053/.045	−.266/−.098 [.767/.907]	.209/.205	.203/.633
Two-Parent Family Structure	.071/.029	.347/.237 [1.415/1.268]	.219/.235	.113/.314
Constants:	NA/NA		NA/NA	NA/NA
cutpoint 1		−3.570/−2.820		
cutpoint 2		−2.622/−2.153		
cutpoint 3		−1.979/−1.595		
cutpoint 4		−1.013/−.690		
cutpoint 5		−.170/−.034		
cutpoint 6		2.072/2.313		
cutpoint 7		3.202/3.502		

Note: τ_b^2 = .063, p = .000, N = 551 for females; τ_b^2 = .048, p = .000, N = 523 for males. NA = not applicable.

bivariate correlates of lower adult net worth, the relationships in table 4.4 are not quite statistically significant, with .05 < p < .10. Minority ethnicity, urban residence, and two-parent family had significant bivariate relationships with adult net worth, but do not have significant relationships controlling for other predictors in table 4.4, suggesting that for females the relationships of adult net worth with neighborhood violence, adolescent general violence victimization, minority ethnicity, urban residence, and two-parent family are spurious with or mediated by other variables in the model. Explained variation in adult net worth for females is 6.3%.

For males, *lower* adult net worth is predicted by adolescent general violence victimization, minority ethnicity, and urban residence. *Higher* adult net worth is predicted by upper/middle parental SES. It is striking that, in this instance, despite the relationship being statistically significant at the .05 level (p = .027), the standardized coefficient is quite small (b* = −.020), but substantively the relationship is consistent with the bivariate relationship. Variables that have significant bivariate relationships with adult net worth but not significant results when controlling for the other predictors in table 4.4 include parental physical abuse, consistent reports of witnessing parental violence, lower parental SES, and two-parent family structure, suggesting that all of those variables may have relationships with adult net worth that are spurious with or mediated by other variables in the model. Explained variation in adult net worth for males is 4.8%, slightly lower than for females. Experiences of direct physical victimization are thus predictive of lower adult net worth for both females and males. For females it is specifically parental physical abuse, but for males it is general violence victimization, that appears to affect adult net worth. An additional difference by gender is that for females but not for males, consistent reports of witnessing parental violence are predictive of lower adult net worth.

Table 4.5 presents the results of the nominal logistic regression analysis for marital status. In the reference category logit model used for the analysis of adult marital status, there are two logistic functions, the first predicting being never married (compared to being currently married, the reference category) and the second predicting being formerly married (again compared to being currently married, the reference category). The bulk of the formerly married respondents are either separated or divorced, with a very small proportion who are widowed. For females in table 4.5, being never married was significantly more likely than being currently married for minority ethnicity and urban respondents, and less likely for rural respondents. For the second logistic function, being formerly married was significantly more likely for urban residents. AEV does not appear to be predictive of the three-way distinction among being never, currently, or previously married for females when we control for other predictors.

Table 4.5   Nominal Logistic Regression Results for Marital Status

Predictors	Coefficients: Female/Male			
	Standardized Coefficient (b*)	Unstandardized Coefficient (b) [Odds Ratio]	Standard Error of b	Statistical Significance (p)
Function 1: **Never Married vs. Currently Married**				
Parental Physical Abuse	.060/.122	.363/.916 [1.438/2.500]	.290/.345	.210/.008
Witnessing Parental Violence (Inconsistent)	−.004/−.056	−.038/−.480 [.963/.619]	.449/.415	.932/.247
Witnessing Parental Violence (Consistent)	−.025/.022	−.217/.180 [.805/1.198]	.418/.339	.604/.594
Neighborhood Violence	.018/.062	.159/.480 [1.172/1.616]	.360/.316	.660/.128
Adolescent General Violence Victimization	.006/−.032	.018/−.075 [1.018/.928]	.142/.105	.902/.476
Minority Ethnicity	.155/.094	1.337/.666 [3.807/1.947]	.360/.314	.000/.034
Upper/Middle Parental SES	−.001/−.014	−.007/−.092 [.993/.911]	.367/.332	.985/.778
Lower Parental SES	−.076/.049	−.492/.271 [.612/1.312]	.337/.275	.144/.324
Urban	.104/.108	.832/.757 [2.298/2.131]	.318/.279	.009/.007
Rural	−.176/−.068	−1.513/−.476 [.220/.621]	.744/.345	.042/.167
Two-Parent Family Structure	−.017/−.004	−139/−.029 [.871/.971]	.364/.344	.703/.933
Constant	NA/NA	−1.913/−1.465 [.148/.231]	.454/.439	.000/.001
Function 2: **Previously Married vs. Currently Married**				
Parental Physical Abuse	.067/.140	.339/1.037 [1.396/2.822]	.207/.331	.107/.002
Witnessing Parental Violence (Inconsistent)	.046/.008	.381/.067 [1.463/1.069]	.322/.348	.238/.847
Witnessing Parental Violence (Consistent)	−.003/−.052	−.019/−.431 [.982/.650]	.313/.390	.953/.269
Neighborhood Violence	−.017/−.040	−.125/−.312 [.883/.732]	.318/.370	.695/.399

(Continued)

Table 4.5   Nominal Logistic Regression Results for Marital Status (Continued)

Predictors	Coefficients: Female/Male			
	Standardized Coefficient (b*)	Unstandardized Coefficient (b) [Odds Ratio]	Standard Error of b	Statistical Significance (p)
Adolescent General Violence Victimization	.077/.112	.195/.259 [1.215/1.296]	.109/.106	.075/.015
Minority Ethnicity	.016/.123	.114/.870 [1.121/2.387]	.337/.322	.732/.007
Upper/Middle Parental SES	.029/.035	.181/.223 [1.198/1.250]	.298/.263	.544/.538
Lower Parental SES	.036/.131	.195/.717 [1.215/2.048]	.260/.292	.454/.014
Urban	.091/−.009	.605/−.061 [1.830/.941]	.285/.334	.034/.855
Rural	.023/−.054	.162/−.375 [1.176/.687]	.294/.327	.581/.251
Two-Parent Family Structure	−.036/−.089	−.248/−.680 [.780/.507]	.294/.324	.399/.036
Constant	NA/NA	−1.586/−1.615 [.205/.199]	.374/.443	.000/.000

Note: R_L^2 = .070, p = .000, N = 573 for females; R_L^2 = .078, p = .000, N = 546 for males. NA = not applicable.

Other variables that are not significantly related to marital status in table 4.5 but have significant bivariate correlations with marital status include parental physical abuse, negatively associated with being currently married and positively associated with being formerly married; exposure to neighborhood violence, positively associated with being never married and negatively associated with being currently married; adolescent general violence victimization, negatively associated with being currently married and positively associated with being formerly married; rural residence, negatively associated with being never married and positively associated with being currently married; and two-parent family, positively associated with being currently married and negatively associated with both being never married and being formerly married. As in other instances of significant bivariate relationships coupled with nonsignificant direct relationships in the multivariate analysis, the suggestion is that these relationships are spurious with or mediated by other variables in the multivariate model. R_L^2 indicates that 7% of the variation in adult marital status is explained by the polytomous nominal logistic regression model.

For males, the results for the first logistic function indicate that parental physical abuse, minority ethnicity, and urban residence are predictive of higher odds of being never married as opposed to currently married. In the second logistic function, parental physical abuse, adolescent general violence victimization, minority ethnicity, and lower parental SES are predictive of higher odds of being formerly married as opposed to currently married, and two-parent family structure is predictive of lower odds of being formerly married as opposed to currently married. Other variables that were not significantly related to adult marital status in the multivariate model results in table 4.5, but had significant bivariate correlations with adult marital status, include exposure to neighborhood violence, positively associated with being never married and negatively associated with being currently married; upper/middle parental SES and rural residence, both positively associated with being currently married; and two-parent family, positively associated with being currently married and negatively associated with being formerly married. Again, these bivariate relationships appear to indicate spurious or mediated relationships, once other predictors are controlled in the model. Explained variation for males is 7.8%, similar to that for females. It appears that for males but not for females, the direct experiences of physical violence in adolescence, both in the form of parental physical abuse and general violence victimization, are predictive of being either never married or formerly married, as opposed to currently married, in adulthood.

DISCUSSION

In this discussion, we begin with a summary of the results for the effects of each of the AEV predictors on the adult outcome variables, including a comparison between the present results and an earlier study with the same data set (Covey et al. 2013). Note that there are important differences in the analysis in the present study compared with the earlier analysis in Covey et al. (2013). To review, Covey et al. examined the same outcomes, with prevalence instead of frequency of parental physical abuse as a predictor, and did not include prevalence or frequency of adolescent general violent victimization as a predictor in any of their models. In addition, although they reported that results did not differ by gender (based on tests for interactions between gender and each of the other predictors in the model), they did not present separate analyses by gender. Bearing those differences in mind, we focus on the multivariate analysis for each of the adult SES outcomes in the discussion of the results. We next examine gender differences in the significance of the different predictors, particularly but not only adolescent exposure to violence, of adult SES. We finish with the broader conclusions that can be drawn from the present study.

Looking only at correlations between AEV and adult outcomes, parental physical abuse appears to be associated with lower education, lower income, lower net worth, not currently being married, and for females but not males, lower likelihood of employment in adulthood. Statistically controlling for other predictors of adult outcomes, physical abuse is associated with lower education for males (but not females), lower employment for females (but not males), lower income for males, lower net worth for females, and lower likelihood of being currently married for males, still a long list of outcomes. In Covey et al. (2013), for females and males combined, prevalence of physical abuse by parents was a significant predictor of lower education, lower income, lower net worth, and lower likelihood of being currently married as opposed to both never married or formerly married, but it was not significant as a predictor of employment. The absence of a significant relationship between adult employment and prevalence of parental physical abuse in Covey et al. (2013) is a difference between the previous study and the present study, which might be a result of the use of frequency instead of prevalence of abuse, or of the inclusion of adolescent general violence victimization, or of the separate analysis by gender, in the present study.

Inconsistent reports of witnessing parental violence are statistically significantly correlated with none of the adult SES. Consistent reports of witnessing parental violence are significantly associated with lower educational attainment, lower adult income, and lower adult net worth for both females and males. Controlling for other predictors, inconsistent reports of witnessing parental violence continue to fail to reach statistical significance as predictors of any of the adult SES, and consistent reports of witnessing parental violence are significantly predictive only of lower net worth for females. In Covey et al. (2013), consistent reporting of witnessing parental violence for the full sample was a significant predictor only of income and net worth, the former result different from and the latter result consistent (at least for females) with the results in the present study.

Exposure to neighborhood violence is significantly associated with lower adult net worth for females, and with lower likelihood of adult employment, lower likelihood of being currently married, and higher likelihood of never having been married, for males in middle adulthood. With controls for other predictors, notably ethnicity and parental SES (which tends to be associated with exposure to violence in the neighborhood; see, for example, Elliott et al. 2006), exposure to neighborhood violence is a statistically significant predictor of lower likelihood of adult employment, for females as well as for males. As noted earlier, the emergence of a significant relationship between exposure to neighborhood violence and adult employment for females, when no significant relationship was indicated in the bivariate relationship, likely reflects a suppressor effect, in which the impact of a predictor on an outcome is evident only when controlling for other variables. In Covey et al. (2013), exposure to neighborhood violence was likewise a significant predictor only of adult employment.

Adolescent general violence victimization has significant bivariate correlations with lower educational attainment, lower net worth, and higher likelihood of being formerly rather than currently married in adulthood for both females and males, and also for females but not quite for males, of lower income in adulthood. In the multivariate models, it is predictive of lower educational attainment for females but not for males, and of lower income, lower net worth, and a higher likelihood of being formerly married rather than currently married, for males but not for females. Neither prevalence nor frequency of adolescent general violence victimization was used as a predictor in Covey et al. (2013).

Two broad patterns seem to emerge here. One is that direct experience of victimization by violence, as represented by parental physical abuse and general violence victimization in adolescence, has more pervasive effects on adult SES than other forms of AEV. The direct effect of adolescent exposure to neighborhood violence is only significant for employment, and witnessing (actually, only consistent and not inconsistent reports of witnessing) parental violence only has a direct effect on net worth for females in adulthood. The second broad pattern is that in the multivariate analyses of the five adult SES outcome variables, there are a total of thirty-nine statistically significant ($p \leq .05$) direct effects, of which twenty-five, or nearly two-thirds, are significant for either females or males but not both (a little over one-third are significant for both). On the surface, this seems to indicate substantial differences between females and males in the significance of different predictors of adult SES.

To further explore this, we performed a formal test (Brame et al.; Paternoster et al. 1998) for differences between females and males for all of the coefficients that were statistically significant for either or both. (There is little point in testing for the statistical significance between two coefficients, neither of which is itself statistically significantly different from zero.) None of the differences between coefficients was statistically significant if a variable was a statistically significant predictor for both females and males. In addition, none of the differences was significant with employment, net worth, or marital status as the dependent variable. The differences that were statistically significant were for the direct effects of (1) parental physical abuse on educational attainment, $z = 1.98$, $p = .048$; (2) minority ethnicity on educational attainment, $z = -2.04$, $p = .041$; (3) minority ethnicity on income, $z = 2.29$, $p = .022$; (4) rural residence on educational attainment, $z = 2.34$, $p = .019$; and (5) urban residence on income, $z = 2.22$, $p = .026$. Note that only one of these differences involves AEV. The other four gender differences involve the relationships of ethnicity and residence to educational attainment and income. Bear in mind, however, that the gender differences in the control variables also have a potential impact on the other results, including results for AEV variables as predictors. The absence of gender differences in Covey et al. (2013) may possibly be explained by the difference in measurement of parental physical abuse—prevalence in Covey et al. (2013), but cumulative frequency in the present study—or by the inclusion here, but not in Covey et al. (2013) of adolescent general violence victimization as a predictor.

CONCLUSIONS

There are three general conclusions to be drawn from the results presented in this chapter. First, as one familiar with social science research in general might expect, simple bivariate correlations between AEV and adult SES outcomes are not adequate to represent the relationships of those two sets of variables and tend to overstate the direct impact of AEV on adult SES outcomes. Correspondingly, to the extent that studies of the impact of AEV on adult outcomes rely on simple bivariate relationships, their results are likely to overstate the impact of AEV on adult outcomes.

Second, consistent with our hypotheses, even with reasonable controls for other influences on adult SES, AEV does have pervasive effects on adult SES outcomes. One can always question whether sufficient controls for other potential influences have been built into any model, but the inclusion in the multivariate model of ethnicity, parental SES, and, for marital status, two-parent family structure at the beginning of the study, is particularly important here. It was noted that some of the significant bivariate relationships for which the coefficients in the multivariate analysis were not statistically significant probably represented spurious or mediated relationships. In the multivariate analysis, for every outcome except employment, at least one of ethnicity, parental SES, or (only for formerly vs. currently married for males) two-parent family was a significant predictor of the outcome. One clearly plausible possibility is that some of the significant-for-bivariate-but-not-multivariate relationships were spurious, with the ascribed status variables (ethnicity, parental SES, two-parent family) in adolescence affecting both AEV (note the several significant correlations involving the AEV variables and the adolescent SES variables in chapter 3, table 3.6) and adult SES outcomes. In contrast to the other outcomes, for both female and male adult employment, the best predictors, based on both statistical significance and the magnitude of the standardized logistic regression coefficients, appear to be forms of AEV.

Third, performing the analysis separately by gender does appear to be justified. In addition, however, formal tests for whether apparent differences by gender are actually statistically significant, of sufficient magnitude that statistical testing indicates that they are unlikely to be attributable to chance, are also important. Of the thirty-nine significant coefficients between the predictors and the outcomes, only a little over one-third involved statistical significance for both females and males for the same predictor. Yet of the twenty-five coefficients that were statistically significant for either females or males but not both, fully 80% of the gender differences in the coefficients were not statistically significant, and of the five differences that were statistically significant, only one was for one of the AEV predictors. Bearing in mind that statistical significance depends on sample size as well as on the magnitude of a relationship or difference, if we look at both the number of gender differences in statistical significance and the number of statistically significant gender differences, we get a range from conservative (based on statistical significance of differences) to liberal (based on number of gender differences in whether a coefficient is statistically significant) estimates of the degree to which the impact of AEV and other predictors differs for female and male respondents.

Multivariate analysis with statistical controls helps us to avoid overstating the extent to which AEV is related to adult SES outcomes, yet still indicates the utility of AEV for predicting adult socioeconomic outcomes. Formal testing for gender differences, similarly, helps us avoid overstating the extent of gender differences in the significance of predictors of adult socioeconomic outcomes, yet still identifies real gender differences that point to the need to consider separate analysis by gender when examining the influences of AEV on adult SES outcomes. The results from the multivariate analysis and the formal tests for gender differences paint a picture in which AEV, particularly direct physical violence victimization, negatively influences adult SES attainment and does so somewhat, but by no means completely, differently for females and males.

Chapter 5

Adolescent Exposure to Violence and Adult Mental Health

There is an extensive literature (Acosta et al. 2001; Boney-McCoy and Finkelhor 1995; Buka et al. 2001; Chen 2010; Fowler et al. 2009; Gewirtz and Edleson 2007; Jones-Webb and Wall 2008; Kendall-Tackett 2013; Kilpatrick et al. 2003; Lynch 2003; Margolin et al. 2010; Merrick et al. 2017; Mills et al. 2013; Mohammed et al. 2015; Ruback and Thompson 2001; Stevens et al. 2013; Turner et al. 2010; Widom 2014) on the relationship of childhood and adolescent exposure to violence (AEV) with subsequent mental health problems, including but not limited to anxiety, depression, and post-traumatic stress disorder (PTSD). A linkage from childhood and adolescent exposure to violence to later mental health problems is implicitly suggested by a combination of the strain theories of Merton (1938) and Agnew (1985, 1992). Combining these perspectives as discussed in chapter 1, AEV is, from Agnew's perspective, a form of noxious stimulus which produces strain. According to Merton, different individuals will respond to strain with one of five different modes of adaptation: conformity, innovation, ritualism, retreatism, or rebellion. The retreatist mode of adaptation, which involves the abandonment of both culturally prescribed goals and the societally approved means of achieving them, is one which Merton suggested would be associated with substance abuse and mental health problems. Thus, based on the combination of Agnew's general strain theory and Merton's anomie theory, we would expect that exposure to noxious stimuli, in this case AEV, will, for some individuals, lead to mental health problems. The expectation would be that the strain of AEV would most likely result in mental health symptoms that were trauma-linked, such as (in the context of the present study) anxiety, depression, and PTSD.

While strain theory forms the primary theoretical basis for the present research, there are other theoretical perspectives that also suggest a link between AEV and adult mental health problems. A theoretical linkage between

AEV and adult anxiety, depression, and PTSD is implied in the literature on the neurobiology of the impact of traumatic events on brain functioning. Anda et al. (2006) and Perry (2001) concluded that the impact of traumatic events and experiences, such as exposure to violence, on brain functioning leads to increased risk for anxiety (see also Weems et al. 2015), depression, PTSD, and other adverse mental health outcomes. According to this perspective, responses to traumatic events individually vary and are often short term or acute, but recollections of some traumatic events, such as physical abuse, are stored deep in the memory and may surface with environmental cues that remind the individual of the previous trauma. Thus, we might expect adolescents, particularly females (Franzese et al. 2014; Merikangas et al. 2009), who have been subjected to violent trauma to have recurrent episodes or lasting effects such as anxiety, depression, and PTSD, and to have a need for mental health services, often later in the life course, including during middle adulthood.

Some research has demonstrated that exposure to violence, including exposure to community violence (Foster et al. 2004), is strongly associated with a variety of mental health symptoms for adolescent girls and boys (Chen 2010). Adverse childhood experiences such as exposure to violence also have been found to have negative effects on the development of brain function (Anda et al. 2006; Teicher et al. 2003). In addition, some studies have found that traumatized individuals with PTSD were more likely to have structural abnormalities in certain regions of their brains (Carrion et al. 2007; Karl et al. 2006; Weems et al. 2015). However, other studies have found no structural differences among post-traumatic children in other regions of the brain (Woon and Hedges 2008). These studies suggest that, in addition to strain theory, research on neurobiology, heterotypic continuity, and the relationship of exposure to violence with behavioral trajectories would lead us to expect a positive relationship between AEV and adult mental health problems and mental health service needs.

Beginning with a consideration of short-term impacts of violent victimization in general, Ruback and Thompson's (2001) review suggests that violent crime victimization is positively associated with anxiety, depression, and PTSD. Menard (2002) found that general violent victimization in adolescence was not significantly associated with past-year anxiety, depression, or PTSD in early adulthood, or with "ever" experiencing anxiety or depression, but was associated with having ever experienced PTSD. Acosta et al. (2001) found that exposure to violence was associated with depression and PTSD. Research has found child abuse in general, and AEV in particular, to be associated with later anxiety, depression, PTSD, and mental health problems (Ciccheti and Rogosch 1977; Dunn et al. 2012; Gewirtz and Edleson 2007; Turner et al. 2006; Yingling 2016). Guterman et al. (2002) found that adolescent victimization was not associated with an increase in mental health services, and might even lower the odds of subsequent mental health service use in adolescence, but Franzese et al. (2014) found that specifically for females, consistent reports of witnessing parental violence were predictive of adult professional and general mental health service use, and exposure to neighborhood violence was predictive of adult general mental health service use. Considering general mental health problems as an outcome of exposure to community violence, several studies have indicated that exposure to community violence may produce negative mental health consequences (e.g., Boney-McCoy and Finkelhor 1995; Durant et al. 1995; Overstreet 2000; Singer et al. 1995). Mueser et al. (1998) in particular found evidence of severe mental illness in adult patients who were victims of exposure to and witnessing community violence as children.

Turning to relationships between specific forms of AEV and specific adult mental health outcomes, anxiety and depression appear to be more closely associated with physical abuse and witnessing violence, and PTSD appears to be more associated with neighborhood violence and, to a lesser extent, with physical abuse (Dunn et al. 2012; Gorman-Smith and Tolan 1998; Luster et al. 2002; Scarpa 2001; Tajima 2004; Vrana and Lauterbach 1994; Widom 2014). Widom's (2014) review suggests that physical abuse by parents is positively related to later PTSD, and that maltreatment more generally is associated with adult depression. Luster et al. (2002) and Tajima (2004) also found physical abuse to be associated with depression. Other studies report that children who have been exposed to community violence experience problems with depression, stress, sleep disorders, anxiety, loneliness, and nervousness (Bell and Jenkins 1993; Gorman-Smith and Tolan 1998; Jaffe et al. 1986; Martinez and Richters 1993; Shakoor and Chalmers 1991). Several studies (Fitzpatrick and Boldizar 1993; Fowler et al. 2009; Guterman and Cameron 1997; Kaminar et al. 2013) have found an association between either or both, direct victimization or more general exposure to violence in the community context, to be associated with PTSD, including longitudinal research that has examined the effects of exposure to community violence that surfaces in young adults as PTSD (Scarpa 2001; Vrana and Lauterbach 1994).

While the results above tend to highlight positive findings, the overall picture is mixed. There is more support for later anxiety and depression being associated with physical abuse and witnessing violence, and less evidence for an association of anxiety and depression with exposure to community violence. For PTSD, on the other hand, there appears to be more evidence for an association with exposure to neighborhood violence and perhaps with physical abuse than with witnessing parental violence. Several of the studies indicate that different stimuli (physical abuse, witnessing parental violence, exposure to neighborhood violence) may be associated with different outcomes (anxiety or depression or PTSD), and that the effects may vary by gender, with females more likely than males to react to stress with internalizing responses such as anxiety or depression (Broidy and Agnew 1997; Watts and McNulty 2013).

In light of these mixed and conditional results, we hypothesize that AEV in at least one of its forms (parental physical abuse, witnessing parental violence, exposure to neighborhood violence, general violence victimization) will be associated with (a) the combined prevalence of adult past-year (to be sure the outcomes are measured subsequently to their purported influences) anxiety, depression, and PTSD, but that the association will vary across the different AEV predictors, and will be stronger for females than for males. We also hypothesize that AEV will be positively associated with (b) adult general mental health service use and (c) adult professional mental health service use, and negatively associated with (d) life satisfaction, all more strongly for females (who are more likely to respond to strain with internalizing behaviors) than for males.

ANALYTICAL APPROACH

As in the previous chapter, the analysis begins with a selective examination of bivariate relationships of AEV and sociodemographic characteristics to the adult outcomes. Following the presentation of significant bivariate results, we move to a more detailed examination of the multivariate models for the adult outcomes, separately by gender. Prevalence of combined anxiety, depression, and PTSD is a dichotomous variable, so binary logistic regression is used to examine the impacts of the AEV variables and the other predictors on the prevalence of the selected adult mental health problems. Frequencies of general and professional mental health service use are ratio-scaled variables, so ordinary least squares (OLS) regression is used for the analysis of those two outcomes. Life satisfaction is an index based on the addition of two ordinal variables, as described in chapter 3. While it might be possible to argue for treating the resulting measure as an ordinal scale, it seems more reasonable to treat it as an interval-scaled variable, and for that reason OLS regression is used in the analysis of life satisfaction. To test for the sensitivity of the results to the assumption of level of measurement, however, an ordinal regression model, not presented in detail here, was also calculated, and the results compared to the OLS regression results.

BIVARIATE RELATIONSHIPS

Figure 5.1 illustrates the relationships of AEV to the four mental health outcome variables. As in the previous chapter, AEV is coded "no" for respondents

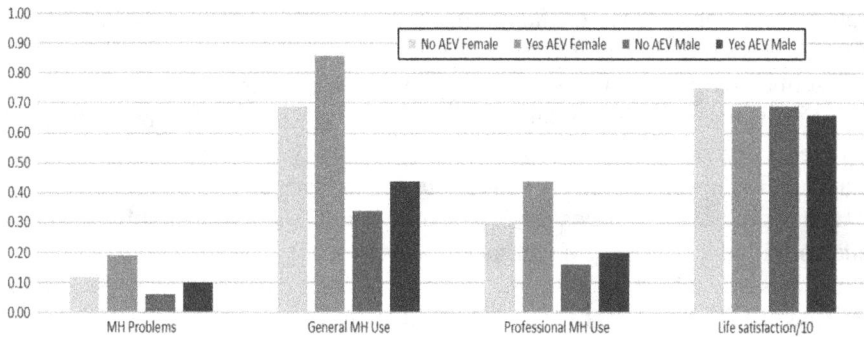

Figure 5.1   AEV and Adult Mental Health. *Source:* Created by the authors.

who reported neither parental physical abuse nor witnessing parental violence, nor exposure to neighborhood violence, nor general violence victimization in adolescence, and "yes" for respondents who reported any one or more of those forms of AEV. Again, the figure is split by gender, going (from left to right within each outcome) from females who reported no AEV to females who reported some (yes) AEV, males who reported no AEV and to males who reported some (yes) AEV. The range of scores for the life satisfaction scale is considerably wider than the range of frequencies for mental health service use, and the mental health problem measure is a prevalence ranging from zero to one, so to make the chart easier to read, given these different scales, the life satisfaction scale score has been divided by 10. Figure 5.1 indicates that for both females and males, the prevalence of mental health problems, the frequency of general mental health service use, and the frequency of professional mental health service use are higher, and life satisfaction is lower, for individuals who have experienced AEV than for individuals who have not.

Breaking down these relationships by specific types of AEV as well as gender, bivariate correlations indicate that the association between adult mental health problems and adolescent general violence victimization is significant and positive for both females (r = .162, p = .000) and males (r = .178, p = .000). For females, adult mental health problems are also associated with parental physical abuse (r = .170, p = .000) and consistent reports of witnessing parental violence (r = .146, p = .001), but not with inconsistent reports of parental violence or exposure to neighborhood violence. For males, none of the other correlations is significant, although the correlation between adult mental health problems and consistent witnessing of parental violence (r = .082, p = .061) nearly meets the p ≤ .05 criterion. The prevalence of mental health problems in adulthood is also significantly positively related to both the scale for parental assessment of adolescent mental health problems (r = .112, p = .008 for females; r = .121, p = .005 for males) and the self-reported prevalence of mental health problems in adolescence (r = .195, p = .000 for females; r = .187, p = .000 for males). For males but not females, being in a two-parent family in adolescence is significantly negatively related to adult mental health problems (r = −.098, p = .024). Adult mental health problems are not significantly related to ethnicity, parental socioeconomic status (SES), or residence for either females or males.

Adult general mental health service use is significantly positively related to adolescent general violence victimization for both females (r = .126, p = .000) and males (r = .121, p = .004). It is also significantly positively related to parental physical abuse (r = .087, p = .033), consistent reports of witnessing parental violence (r = .132, p = .001), and exposure to neighborhood violence (r = .099, p = .019) for females but not for males, and is not significantly related to inconsistent reports of witnessing parental violence for either females or males. For females, adult general mental health service use is positively related to both parent assessments (r = .090, p = .029) and self-reports (r = .134, p = .000) of adolescent mental health problems, but for males, it is significantly positively related (more weakly than for females) only to adolescent self-reports (r = .089, p = .035), not to parental assessments of adolescent mental health problems. Ethnicity, parental SES, and residence are not significantly related to adult general mental health service use for females or for males. Being in a two-parent family is significantly negatively associated with adult general mental health service use for males (r = −.105, p = .013) but not for females.

Adult professional mental health service use follows a similar, but not identical, pattern. For females, adult professional mental health service use is significantly positively related to consistent reports of witnessing parental violence (r = .127, p = .002) and to adolescent general violence victimization (r = .106, p = .010), but the association with parental physical abuse (r = .069, p = .093) does not quite meet the p ≤ .05 cutoff for statistical significance, in contrast to the result for general mental health service use. For males, adult frequency of professional mental health service use, like general mental health service use, is significantly positively related to adolescent general violence victimization (r = .116, p = .006), but not to parental physical abuse, witnessing parental violence, or exposure to neighborhood violence. Adult professional mental health service use, like general mental health service use, is significantly positively related to self-reported adolescent mental health problems for both females (r = .136, p = .001) and males (r = .107, p = .011), and to parental assessments of mental health problems for females (r = .080, p = .053) but not for males. Urban residence in adulthood is significantly positively associated with adult professional mental health service use for males (r = .089, p = .035), but ethnicity, parental SES, residence, and being in a two-parent family are otherwise not significantly associated with adult professional mental health service use.

Adult life satisfaction is significantly and negatively related to parental physical abuse, more strongly for females ($r = -.197$, $p = .000$) than for males ($r = -.091$, $p = .021$); to consistent reports of witnessing parental violence, more strongly for males ($r = -.139$, $p = .001$) than for females ($r = -.096$, $p = .015$); and to exposure to neighborhood violence, more strongly for females ($r = -.121$, $p = .003$) than for males ($r = -.087$, $p = .034$). It is not significantly related to inconsistent reports of witnessing parental violence. Adult life satisfaction is also significantly negatively associated with both parental assessments ($r = -.143$, $p = .000$ for females; $r = -.193$, $p = .000$ for males) and self-reports ($r = -.146$, $p = .000$ for females; $r = -.206$, $p = .000$ for males) of mental health problems in adolescence. For both females and males, adult life satisfaction is negatively associated with minority ethnicity ($r = -.114$, $p = .004$ for females; $r = -.129$, $p = .001$ for males). For males but not females, adult life satisfaction is associated with lower parental SES ($r = -.112$, $p = .006$). For both females and males, life satisfaction is positively associated with upper/middle parental SES ($r = .140$, $p = .001$ for females; $r = .147$, $p = .000$ for males) and with being in a two-parent family in adolescence ($r = .136$, $p = .001$ for females; $r = .164$, $p = .000$ for males).

In general, the bivariate results indicate that AEV is positively related to adult mental health problems and mental health service use, and negatively related to adult life satisfaction. General violence victimization is predictive of adult mental health outcomes for both females and males, but parental physical abuse and consistent reports of witnessing parental violence are more predictive of adult mental health outcomes for females than for males, consistent with our expectation that AEV would be more associated with adult mental health outcomes for females. Exposure to neighborhood violence was related more to life satisfaction than to the other mental health outcomes, and inconsistent reports of witnessing parental violence were not significantly related to any of the mental health outcomes. If we judged only by the bivariate results, both the hypothesis that AEV would be related to increased mental health problems and mental health service use, and to lower life satisfaction, and also the hypothesis that the relationship would be more pronounced for females than for males, would be supported. In order to obtain a clearer picture of the relationship of AEV to adult mental health outcomes, however, we need to examine the relationships controlling for the other predictors.

MULTIVARIATE ANALYSIS

Tables 5.1–5.4 follow the same format as the tables in the previous chapter, as described in the first two paragraphs in the Multivariate Analysis section in chapter 4. Table 5.1 presents the binary logistic regression analysis for the analysis of the combined prevalence of mental health problems (anxiety, depression, and PTSD). For females, significant predictors of higher prevalence of adult mental health problems include adolescent general violence victimization, self-reported adolescent mental health problems, and, marginally (p = .055), consistent reports of witnessing parental violence. Prevalence of adult mental health problems for females also had a significant bivariate association with parental physical abuse and parent reports of adolescent mental health problems, but those relationships are not statistically significant in table 5.1, and likely reflect relationships that are spurious with or mediated by other variables in the multivariate model. The R_L^2 statistic for explained variation (Menard 2010) indicates that the model explains a little over 10% of the variation in the prevalence of adult mental health problems in table 5.1.

For males, significant predictors of higher prevalence of adult mental health problems include adolescent general violence victimization and adolescent self-reports of mental health problems. In contrast to females, consistent reports of witnessing parental violence are significant predictors of adult prevalence of mental health problems in neither the bivariate correlations nor the multivariate analysis for males in table 5.1. In the bivariate analysis, parent reports of adolescent mental health problems were associated with higher, and two-parent family with lower, prevalence of adult mental health problems, but neither of those relationships is significant controlling for other predictors in the multivariate analysis in table 5.1, suggesting that those relationships are spurious with or mediated by other variables in the multivariate analysis. For both females and males, the strongest predictor of adult mental health problem prevalence is the self-reported prevalence of mental health problems in adolescence (indicating continuity in mental health problems from adolescence to adulthood), followed by adolescent general violence victimization. Similarly to the results for females, a little under 10% of the variation is explained in the adult mental health problems analyzed in table 5.1 for males.

Table 5.2 presents the OLS regression results for the frequency of general mental health service use. Significant predictors of higher frequency of female mental health service use in middle adulthood include consistent reports of witnessing parental violence and exposure to neighborhood violence in adolescence, but surprisingly neither of the adolescent mental health problem variables. In the bivariate correlations, both self-reports and parent assessments of adolescent mental health problems, along with adolescent general violence victimization, were also significant predictors of adult mental health problems, but controlling for the other predictors in table 5.2, it appears that those variables have spurious or mediated relationships with adult general mental health service use. Just under 7% of the variance in adult general mental health service use is explained for females.

Table 5.1   Binary Logistic Regression Results for Prevalence of Mental Health (ADP) Problems

Predictors	Coefficients: Female/Male			
	Standardized Coefficient (b*)	Unstandardized Coefficient (b) [Odds Ratio]	Standard Error of b	Statistical Significance (p)
Parental Physical Abuse	.071/−.015	.336/−.112 [1.399/.894]	.238/.427	.159/.793
Witnessing Parental Violence (Inconsistent)	−.081/.072	−.618/.621 [.539/1.861]	.483/.467	.201/.183
Witnessing Parental Violence (Consistent)	.101/.019	.652/.158 [1.920/1.172]	.340/.475	.055/.739
Neighborhood Violence	−.040/−.005	−.279/−.037 [.756/.963]	.393/.459	.478/.935
Adolescent General Violence Victimization	.112/.127	.263/.286 [1.300/1.331]	.129/.141	.042/.042
Parental Assessment: Mental Health Problems	.056/.070	.047/.067 [1.048/1.069]	.043/.059	.277/.252
Self-report: Mental Health Problems	.160/.169	.948/1.197 [2.580/3.309]	.301/.400	.002/.003
Minority Ethnicity	−.069/.002	−.456/.015 [.634/1.016]	.434/.465	.293/.973
Upper/Middle Parental SES	.031/.064	.178/.403 [1.194/1.496]	.330/.456	.591/.376
Lower Parental SES	−.058/−.049	−.345/−.266 [.708/.766]	.307/.427	.261/.533
Urban	−.018/.047	−.113/.318 [.893/1.375]	.357/.432	.752/.461
Rural	.009/.027	.062/.184 [1.064/1.202]	.353/.456	.861/.686
Two-Parent Family Structure	.083/−.031	.543/−.247 [1.722/.781]	.390/.448	.164/.582
Constant	NA/NA	−2.968/−3.719 [.051/.024]	.613/.810	.000/.000

Note: R_L^2 = .103, p = .000, N = 503 for females; R_L^2 = .097, p = .007, N = 471 for males. NA = not applicable.

For males, the only predictor of adult general mental health service use that is statistically significant at the .05 level is self-reported adolescent mental health problems. In the bivariate analysis, adolescent general violence victimization and two-parent family also had significant correlations with adult general mental health services, but controlling for the other variables in the model in table 5.2, it appears that those relationships may be spurious with or mediated by other predictors. Given that self-reported prevalence of

Table 5.2   OLS Regression Results for Frequency of General Mental Health Service Use

Predictors	Coefficients: Female/Male			
	Standardized Coefficient (b*)	Unstandardized Coefficient (b)	Standard Error of b	Statistical Significance (p)
Parental Physical Abuse	.008/−.064	.023/−.157	.126/.117	.855/.180
Witnessing Parental Violence (Inconsistent)	−.065/.048	−.277/.136	.186/.131	.137/.298
Witnessing Parental Violence (Consistent)	.114/.040	.412/.111	.170/.129	.016/.389
Neighborhood Violence	.097/−.089	.368/−.228	.169/.123	.030/.064
Adolescent General Violence Victimization	.079/.067	.102/.050	.062/.035	.102/.162
Parental Assessment: Mental Health Problems	.052/.005	.025/.002	.021/.015	.243/.920
Self-report: Mental Health Problems	.086/.113	.279/.260	.153/.116	.069/.025
Minority Ethnicity	−.006/−.026	−.023/−.062	.176/.120	.895/.606
Upper/Middle Parental SES	.041/.015	.133/.031	.155/.112	.394/.783
Lower Parental SES	−.082/−.051	−.225/−.093	.138/.099	.103/.347
Urban	.039/.067	.131/.151	.159/.109	.408/.166
Rural	.034/−.083	.123/−.189	.161/.108	.445/.080
Two-Parent Family Structure	.028/−.033	.102/−.087	.171/.128	.551/.198
Constant	NA/NA	.280/.408	.271/.205	.301/.047

Note: R^2 = .068, p = .000, N = 533 for females; R^2 = .046, p = .046, N = 491 for males. NA = not applicable.

mental health problems is the only significant predictor in the model, it seems likely that this is the mediating variable, but absent clear time ordering for the predictors measured in adolescence, that possibility cannot be adequately assessed with the present data. Explained variation for adult general mental health services for males is fairly low at 4.6%.

Table 5.3 presents the OLS regression results for frequency of professional mental health services. The significant predictors of higher frequency of professional health services in adulthood for females are consistent reporting of parental violence and self-reported adolescent mental health problems. In the bivariate analysis, adolescent general violence victimization and, marginally, parental assessment of adolescent mental health problems were also significantly correlated with adult professional services use for females, but controlling for the other variables in the model in table 5.3, it appears

Table 5.3   OLS Regression Results for Frequency of Professional Mental Health Service Use

Predictors	Coefficients: Female/Male			
	Standardized Coefficient (b*)	Unstandardized Coefficient (b)	Standard Error of b	Statistical Significance (p)
Parental Physical Abuse	.013/−.058	.022/−.082	.081/.067	.791/.226
Witnessing Parental Violence (Inconsistent)	−.031/.034	−.085/.055	.120/.075	.480/.468
Witnessing Parental Violence (Consistent)	.108/.019	.251/.030	.110/.074	.023/.687
Neighborhood Violence	.032/−.095	.078/−.139	.109/.070	.478/.049
Adolescent General Violence victimization	.066/.054	.054/.023	.040/.020	.176/.261
Parental Assessment: Mental Health Problems	.036/.008	.011/.001	.014/.009	.423/.872
Self-report: Mental Health Problems	.102/.140	.213/.185	.099/.067	.032/.006
Minority Ethnicity	.027/−.037	.062/−.050	.114/.069	.586/.468
Upper/Middle Parental SES	.049/.000	.100/.000	.101/.064	.323/.995
Lower Parental SES	−.068/−.033	−.119/−.035	.089/.057	.181/.542
Urban	.038/.097	.082/.124	.103/.063	.424/.047
Rural	.063/−.073	.146/−.096	.104/.062	.161/.123
Two-Parent Family Structure	.026/.037	.061/.055	.111/.073	.584/.458
Constant	NA/NA	.080/.078	.175/.118	.648/.506

Note: R^2 = .052, p = .009, N = 533 for females; R^2 = .044, p = .057, N = 491 for males. NA = not applicable.

that those relationships are spurious with or mediated by other variables in the model. Explained variation for professional mental health service use in middle adulthood by females is fairly low at 5.2%.

The frequency of professional mental health services for males in middle adulthood is significantly higher for respondents who are urban residents in adulthood and who self-reported having mental health problems in adolescence; and surprisingly, professional mental health service use is lower for males who report experiencing exposure to neighborhood violence in adolescence. In the bivariate analysis, the correlation between exposure to neighborhood violence was negative but not statistically significant, so the significant negative relationship of exposure to neighborhood violence and adult professional mental health service use only emerges in the presence of controls for other predictors. Two-parent family was also significantly associated with lower adult professional mental health service use for males in the bivariate analysis, but its relationship in table 5.3 with adult mental health service use is no longer significant once controls are included for other predictors. Explained variation for adult professional mental health services is fairly low at 4.4%.

Table 5.4 presents the results of the OLS regression for life satisfaction. Significant predictors of *lower* adult life satisfaction for females include parental physical abuse, exposure to neighborhood violence, adolescent general violence victimization, and parental assessment of adolescent mental health problems. Upper/middle parental SES is significantly predictive of *higher* adult life satisfaction. In the bivariate analysis, consistent reports of witnessing parental violence, self-reported mental health problems, and minority ethnicity were also significantly associated with *lower*, and two-parent family with *higher*, adult life satisfaction for females. Controlling for the other predictors, it appears that the relationships of these variables

Table 5.4   OLS Regression Results for Life Satisfaction

Predictors	Coefficients: Female/Male			
	Standardized Coefficient (b*)	Unstandardized Coefficient (b)	Standard Error of b	Statistical Significance (p)
Parental Physical Abuse	−.090/−.017	−.303/−.085	.153/.224	.048/.704
Witnessing Parental Violence (Inconsistent)	−.029/−.048	−.162/−.283	.233/.249	.487/.255
Witnessing Parental Violence (Consistent)	−.017/−.065	−.082/−.369	.214/.245	.700/.132
Neighborhood Violence	−.090/−.009	−.450/−.047	.210/.234	.032/.841
Adolescent General Violence Victimization	−.136/−.054	−.230/−.087	.078/.070	.003/.212
Parental Assessment: Mental Health Problems	−.092/−.128	−.057/−.086	.027/.029	.032/.004
Self-report: Mental Health Problems	−.026/−.108	−.108/−.520	.190/.217	.572/.017
Minority Ethnicity	−.012/−.046	−.058/−.226	.221/.225	.795/.315
Upper/Middle Parental SES	.106/.051	.442/.227	.195/.217	.024/.295
Lower Parental SES	.064/−.056	.233/−.213	.173/.189	.179/.260
Urban	−.033/−.083	−.146/−.397	.197/.210	.459/.059
Rural	−.050/.020	−.241/.095	.202/.205	.233/.632
Two-Parent Family Structure	.010/.071	.046/.375	.207/.234	.823/.109
Constant	NA/NA	7.832/7.611	.328/.394	.000/.000

Note: R^2 = .089, p = .000, N = 573 for females; R^2 = .117, p = .000, N = 547 for males. NA = not applicable.

are spurious with or mediated by other predictors in table 5.4. Just under 9% of the variance in adult life satisfaction for females is explained by the predictors in the model, with adolescent general violence victimization and upper/middle parental SES having the strongest influences, followed by the parental assessment of adolescent mental health problems and parental physical abuse.

For males, the only significant predictors of adult life satisfaction are parental assessments and self-reports of adolescent mental health problems, both predictive of lower adult life satisfaction. In the bivariate analysis, parental physical abuse, consistent reports of witnessing parental violence, exposure to neighborhood violence, and adolescent general violence victimization were all significantly negatively related to adult life satisfaction, as were minority ethnicity, lower parental SES, and urban residence. Upper/middle parental SES and two-parent family were significantly positively correlated with adult life satisfaction. That all of these relationships would fail to be statistically significant in the presence of controls for other predictors in the model is somewhat striking, but it does suggest that those bivariate relationships are spurious with or mediated by other predictors in the model in table 5.4, and most likely by their association with adolescent mental health problems, as reported by the respondents themselves and by the parents of the respondents. Explained variance for adult life satisfaction for males is just under 12%.

DISCUSSION

As in the previous chapter, we begin with a summary of the results for each of the AEV predictors of adult mental health problems. For each of the predictors, we also draw comparisons with our previous work on the relationship of AEV with adult mental health problems (Covey et al. 2017; Franzese et al. 2014). Covey et al. (2017) include the prevalence of adult anxiety, depression, and PTSD as outcomes, but analyze them separately, in contrast to the present study which combines them into a single mental health problem index. Franzese et al. (2014) use prevalence, while the present study uses frequency, of adult general and professional mental health service use as outcomes. As predictors, Covey et al. (2017) and Franzese et al. (2014) use prevalence rather than (as in the present study) frequency of parental physical abuse and adolescent general violence victimization as predictors. The present study includes life satisfaction as an outcome, which was not included in either of the previous studies, but the present study does not include physical health problems, which were covered in Franzese et al. (2014). The prior results on physical health problems will be briefly reviewed in this discussion for the sake of completeness. Again paralleling the previous chapter, we continue with an examination of gender differences in the effects of AEV on adult mental health outcomes, and finish with general conclusions that can be drawn based on the combination of the present study with previous results from the NYSFS on the relationship of AEV with adult mental health.

In the bivariate correlations, parental physical abuse appears to be significantly negatively related to adult life satisfaction for both females and males, and positively related to the prevalence of the selected adult mental health problems (anxiety, depression, PTSD) and adult general mental health service use for females. In the multivariate analysis, the only significant direct of effect parental physical abuse is its negative effect on adult life satisfaction for females. Covey et al. (2017) found parental physical abuse to have a significant positive correlation with adult anxiety for females (and marginally for males) and adult depression and PTSD for males, but it was not a significant predictor of anxiety, depression, or PTSD in the multivariate analysis. In Franzese et al. (2014), parental physical abuse was not significantly associated with the prevalence of adult general or professional mental health service use for either females or males in either the bivariate or the multivariate analysis. It was significantly positively associated with adult physical health problems for females but not for males in both the bivariate and the multivariate analysis. Combining the current and prior results, when we control for other predictors, parental physical abuse does not appear to be predictive of more conventional mental health measures (anxiety, depression, PTSD, mental health service use) for either females or males, but it is predictive of physical health problems and lower life satisfaction for females, but not for males.

In both the bivariate and multivariate analysis, inconsistent reporting of witnessing parental violence was not significantly associated with any of the outcomes in the present chapter. It was also not significantly associated with anxiety, depression, PTSD, or adult general or professional mental health service use in Covey et al. (2017) and Franzese et al. (2014), but in both the bivariate and multivariate analyses in Franzese et al., it was positively associated with adult physical health problems. In the present study, consistent reports of witnessing parental violence are negatively associated with adult life satisfaction for both females and males in the bivariate but not the multivariate analysis, and with adult prevalence of mental health problems and adult frequency of general and professional mental health service use for females in both the bivariate and multivariate analysis (marginally for adult mental health problems, at p = .055). In the bivariate analysis in Covey et al. (2017), consistent reporting of witnessing parental violence was positively correlated with depression and PTSD but not anxiety, for females but not for males, and also had a positive direct effect on adult depression for females. In both the bivariate and multivariate analysis in Franzese et al. (2014), consistent reports of witnessing parental violence were positively associated with, and had positive direct influences on, the prevalence of adult general and professional mental health service use, and with adult physical health problems, for females but not for males. Again combining present and prior results with this sample, it appears that consistent reporting of witnessing parental violence is predictive of adult mental health problems (particularly depression), mental health service use, and physical problems for females but not for males.

In both Covey et al. (2017), using separate variables for anxiety, depression, and PTSD, and in the present analysis, using a single prevalence measure that combines the three, exposure to neighborhood violence is significantly related to these mental health problems in neither the bivariate nor the multivariate analysis. Adolescent exposure to neighborhood violence is negatively associated with adult life satisfaction for both females and males, and has a direct negative effect on adult life satisfaction for females but not for males. In Franzese et al. (2014), there is a significant positive bivariate correlation and a significant positive direct effect between exposure to neighborhood violence and the prevalence of adult general mental health service use for females but not for males. In the present study, exposure to neighborhood violence has a significant positive bivariate association with, and a significant positive direct effect on, the frequency of adult general mental health service use for females but not for males. Although exposure to neighborhood violence does not have a significant bivariate correlation with the frequency of adult professional mental health service use for males, it does have a significant, but unexpectedly negative, direct effect on frequency of adult professional mental health service use in the multivariate analysis. It is not clear whether this represents a statistical artifact, a problem with an important variable being omitted from the analysis, or possibly a suppression effect in which the impact of exposure to neighborhood violence in adolescence is genuinely predictive of a lower frequency of adult professional mental health services by males. Aside from this anomalous finding, it appears that exposure to neighborhood violence is predictive of lower life satisfaction and greater mental health service use in adulthood for females but not for males.

Adolescent general violence victimization has significant positive bivariate correlations with adult prevalence of mental health problems and with adult frequency of mental health service use, plus significant negative correlations with adult life satisfaction, for both females and males. In the multivariate analyses, it has a significant positive direct effect on the combined prevalence of anxiety, depression, and PTSD for both females and males, and a significant negative direct effect on adult life satisfaction for females, but no significant direct effect on adult mental health service use for females or males. In contrast to the present results, Covey et al. (2017) found no direct effect of adolescent general violence victimization on prevalence of anxiety, depression, and PTSD, considered as separate outcomes, rather than the combined prevalence of the three in the present analysis. In Franzese et al. (2014), adolescent general violence victimization had no significant direct effect on the prevalence physical health problems or on the prevalence of general or professional mental health service use (although the positive effect on general mental health service use for females was marginally significant at p = .055). Taken together these results indicate that adolescent general violence victimization does not appear to be predictive of adult mental health service use or physical problems, but it is predictive of lower life satisfaction for females, and of the combined (but not separately measured) prevalence of adult anxiety, depression, and PTSD for both females and males. Put another way, adolescent general violence victimization is more predictive of having some sort of mental health problem in general than it is of having any one specific mental health problem in particular.

Tests were performed for gender differences in coefficients when the coefficient in the multivariate analysis for either females or males or both was statistically significant. As in chapter 4, about one-third of the significant coefficients involved females and males both having significant coefficients for the same outcome, and about two-thirds involved either females or males but not both having significant coefficients for the same outcome. Of the eighteen comparisons, there was only one pair of coefficients that was significantly different for females and males. The unstandardized coefficients for the direct effects of neighborhood violence on frequency of adult general mental health service use were .368 (p = .030) for males and −.228 (p = .064) for females, and the test for the difference in the two coefficients resulted in z = 2.85 (p = .004). We also tested to see whether treating life satisfaction as an ordinal variable would have an effect on the substantive conclusions. There were no changes in the signs of any of the significant coefficients for females or males, and the only change in statistical significance was that the negative direct effect of parental physical abuse on life satisfaction for females was (just barely) significant at the .05 level with life satisfaction treated as an interval variable (p = .048), but not quite statistically significant at the .05 level with life satisfaction treated as an ordinal variable and analyzed using ordinal logistic regression (p = .065). The hypothesis that AEV will be predictive of adult mental health problems, mental health service use, and life satisfaction is supported for males for all except life satisfaction (but at best only marginally for adult general mental health service use at $p = .064$), and more strongly, as hypothesized, for females, for all of the mental health outcome measures.

CONCLUSIONS

Three general conclusions can be drawn from the results in the present chapter for the relationships between AEV and adult mental health outcomes. First, there appears to be substantial and pervasive continuity in mental health problems from adolescence to middle adulthood, particularly for the adolescent self-reported mental health problem measure used here and in prior research with this sample. Covey et al. (2017) found that self-reported adolescent mental health problems were predictive of the prevalence of anxiety and depression in middle adulthood for both females and males, and of adult PTSD for females but not males; and the results in the present chapter indicate that self-reported adolescent mental health problems are also significant predictors of the combined prevalence of anxiety, depression, and PTSD for both females and males. Franzese et al. (2014) found that adolescent self-reported mental health problems were predictive of the prevalence of adult general mental health service use for females (for males, $p = .100$), and of adult professional mental health service use for both females and males. In the present chapter, we find adolescent self-reported mental health problems to be predictive of the frequency of adult general and professional mental health service use, and also of life satisfaction for males. For females, adolescent self-reported mental health problems are not quite significant ($p = .069$) in predicting the frequency of adult general mental health service use, and significant in predicting adult professional mental health service use. Also for females, it is the parental assessment, rather than the self-report, of adolescent mental health problems that is predictive of adult life satisfaction.

Second, as with adult SES in the previous chapter, although there are coefficients that are statistically significant for one but not the other of females and males, merely noting those differences without formal testing for their significance may overstate gender differences in the influences on adult outcomes. Twice as many of the statistically significant direct effects found in the analyses in the present chapter are for females alone (8) as for males alone (4), with the remainder (8) being for both females and males. Life satisfaction, in particular, appears on the surface to be more affected by AEV for females than for males. These findings are consistent with the expectation, based on past studies, that females are more likely than males to react to strain with internalizing responses such as anxiety and depression. Yet of the apparent gender differences in the statistical significance of coefficients for the same outcome, only one, the coefficient for the direct effect of exposure to neighborhood violence on adult general mental health service use, is statistically significant at the .05 level. As noted in chapter 4, the number of differences in whether coefficients are statistically significant provides a more liberal estimate, and the number of statistically significant differences in coefficients provides a more conservative estimate, of the existence of gender differences in the impact of AEV on adult mental health outcomes. The broad pattern of the results, here, and the specific existence of a gender difference in the direct effect of exposure to neighborhood violence on adult general mental health service use do suggest that is useful to consider both separate analysis for females and males, and formal testing for gender differences.

Third, in contrast to the previous chapter, in which it appeared that the more direct experiences of violence in adolescence (parental physical abuse, adolescent general violence victimization) had more of an impact than the more indirect experiences (witnessing parental violence, exposure to violence in the neighborhood) on adult SES, in the present chapter, it is the more indirect forms of AEV that appear to have the more pervasive effects on adult mental health. Combining the results in this chapter with the earlier results of Covey et al. (2017) and Franzese et al. (2014), parental physical abuse has two significant direct effects, on adult life satisfaction and adult physical health problems for females, but not for males. Adolescent general violence victimization has three significant direct effects, on the combined index of adult mental health problems for both females and males, and on adult life satisfaction for females. The direct experience of violence thus has a total of four direct effects on the adult mental and physical health outcome measures.

Exposure to neighborhood violence has four direct effects, on adult life satisfaction, on both prevalence and frequency of adult general mental health service use for females, and on frequency of adult professional mental health service use for males. Witnessing parental violence has eight direct effects: (1) inconsistent reports of witnessing parental violence on adult physical health problems (the only direct effect of inconsistent reports of witnessing parental violence on the physical or mental health outcomes analyzed here), plus consistent reports of witnessing parental violence on (2) prevalence of the combined (anxiety, depression, PTSD) index of adult mental health problems, (3) prevalence of adult depression, both (4) prevalence and (5) frequency of general mental health services in adulthood, both (6) prevalence and (7) frequency of professional mental health service use in adulthood, and (8) prevalence of adult physical health problems, all for females and not for males. In total, there are three times as many significant effects of indirect exposure to violence as for direct victimization by violence in adolescence on the adult mental and physical health outcomes. Put another way, the present results suggest that, particularly for females, mental health outcomes appear to be more sensitive to what one has seen done to others than to what one has directly experienced being done to oneself.

Chapter 6

Adolescent Exposure to Violence and Adult Substance Use

Although no theoretical perspective has been specifically developed to explain the relationship of adolescent exposure to violence (AEV) with illicit and problem substance use in adulthood, the broad category denoted as strain theories (Agnew 1985, 1992; Merton 1938) is straightforwardly applicable to this relationship, as it was for the relationship between AEV and mental health problems in the previous chapter. Once again, adolescent AEV constitutes the noxious stimulus. As with mental health problems, Merton's (1938) retreatist mode of adaptation, which involves the abandonment of both culturally prescribed goals and the societally approved means of achieving them, is the one most clearly linked to illicit substance use (including softer drugs like marijuana and harder drugs like hallucinogens, whose possession and use are themselves crimes) and problem use (including problem use of alcohol as well as problem use of illicit drugs). Based on this perspective, we would expect that AEV in adolescence would, for some individuals, lead to substance use problems, but as described in chapter 1, there are other modes of adaptation possible, and these would result in different outcomes in response to AEV.

Worth noting is that research by Menard (1995, 1997) supports the relationship of strain via retreatism to illicit drug use. Menard, like Merton, however, focused on economic strains (inability to achieve positively valued goals) rather than experiences of AEV (noxious stimuli) that are of concern here. Once again, the different types of AEV constitute the noxious stimuli, in the context of Agnew's (1985, 1992) general strain theory, which produce the strain to which the retreatist adaptation is one possible response. There has been extensive research testing general strain theory in relationship to juvenile delinquency (e.g., Broidy 2001), but the theory has not been extensively applied to the relationship of AEV with subsequent illicit and problem drug use. However, there have been a few exceptions, such as Zimmerman and Kushner's (2017) research that relies on Agnew's general strain theory to explain the relationships between secondary exposure to violence and substance use.

Strain theories vary in how they suggest a linkage between exposure to violence, including AEV, and substance use problems. As noted in chapter 1, Merton's (1938) anomie theory allows for different modes of adaptation, not all of which lead to substance use. Agnew's (1985) general strain theory suggests that strain is mediated by negative emotionality, including feelings of depression and anger, but does not specify how negative emotionality might lead to substance use problems, as opposed to violence (external-izing) or mental health problems (internalizing). Anda et al. (2006) and Perry (2001) suggest a neurobiological approach in which trauma affects brain functioning in ways that lead to adverse behavioral and mental health outcomes, but are not specific in describing how AEV would result in substance use problems. Other theoretical perspectives might be suggested here, but to our knowledge none provides a clearer explanation than strain theory for the relationship of AEV to illicit drug use. Moreover, of the theories linking victimization and offending discussed in Menard (2012), some would clearly not apply here. Learning theories would expect AEV to result in further violence, not substance use, and self-control theories, which emphasize voluntarily placing oneself in risky situations, would not appear to be applicable to the (presumably involuntary) situation of witness-ing parental violence (although an argument might be made for self-control provoking physical abuse or resulting in greater exposure to neighborhood violence).

Studies of the relationship of childhood and adolescent exposure to vio-lence with illicit drug use have been marked by methodological limitations and inconsistency of results (Kendall-Tackett 2013; Lynch 2003; Widom 2014; Wolfe et al. 2003), particularly with respect to the relationship of witnessing parental violence to illicit substance use; compare, for example, Fergusson and Lynskey (1997) and Herrenkohl et al. (2008) with Zinzow et al. (2009). Zimmerman and Kushner (2017) noted the absence of multi-wave research focused on the relationship between secondary exposure to violence and substance abuse. Widom (2014) summarized the state of this research by noting that

> hundreds of papers have been published describing a relationship between child maltreatment and *substance abuse*, primarily based on cross-sectional designs. Few longitudinal studies have followed abused and/or neglected children into adulthood, and, based on these few studies . . . the evidence linking child abuse and substance abuse is mixed. (p. 231, italics in original)

While there may be hundreds of studies of maltreatment (a term including but not limited to physical abuse) in childhood (sometimes including adolescence, under age 18, but often limited to younger ages), and short-term associations with substance abuse, there are far fewer studies of specifically AEV and its long-term relationship to illicit and problem substance use.

Kendall-Tackett (2013) cites several studies that suggest a positive relationship between physical abuse and later alcohol problems and illicit drug use, including Harrison et al. (1997), who found that physical abuse was associated with increased likelihood of marijuana and other drug use, and that victims indicated that they were using substances as a form of self-medication, a pattern consistent with the retreatist adaptation in anomie theory. Widom (2014; see also Widom and White 1997) found that physical abuse was associated with substance use, abuse, and dependence, particularly with excessive drinking and early onset of marijuana use for girls. Fuller-Thomson et al. (2016) found that for respondents in the Canadian Community Health Survey-Mental Health, sexual abuse, physical abuse, and witnessing domestic violence were all predictive of alcohol and drug dependence. They also found that there was no strong evidence for differences in behavior based on gender in the relationship between exposure to violence and substance dependence. Lynch (2003) cites evidence that assault victimization, witnessing violence, and exposure to neighborhood violence generally place individuals at increased risk of substance use and abuse. Beardslee et al. (2020) found that controlling for adolescent substance use, adolescents who were injured or threatened with injury had more alcohol use symptoms in adulthood than nonvictims, more so for women than for men, but that the effects of adolescent victimization were attenuated when controlling for more recent (young adult) victimization.

Kendall-Tackett (2013) also cites research that supports a positive relationship between substance abuse and, variously phrased, witnessing violence or exposure to violence in the home, including the study by Fergusson and Lynskey (1997) in New Zealand, which found that exposure to parental violence was related to marijuana use and dependence, and also to abuse of other substances. Herrenkohl et al. (2008) also reported a number of behavioral consequences of children exposed to domestic violence, including substance abuse. In contrast, however, Zinzow et al. (2009) found that although exposure to community violence was positively related to substance abuse, witnessing parental violence was not predictive of substance abuse. Wright et al. (2013) also found that community violence and child abuse, but not school violence or exposure to intimate partner violence, were predictive of alcohol and marijuana use. In a longitudinal study of exposure to community violence, Pinchevsky et al. (2013) found that AEV increased both male and female use of alcohol, and that females were more likely to have engaged in binge drinking than males. This study further underscores the suggestion that gender must be taken into account when considering the relationship between violence and substance use.

In summary, the literature on the relationships of adolescent physical abuse, witnessing parental violence, and exposure to neighborhood violence to subsequent illicit drug use generally seem to suggest a positive relationship, but the evidence is not entirely consistent. Some evidence fails to find such a relationship, particularly when controlling for prior illicit drug use. There is some suggestion that the relationship may be gender specific, applying more to females than to males, but this, too, is not consistent across all studies. Finally, there is some indication that the relationship may be stronger for adolescent, as opposed to childhood, exposure to violence, further reinforcing the focus on adolescence in the present study.

Based on strain theory, and also on past empirical results, we therefore hypothesize that AEV in at least one of its forms (physical abuse, witnessing parental violence, exposure to neighborhood violence, general violence victimization) will be positively associated with illicit and problem substance use, including (a) frequency of hard drug use, (b) frequency of marijuana use, (c) problem drug use, (d) problem marijuana use, and (c) problem alcohol use in middle adulthood.

ANALYTICAL APPROACH

As in the previous two chapters, the analysis begins with a selective examination of bivariate relationships of AEV and sociodemographic characteristics to the adult outcomes. Following the presentation of significant bivariate results, we move to a more detailed examination of the multivariate models for the adult outcomes, separately by gender. For frequency of hard drug use and frequency of marijuana use, the dependent variable is a highly skewed ratio-scaled variable that includes outlying cases with very high, but evidently valid, numerical values. For this reason, we use ordinary least squares (OLS) regression, but before performing the analysis, we apply a nonlinear transformation, the natural logarithmic transformation. This transformation, $LogY = ln(Y + 1)$, produces a less skewed dependent variable that still has a minimum value of zero. Two other reasons for using this transformation are that the relationship may be genuinely nonlinear, and the natural logarithmic transformation is a reasonable transformation for modeling that nonlinearity, and also that the lower frequencies for substance use (and for other illegal behavior as well) tend to be more reliable than the higher numeric values (Huizinga and Elliott 1986). The logarithmic transformation results in reducing the influence of the (more unreliable) higher numeric values of the dependent variable on the reliability of the dependent variable. OLS regression is also used in the analysis of problem hard drug, marijuana, and alcohol use, but these scales do not have the issues of high skewness or higher unreliability associated with higher values that characterize frequency of hard drug and marijuana use, so no transformation is applied prior to the analysis of these two outcomes.

For both frequency of hard drug use and frequency of marijuana use in adulthood, we include the logarithmically transformed frequencies of both hard drug use and marijuana use in adolescence as controls. Similarly, for all three of adult problem hard drug use, problem marijuana use, and problem alcohol use, we include both problem drug use and problem alcohol use in adolescence as controls. One may question why we use only frequency as a control for frequency, and problem use as a control for problem use. One could equally well question why we do not use adolescent substance use as a predictor of adult crime (in chapter 7), or adolescent mental health problems as a predictor of adult substance use in the present chapter. The short answer is that for adult frequency of substance use and, separately, adult problem substance use, we are selecting as adolescent controls those available predictors that most closely parallel the adult outcomes we are modeling. To reiterate the point made in chapter 1, our focus is on the utility of the predictors for a broad range of outcomes, not the relationship of the outcomes to the broadest or most inclusive range of predictors. The broader issue of the completeness of the models for each of our outcomes in chapters 4–8 will be revisited in chapter 9.

BIVARIATE RELATIONSHIPS

Figure 6.1 illustrates the relationships of AEV to the five substance use outcome variables. As in the previous chapters, AEV is coded "no" for respondents who

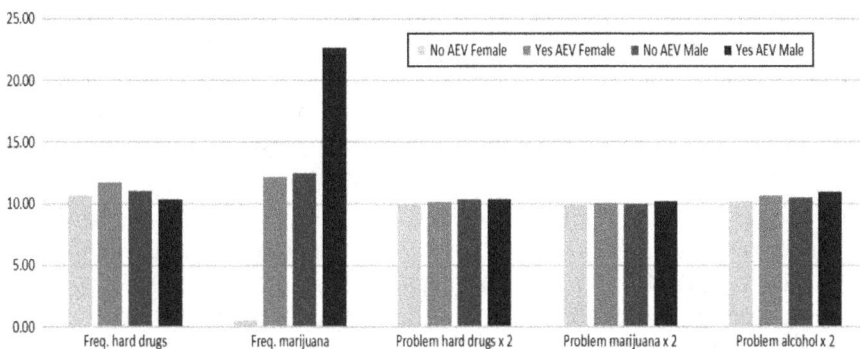

Figure 6.1   AEV and Adult Substance Use. *Source:* Created by the authors.

reported neither parental physical abuse nor witnessing parental violence, nor exposure to neighborhood violence, nor general violence victimization in adolescence, and "yes" for respondents who reported any one or more of those forms of AEV. Again, the figure is split by gender, going (from left to right within each outcome) from females who reported no AEV to females who reported some (yes) AEV, males who reported no AEV and to males who reported some (yes) AEV. The range for frequency of hard drug and marijuana use is wider than the range for the problem substance use scales, so to improve readability, the problem substance use scale scores have been multiplied by two in figure 6.1. In figure 6.1, frequency of hard drug use and frequency of marijuana use are higher for females who have experienced AEV than for females who have not, and frequency of marijuana use is higher for males who have experienced AEV than for males who have not, but frequency of hard drug use appears to be lower for males who have experienced AEV than for males who have not. For both females and males, for problem hard drug, marijuana, and alcohol use, there appears to be little difference between those who have experienced AEV and those who have not. What little difference does exist indicates higher scores on all three of the problem substance use scales for those who have experienced AEV than for those who have not.

Breaking down these relationships by specific types of AEV as well as gender, bivariate correlations indicate that female adult frequency of hard drug use is significantly positively associated with parental physical abuse ($r = .130$, $p = .001$), consistent witnessing of parental violence ($r = .108$, $p = .008$), and adolescent general violence victimization ($r = .120$, $p = .003$), but not with inconsistent reports of witnessing parental violence, exposure to neighborhood violence, or adolescent frequency of hard drug or marijuana use. It is also significantly and negatively associated with rural residence in adulthood ($r = -.092$, $p = .024$), and significantly positively associated with adolescent problem alcohol use ($r = .093$, $p = .028$), but it is not significantly associated with adolescent problem drug use, ethnicity, parental socioeconomic status (SES), residence, or having been in a two-parent family. Male adult hard drug use is significantly positively associated with exposure to neighborhood violence ($r = .102$, $p = .018$), frequency of hard drug use ($r = .164$, $p = .000$), frequency of marijuana use ($r = .131$, $p = .002$), problem drug use ($r = .138$. $p = .002$), and problem alcohol use in adolescence ($r = .110$, $p = .013$), but not with parental physical abuse, witnessing parental violence, or adolescent general violence victimization. Male adult hard drug use is also significantly negatively associated with upper/middle parental SES ($r = -.085$, $p = .047$), but not significantly associated with ethnicity, lower parental SES, residence, or two-parent family status in adolescence.

For both females and males, adult frequency of marijuana use is significantly positively associated with frequency of general violence victimization (r = .187, p = .000 for females; r = .127, p = .002 for males), frequency of hard drug use (r = .198, p = .000 for females; r = .333, p = .000 for males), frequency of marijuana use (r = .236, p = .000 for females; r = .309, p = .000 for males), problem drug use (r = .166, p = .000 for females; r = .282, p = .000 for males), and problem alcohol use (r = .108, p = .011 for females; r = .177, p = .000 for males) in adolescence. For females, adult frequency of marijuana use is also associated with consistent (but not inconsistent) reports of witnessing parental violence (r = .085, p = .038) and just barely significantly (to two decimal places; p = .05) positively associated with parental physical abuse (r = .079, p = .054). For males, adult frequency of marijuana use is not significantly associated with parental physical abuse, or with either consistent or inconsistent reports of witnessing parental violence. For both females and males, adult frequency of marijuana use is not significantly associated with neighborhood violence, minority ethnicity, parental SES, residence, or having been in a two-parent family.

The relationships of female adult problem hard drug use are significantly positive with parental physical abuse (r = .099, p = .016), adolescent general violence victimization (r = .152, p = .000), adolescent frequency of marijuana use (r = .127, p = .002), and adolescent problem alcohol use (r = .089, p = .036), but not with witnessing parental violence, neighborhood violence, adolescent hard drug use, or adolescent problem drug use. For males, adult problem hard drug use is significantly positively related to adolescent frequency of hard drug (r = .105, p = .013) and marijuana (r = .098, p = .020) use and to adolescent problem drug use (r = .154, p = .001), but not to parental physical abuse, witnessing parental violence, exposure to neighborhood violence, adolescent general violence victimization, or adolescent problem alcohol use. For both females and males, adult problem hard drug use is not significantly related to ethnicity, parental SES, residence, or two-parent family structure in adolescence.

Adult problem marijuana use for females is significantly positively related to adolescent frequency of marijuana use (r = .086, p = .036) and minority ethnicity (r = .108, p = .008), and not to adolescent hard drug use, adolescent problem drug or alcohol use, parental SES, residence, or two-parent family structure. For males, the positive relationship of adult problem marijuana use with inconsistent reports of witnessing parental violence is statistically significant (r = .139, p = .001). Adult problem marijuana use also has significant positive relationships with adolescent general violence victimization (r = .112, p = .008), frequency of hard drug use (r = .206, p = .000), frequency of marijuana use (r = −.116, p = .006), problem drug use (r = .237, p = .000), and problem alcohol use (r = .171, p = .000). The correlations of adult problem marijuana use with physical abuse, consistent reports of witnessing parental violence, exposure to neighborhood violence, ethnicity, parental SES, residence, and two-parent family are not statistically significant.

For both females and males, adult problem alcohol use is significantly pos-itively related to adolescent general violence victimization (r = .130, p = .002 for females; r = .090, p = .036 for males), marijuana use (r = .148, p = .000 for females; r = .126, p = .003 for males), problem drug use (r = .104, p = .015 for females; r = .200, p = .000 for males), problem alcohol use (r = .118, p = .006 for females; r = .183, p = .000 for males), and for males but not females, ado-lescent hard drug use (r = .187, p = .000). For both females and males, adult problem alcohol use is not significantly associated with ethnicity, parental SES, residence, or two-parent family.

In summary, based on the results of the bivariate correlation analysis, the hypothesis that AEV will be related to all of the adult substance use outcomes is supported except for problem drug use for males and problem marijuana use for females. We turn now to the multivariate analysis to see whether these relationships persist once other predictors are statistically controlled.

MULTIVARIATE ANALYSIS

Tables 6.1–6.5 follow the same format as the tables in the previous chapters, as described in the first two paragraphs in the Multivariate Analysis section in chapter 4. Table 6.1 presents the OLS regression results for the frequency of hard drug use. Significant predictors of *higher* frequency of hard drug use in adulthood for females include parental physical abuse and consistent reports of witnessing parental violence, while rural residence is predictive of *lower* hard drug use. Perhaps surprisingly, adolescent hard drug and marijuana use are not significant predictors of adult hard drug use for females, but neither were they in the bivariate analysis. In the bivariate analysis, adolescent general violence victimization was significantly positively correlated with adult hard drug use for females, but controlling for the other predictors in the multivariate model in table 6.1, the relationship of adult hard drug use and adolescent general violence victimization is not statistically significant. This suggests that the relationship of adolescent violence victimization with adult frequency of hard drug use is either spurious with or mediated by other variables in the model, with spuriousness with parental abuse being one pos-sibility. The predictors in table 6.1 explain 6.2% of the variance in the adult frequency of hard drug use for females.

Significant predictors of higher frequency of hard drug use in adulthood for males include only exposure to neighborhood violence and adolescent hard drug use. In the bivariate analysis, adolescent marijuana use was also significantly positively, and upper/middle parental SES significantly nega-tively, related to adult hard drug use, but those relationships are not statisti-cally significant when controlling for other predictors in the multivariate

Table 6.1 OLS Regression Results for Logged Frequency of Hard Drug Use

Predictors	Coefficients: Female/Male			
	Standardized Coefficient (b*)	Unstandardized Coefficient (b)	Standard Error of b	Statistical Significance (p)
Parental Physical Abuse	.115/−.017	.254/−.050	.108/.142	.019/.723
Witnessing Parental Violence (Inconsistent)	−.010/−.017	−.036/−.061	.157/.162	.817/.708
Witnessing Parental Violence (Consistent)	.137/.037	.418/.126	.144/.157	.004/.425
Neighborhood Violence	−.032/.120	−.103/.379	.143/.151	.470/.012
Adolescent General Violence Victimization	.064/−.018	.070/−.017	.053/.046	.189/.713
Adolescent Hard Drug Use	.011/.131	.009/.096	.050/.048	.855/.048
Adolescent Marijuana Use	−.075/.011	−.041/.005	.031/.031	.196/.870
Minority Ethnicity	−.001/.031	−.002/.091	.151/.149	.989/.542
Upper/Middle Parental SES	.081/−.082	.216/−.211	.132/.139	.101/.128
Lower Parental SES	.056/.004	.130/.009	.116/.120	.261/.939
Urban	.055/.018	.158/.050	.135/.135	.242/.710
Rural	−.100/−.003	−.307/−.009	.136/.134	.025/.947
Two-Parent Family Structure	.067/.080	.204/.258	.146/.157	.165/.101
Constant	NA/NA	.003/.015	.184/.204	.987/.942

Note: R^2 = .062, p = .001, N = 534 for females; R^2 = .046, p = .047, N = 490 for males. NA = not applicable.

model in Table 6.1, suggesting that the relationships of adolescent marijuana use and upper/middle parental SES are spurious with or mediated by other variables in the multivariate model. Here it seems likely that it is specifically adolescent hard drug use that accounts for the absence of a significant effect of adolescent marijuana use on adult hard drug use, given the high correlation between adolescent marijuana and hard drug use and the typical sequencing of marijuana and hard drug use in adolescence (Elliott et al. 1989). Those results indicate that marijuana use was typically initiated prior to, and increased the subsequent risk of, hard drug use. Taken together with the present results, it seems likely that marijuana use leads to hard drug use in adolescence, and that subsequent hard drug use in adulthood reflects continuity in hard drug use from adolescence to adulthood for males. The predictors in table 6.1 explain 4.6% of the variance in the adult frequency of hard drug use for males.

Table 6.2 presents the OLS regression results for the frequency of marijuana use. Significant predictors of higher frequency of marijuana use in adulthood for females include only adolescent general violence victimization and adolescent marijuana use. In the bivariate analysis, other significant pre-dictors of higher frequency of adult marijuana use included parental physical abuse (marginally, with p = .054), consistent reports of witnessing parental violence, adolescent hard drug use, and adolescent marijuana use. As with hard drug use for males, it appears that for females there is continuity in marijuana use from adolescence to adulthood, and that adolescent hard drug use may be spuriously related to adult marijuana use through adolescent mari-juana use. The other variables that have significant relationships with adult marijuana use in the bivariate analysis but not in the multivariate analysis in table 6.2 may also involve either spurious or mediated relationships with adult marijuana use. The predictors in table 6.2 explain 10.4% of the variance in the adult frequency of marijuana use for females.

Significant predictors of higher frequency of marijuana use in adulthood for males include both marijuana use and hard drug use in adolescence. Minority ethnicity has a significant negative relationship with adult marijuana use for males, a relationship that was not quite statistically significant (p = .079) in the bivariate analysis, but which emerges as statistically significant (p = .021)

Table 6.2   OLS Regression Results for Logged Frequency of Marijuana Use

Predictors	Coefficients: Female/Male			
	Standardized Coefficient (b*)	Unstandardized Coefficient (b)	Standard Error of b	Statistical Significance (p)
Parental Physical Abuse	−.053/−.006	−.104/−.023	.093/.173	.264/.892
Witnessing Parental Violence (Inconsistent)	.021/.056	.065/.254	.135/.197	.628/.198
Witnessing Parental Violence (Consistent)	.074/.058	.199/.254	.124/.192	.110/.185
Neighborhood Violence	−.047/−.005	−.134/−.020	.124/.184	.280/.913
Adolescent General Violence Victimization	.137/.002	.130/.002	.045/.055	.004/.967
Adolescent Hard Drug Use	.090/.215	.068/.204	.043/.059	.115/.001
Adolescent Marijuana Use	.181/.159	.086/.096	.027/.037	.002/.010
Minority Ethnicity	.047/−.110	.127/−.420	.131/.182	.329/.021
Upper/Middle Parental SES	.026/−.018	.062/−.059	.113/.169	.588/.726
Lower Parental SES	.069/.073	.141/.210	.100/.146	.158/.151
Urban	.020/.031	.051/.110	.117/.164	.662/.504
Rural	.014/−.033	.037/−.119	.117/.164	.754/.466
Two-Parent Family Structure	.056/−.079	.150/−.327	.126/.191	.235/.088
Constant	NA/NA	−.259/.424	.158/.249	.102/.089

Note: R^2 = .104, p = .000, N = 532 for females; R^2 = .160, p = .000, N = 490 for males. NA = not applicable.

after controlling for the other predictors in the multivariate model in table 6.2. The only other variable with a significant bivariate relationship with adult marijuana use is adolescent general violence victimization, a relationship which, given the absence of a significant relationship in the multivariate analysis, appears to be spurious with or mediated by other variables in table 6.5. The predictors in table 6.2 explain 16% of the variance in the adult frequency of marijuana use for males.

Table 6.3 presents the OLS regression results for problem hard drug use. The two significant predictors of higher problem hard drug use in adulthood for females are adolescent general violence victimization and urban residence, the latter of which was not quite statistically significant (p = .060) in the bivariate correlations. Also in the bivariate analysis, adult problem hard drug use for females was significantly positively correlated with parental physical abuse and adolescent problem alcohol use. Those two relationships are not statistically significant at the .05 level in table 6.3, suggesting that their relationships are either indirect or spurious. Frequency of marijuana use is not included in the model for adult problem hard drug use because we use

Table 6.3   OLS Regression Results for Problem Hard Drug Use

Predictors	Coefficients: Female/Male			
	Standardized Coefficient (b*)	Unstandardized Coefficient (b)	Standard Error of b	Statistical Significance (p)
Parental Physical Abuse	.083/.043	.065/.143	.040/.160	.104/.372
Witnessing Parental Violence (Inconsistent)	−.039/−.002	−.048/−.008	.055/.179	.377/.966
Witnessing Parental Violence (Consistent)	−.081/.077	−.088/.282	.052/.172	.089/.101
Neighborhood violence	.031/−.006	.035/−.019	.051/.167	.491/.909
Adolescent General Violence Victimization	.190/−.033	.073/−.033	.019/.052	.000/.527
Adolescent Problem Drug Use	−.046/.213	−.008/.094	.013/.025	.535/.000
Adolescent Problem Alcohol Use	.034/−.077	.005/−.023	.011/.017	.649/.174
Minority Ethnicity	−.083/−.043	−.090/−.136	.053/.165	.092/.408
Upper/Middle Parental SES	.042/−.067	.040/−.188	.046/.154	.394/.224
Lower Parental SES	.068/−.065	.055/−.157	.041/.133	.178/.239
Urban	.156/.095	.157/.287	.047/.149	.001/.055
Rural	.079/.079	.084/.242	.048/.148	.080/.103
Two-Parent Family Structure	.039/.055	.041/.192	.051/.175	.426/.273
Constant	NA/NA	4.915/4.302	.108/.325	.000/.000

Note: R² = .076, p = .000, N = 516 for females; R² = .056, p = .015, N = 467 for males. NA = not applicable.

problem substance use rather than frequency of substance use in adolescence as the controls for adult problem use, but in the bivariate analysis, adult problem drug use was significantly associated with the frequency of adolescent marijuana use. The predictors in table 6.3 explain 7.6% of the variance in the adult problem hard drug use for females.

In the bivariate analysis, adolescent problem drug use was significantly positively correlated with adult problem hard drug use for males, and the relationship is also significantly positive in the multivariate results in table 6.3. Two variables not in the model in table 6.3, adolescent hard drug and marijuana use, were also significantly positively correlated with adult problem hard drug use for males. Again, we limit the adolescent controls for adult problem substance use to the conceptually most similar variables in adolescence. Also in table 6.3, while only adolescent problem drug use has a significant positive relationship with adult problem drug use, the positive relationship with urban residence is close at p = .055. The predictors in table 6.3 explain 5.6% of the variance in adult problem hard drug use.

Table 6.4 presents the OLS regression results for problem marijuana use. The significant predictors of higher problem marijuana use in adulthood for females are adolescent general violence victimization and minority ethnicity, the latter of which also had a significant positive bivariate association with adult problem marijuana use. Adolescent general violence victimization was not quite significant at the .05 level (p = .072) in the bivariate analysis, but it does have a significant direct effect when controlling for the other predictors in the model. Of the remaining predictors, only adolescent marijuana use, which is not included as a control in the model for adult problem use of marijuana, had a significant positive relationship with adult problem marijuana use for females. The predictors in table 6.4 explain only 2.8% of the variance in adult problem marijuana use for females, and this level of explained variance is not statistically significant (p = .332).

The two significant predictors of higher adult problem marijuana use for males are inconsistent reports of witnessing parental violence and adolescent problem drug use. In the bivariate analysis, adolescent violence victimization and problem alcohol use were also significantly positively associated with male adult problem marijuana use, but based on the results in table 6.4, their effects on adult problem marijuana use appear to be spurious or indirect. For general violence victimization, one possibility is that the effect is indirect via adolescent problem drug use. It is possible that adolescent frequencies of marijuana and hard drug use are also involved, possibly as mediators between general violence victimization and problem drug use, but that possibility is speculative, and it is beyond the scope of the present study (and probably the present data) to fully test it. The impact of problem alcohol use may more plausibly be spurious, with similar etiologies for problem alcohol

Table 6.4   OLS Regression Results for Problem Marijuana Use

Predictors	Coefficients: Female/Male			
	Standardized Coefficient (b*)	Unstandardized Coefficient (b)	Standard Error of b	Statistical Significance (p)
Parental Physical Abuse	−.066/−.028	−.044/−.035	.035/.060	.204/.556
Witnessing Parental Violence (Inconsistent)	.024/.119	.025/.174	.048/.068	.596/.011
Witnessing Parental Violence (Consistent)	−.023/.063	−.022/.086	.045/.064	.633/.181
Neighborhood Violence	−.015/.007	−.015/.009	.044/.062	.740/.885
Adolescent General Violence Victimization	.107/.031	.035/.012	.017/.019	.037/.542
Adolescent Problem Drug Use	.017/.226	.003/.038	.011/.009	.823/.000
Adolescent Problem Alcohol Use	−.004/.019	−.000/.002	.009/.006	.958/.737
Minority Ethnicity	.127/−.057	.116/−.069	.046/.061	.012/.265
Upper/Middle parental SES	−.044/.005	−.035/.006	.041/.058	.390/.921
Lower Parental SES	−.051/−.011	−.035/−.010	.036/.050	.329/.838
Urban	−.017/−.008	−.015/−.009	.042/.056	.727/.873
Rural	.040/.039	.036/.045	.042/.055	.390/.416
Two-Parent Family Structure	.015/.026	.013/.034	.045/.066	.766/.608
Constant	NA/NA	4.973/4.558	.094/.122	.000/.000

Note: R^2 = .028, p = .332, N = 517 for females; R^2 = .083, p = .000, N = 466 for males. NA = not applicable.

use and problem drug use (Elliott et al. 1989). Adolescent frequency of hard drug use and marijuana use also had significant positive correlations with adult problem marijuana use for males, but as frequency rather than problem use measures, they are not included as controls in the model for problem marijuana use. The explained variance in adult problem marijuana use in Table 6.4 is 8.3%.

Table 6.5 presents the OLS regression results for adult problem alcohol use. Adolescent general violence victimization has a significant positive relationship with adult problem alcohol use for females, and is the single statistically significant predictor for females in table 6.5. In the bivariate analysis, other predictors with significant positive relationships with female adult problem alcohol use include adolescent problem drug use and adolescent problem alcohol use. The effects of adolescent problem drug and alcohol use appear to be spurious or indirect, possibly spurious, with adolescent general violence victimization as a common cause. Frequencies of adolescent hard drug and marijuana use were also significantly positively related to adult problem alcohol use for females, but as frequency rather than problem use

Table 6.5   OLS Regression Results for Problem Alcohol Use

Predictors	Coefficients: Female/Male			
	Standardized Coefficient (b*)	Unstandardized Coefficient (b)	Standard Error of b	Statistical Significance (p)
Parental Physical Abuse	−.059/−.077	−.119/−.260	.108/.162	.268/.110
Witnessing Parental Violence (Inconsistent)	.041/.034	.135/.138	.150/.190	.369/.467
Witnessing Parental Violence (Consistent)	.041/.026	.120/.096	.143/.175	.402/.585
Neighborhood Violence	−.010/−.037	−.031/−.134	.140/.178	.826/.454
Adolescent General Violence Victimization	.109/.004	.110/.004	.053/.053	.037/.943
Adolescent Problem Drug Use	.016/.153	.007/.069	.036/.026	.839/.007
Adolescent Problem Alcohol Use	.104/.150	.039/.047	.030/.017	.190/.007
Minority Ethnicity	.067/−.063	.191/−.207	.147/.170	.195/.224
Upper/Middle Parental SES	.014/−.083	.035/−.240	.129/.160	.786/.135
Lower Parental SES	.033/−.040	.072/−.100	.114/.137	.527/.469
Urban	−.076/−.017	−.206/−.052	.133/.152	.124/.733
Rural	−.007/−.082	−.018/−.256	.131/.150	.888/.088
Two-Parent Family Structure	.071/−.054	.200/−.191	.141/.180	.157/.291
Constant	NA/NA	4.417/4.439	.296/.340	.000/.000

Note: R^2 = .040, p = .097, N = 502 for females; R^2 = .095, p = .000, N = 449 for males. NA = not applicable.

variables, they were not included as controls for adult problem alcohol use. Explained variance for the model in table 6.5 is 4.0%, which at p = .097 is not statistically significant.

Both adolescent problem drug use and adolescent problem alcohol use have significant positive effects on adult male problem alcohol use, and are the only predictors with significant effects in the model for males in table 6.5. In the bivariate correlations for males, adolescent general violence victimization also had a significant positive relationship with adult male problem alcohol use. The effect of adolescent general violence victimization appears to be spurious or indirect, possibly via adolescent problem drug or alcohol use, and possibly with frequency of hard drug or marijuana use also in the causal sequence, perhaps between adolescent general violence victimization and adolescent problem drug or alcohol use. As with adult male problem marijuana use, this suggestion is entirely speculative, and it is beyond the scope of the present study (and probably the present data) to fully test it. Adolescent frequencies of hard drug and marijuana use were significantly positively correlated with adult male problem alcohol use, but as frequency rather than problem use variables, they were not included as controls for adult problem alcohol use. Explained variance for the model in table 6.5 is 9.5%.

DISCUSSION

We begin this section with a summary of the effects of each of the AEV predictors, followed by an examination of gender differences in the effects of AEV on adult illicit drug use and problem substance use, and follow this section with general conclusions that can be drawn based on the combination of the present study with previous results from the NYSFS on the relationship of AEV with adult illicit drug use and problem substance use (Menard et al. 2015). Menard et al. (2015) examined the prevalence (whether) as opposed to the frequency (how many times) of adult hard drug use and marijuana use, and one would expect that those results would be similar to the results for frequency of adult hard drug and marijuana use in the present chapter, but they did not analyze the impact of AEV on adult problem hard drug, marijuana, or alcohol use.

In the bivariate analysis, parental physical abuse is significantly positively associated with frequency of hard drug use, frequency of marijuana use (marginally, p = .054), and problem hard drug use, all for females but not for males. In the multivariate analysis, it has a significant positive direct effect only on adult hard drug use for females. In Menard et al. (2015), parental physical abuse had significant positive bivariate correlations with the prevalence of adult hard drug use for females and with the prevalence of adult marijuana use for both females and males. In the multivariate analysis, however, parental physical abuse was not statistically significant as a predictor of adult marijuana or hard drug use for females or males.

Inconsistent reports of witnessing parental violence were significantly positively associated with adult problem marijuana use for males in both the bivariate and multivariate analyses. Consistent reports of witnessing parental violence for females, but not for males, are significantly positively associated with the frequency of adult hard drug use and marijuana use in both the bivariate correlations and the multivariate analysis for the frequency of adult hard drug use, but not with the frequency of adult marijuana use. In Menard et al. (2015), inconsistent reports of witnessing parental violence were not significantly related to adult prevalence of hard drug or marijuana use, for females or males, in either the bivariate correlations or the multivariate analysis. Menard et al. (2015) also found that consistent reports of witnessing parental violence were significantly positively associated with adult prevalence of both hard drug and marijuana use, in both the bivariate and the multivariate analysis, only for females and not for males.

Exposure to neighborhood violence was significantly positively associated with the frequency of adult hard drug use for males but not for females, in both the bivariate correlations and the multivariate analysis, but was otherwise not significantly associated with any of the adult substance use outcomes in the present chapter. The same pattern of a positive relationship in both bivariate and multivariate analysis between exposure to neighborhood violence and adult hard drug use (but not marijuana use) for males (but not females) was found in Menard et al. (2015).

In the bivariate analysis, adolescent general violence victimization was significantly positively associated with the frequency of adult hard drug and marijuana use and with adult problem marijuana use and problem alcohol use for females; and also with frequency of adult marijuana use, adult problem marijuana use, and adult problem alcohol use for males. In the multivariate analyses, adolescent general violence victimization had significantly positive relationships with adult frequency of marijuana use, problem drug use, problem marijuana use, and problem alcohol use for females, but had no significant direct effect for any of the outcomes for males. For prevalence rather than frequency of adult hard drug and marijuana use, the multiple logistic regression analysis in Menard et al. (2015) found that adolescent general violence victimization was significantly positively related to the prevalence of hard drug and marijuana use for females, but not for males.

Of the twenty significant relationships found in the multivariate analyses in the present chapter, there were only two coefficients (one relationship) that were significant for both females and males, the effect of adolescent marijuana use on adult marijuana use. The impact of urban residence on adult problem hard drug use came close (p = .001 for females, p = .055 for males), and could arguably be considered to count as a twenty-first significant coefficient and a second relationship that was the same for females and males. The remaining eighteen significant relationships were significant for either females (nine) or males (nine), but not both. Of those relationships, six were significantly different for females and males: (1) the direct effect of adolescent general violence victimization on adult problem hard drug use (z = 4.03, p = .000); (2) the direct effect of adolescent problem drug use on adult problem hard drug use (z = −10.35, p = .000); (3) the direct effect of adolescent general violence victimization on adult problem marijuana use (z = 2.98, p = .003); (4) the direct effect of adolescent problem drug use on adult problem marijuana use (z = −14.71, p = .000); (5) the direct effect of minority ethnicity on adult problem marijuana use (z = 2.41, p = .016); and the direct effect of adolescent problem drug use on adult problem alcohol use (z = -3.09, p = .002). Notice that of the six significant differences, three involve effects of adolescent problem drug use that were significant for males but not for females, and two involve effects of adolescent general violence victimization that were significant for females but not for males.

To summarize, the hypothesis regarding the impact of AEV on adult illicit and problem substance use is supported for all five outcomes for females, but only for frequency of hard drug use and for problem marijuana use for males. Of the four AEV measures, to the extent that AEV has an impact on adult illicit and problem substance use, it appears to be adolescent general violence victimization, rather than parental physical abuse, witnessing parental violence, or exposure to neighborhood violence, that is the principal risk factor.

CONCLUSIONS

The first conclusion that can be drawn from the results in the present chapter is that there appear to be real and substantial gender differences in the impact of AEV on the frequency (and also, based on Menard et al. 2015, the prevalence) of adult hard drug and marijuana use, and on adult problem hard drug, problem marijuana, and problem alcohol use. In the multivariate analyses for females, the frequency of parental physical abuse and consistent reports of witnessing parental violence have significant direct effects on the frequency of adult hard drug use, and the frequency of adolescent general violence victimization has significant direct effects on frequency of adult marijuana use, and on problem hard drug use, problem marijuana use, and problem alcohol use. Those same variables are not significant predictors for males. Instead, for males but not for females, neighborhood violence and adolescent frequency of hard drug use are significant as predictors of adult hard drug use, adolescent frequency of hard drug use is a predictor of adult frequency of marijuana use, and adolescent problem drug use is a significant predictor of adult problem hard drug use, problem marijuana use, and along with adolescent problem alcohol use as a second predictor that is significant for males but not for females, problem alcohol use. More than was the case for adult SES or mental health, the results for adult illicit drug use and problem substance use reinforce the need to consider gender differences when examining the relationship of AEV with adult outcomes.

Second, returning to theoretical considerations raised earlier in this chapter, the pattern of a more pervasive impact of AEV on drug use and problem use for females as opposed to males, combined with prior research indicating that females are more likely than males to respond to strain with internalizing behaviors (such as anxiety or depression) rather than externalizing behaviors (such as violence), suggests that females, more than males, may be self-medicating in response to anxiety or depression produced by AEV. For females, every one of the five outcomes has a significant positive direct effect from some form of adolescent direct physical violence victimization as a predictor (parental abuse for frequency of hard drug use; general violence victimization for the other four outcomes), and consistent witnessing of parental violence also has a significant positive direct effect on frequency of adult hard drug use for females. For males, the primary pattern is one of continuity from adolescence to adulthood, with adolescent hard drug use as a significant predictor of adult hard drug use; adolescent marijuana use, and also hard drug use, as predictors of adult marijuana use; adolescent problem drug use as a predictor of adult problem drug use, problem marijuana use, and problem alcohol use; and adolescent problem alcohol use as a predictor of adult problem alcohol use. The only indications of direct effects from AEV to adult substance use and problem substance use outcomes for males are the positive direct effects of exposure to neighborhood violence on adult frequency of hard drug use, and of inconsistent reports of witnessing parental violence on adult problem marijuana use.

Third and finally, to the extent that a distinction can be drawn between more direct exposure to violence (actual victimization by parental physical abuse or general violence in adolescence) and less direct exposure (witnessing parental violence, exposure to neighborhood violence), the effects of direct exposure are more important for females, and to the extent that AEV matters for males, it is the more indirect forms of AEV that are predictive of adult substance use frequency and problem use. The two significant direct effects of AEV for males involve more indirect exposure (direct effects of inconsistent reports of witnessing parental violence on problem marijuana use, and of exposure to neighborhood violence on frequency of hard drug use). For females, in contrast, of the six direct effects of AEV, five involve direct physical victimization and only one (the direct effect of consistent reports of witnessing parental violence on frequency of hard drug use) involves more indirect exposure. Again, there is an effect of a more direct form of AEV (parental physical abuse for adult frequency of hard drug use; adolescent general violence victimization for the other four outcomes) on every one of the adult drug-related outcomes for females. For males, then, indirect exposure to violence has an impact for adult frequency of hard drug use and problem marijuana use, while for females, direct exposure to violence has a more pervasive impact, affecting frequency of hard drugs and marijuana use and also problem use of hard drugs, marijuana, and alcohol in adulthood.

Chapter 7

Adolescent Exposure to Violence and Adult General Violence Victimization and Perpetration

The theoretical framework for predicting that adolescent exposure to violence will be associated with subsequent violence victimization and perpetration is, as in previous chapters, based on strain theory, but also, for violence victimization and perpetration, on social learning theory. Agnew's (1985, 1992, 2002) general strain theory predicts that exposure to and/or inability to avoid noxious stimuli, including but not limited to AEV, may provoke perpetration of violence, and this may occur to gain revenge, to express frustration, to try to exercise or regain a sense of control over one's circumstances, or, by projecting an image of toughness, to deter further victimization (Baron 2009; Hay and Evans 2006; Rebellon and Van Gundy 2005). With reference to the modes of adaptation in Merton's (1938) anomie theory, including the extension of anomie theory by Cloward and Ohlin (1960), either the innovation or the rebellion mode of adaptation may lead to criminal or delinquent violence perpetration. This does not, however, address the relationship of strain to violence victimization.

Social learning theory (Akers 1985; Bandura 1977) predicts that exposure to violence will affect both perpetration and victimization, a prediction consistent with the intergenerational cycle of violence perspective and research (e.g., Straus et al. 1980; Widom 1989b). Children who witness the use of violence in the family and neighborhood contexts may interpret aggressive behavior as an appropriate response to conflict and may more readily take on the roles of either or both, victim or perpetrator. It is not clear from the theory whether we should expect only short-term effects, or whether the effects should persist later in life, and whether exposure to violence of a particular form in the home or community, for example, intimate partner violence (IPV), should be associated with the same forms of violence in those same specific contexts (again, for example, IPV), or should be associated with violence more generally (perpetration of violence other than IPV).

The relationship of adolescent exposure to arrest is more complicated. Arrest, like victimization, is an involuntary and generally undesired behavior, contingent on the actions of others. Like victimization, it could in principle be modeled in the family or neighborhood context, but in contrast to violence, there is nothing in the literature to suggest that being arrested is itself a learned behavior. Arrest is not uniquely associated with violence, but may instead occur for offenses such as theft or public order offenses, in which no violence occurs. This raises the question of whether we should expect adolescent exposure to violence to result in non-violent, as opposed to or in addition to violent, behavior that could result in arrest. Finally, although we would expect arrest to be associated with actual illegal behavior, illegal behavior is not by any means the sole influence on arrest. In addition to being influenced by, and controlling for, current illegal behavior, the likelihood of arrest is also increased by prior arrest record ("the usual suspects"), association with others who are involved in illegal behavior ("guilt by association"), being male, having lower academic achievement (performance in school, which continues to have an effect on arrest even in adulthood after the completion of formal education), lower parental socioeconomic status (SES), and minority ethnic group membership (specific to the sample used in the present study, see Pollock and Menard 2014; Pollock et al. 2012, 2016). Although there is an extensive literature on theories to explain illegal behavior, no such literature exists to explain arrest as distinct from illegal behavior. Instead, arrest has often been used as a proxy for actual illegal behavior (inappropriately; see the review in Elliott et al. 1989) in research on crime and delinquency.

Existing evidence on the specific predictors considered here is limited for adolescence, and sometimes includes more general victimization or extends beyond adolescence to childhood; or to specific (e.g., IPV) rather than general violent victimization in adulthood. Regarding the impact of physical abuse on subsequent violence, Rebellon and Van Gundy (2005) used National Youth Survey data over a 3-year span from 1976 to 1978. About 6% of their respondents indicated a parent had beaten them up in the previous year. Those respondents reporting having been physically abused were more likely to have reported both property and violent offending than those reporting no physical abuse. They also found that abuse was equally associated with male and female delinquency. Widom (1989a) found that physical abuse (and also neglect) increased the likelihood of adult arrests for violent offenses (in contrast to sexual abuse, which was actually associated with lower rates of arrest for violent offenses). Widom and Maxfield (1996) further specified that abused and neglected children had a higher likelihood of arrest for delinquency, adult criminality, and violent criminal behavior than controls.

Further, abused and neglected children were arrested earlier, committed more offenses, and more often became chronic or repeat offenders. Zingraff et al. (1993) found similar results in an analysis of violent crime arrest rates for youth with a history of abuse or neglect and those with no record of maltreatment, using North Carolina's central registry of child abuse and neglect. In a similar vein, Currie and Tekin (2012) measured the impact of maltreatment on the tendency to commit crimes in adulthood. They found that child abuse and neglect experiences, for females and males, doubled the likelihood of committing crimes in young adulthood.

Ireland et al. (2002) and Thornberry et al. (2001) found evidence for effects of adolescent but not earlier childhood maltreatment (substantiated physical abuse, sexual abuse, and neglect) on later arrest, drug use, street crimes, and violent crimes in early and late adolescence. Specific to adolescence but not specific to parental physical abuse, Menard (2002) found that violent victimization in adolescence was predictive of both violent offending and violent victimization in early adulthood. Overall, these findings suggest that physical abuse should be predictive of adult violence perpetration and victimization. The question is whether adolescent physical abuse by parents is predictive of both offending and victimization, and is predictive in the long term (for older respondents) as well as the short term.

Evidence regarding the impact of witnessing parental violence during adolescence on adult violent offending and victimization is limited, and tends to focus largely on the impact of witnessing parental violence on adult IPV, discussed in the next chapter, or on more diffuse and diverse measures of behavior or adjustment, including anxiety, internalizing behaviors, physical development, and delinquency, primarily over the short term rather than from adolescence to adulthood (e.g., Herrenkohl et al. 2008; Kolbo et al. 1996; Wolfe et al. 2003). To the extent that aggression or violence is included as an outcome, the results tend to be mixed or equivocal (Kolbo et al. 1996). For example, Weir et al. (2019) found in a longitudinal study of childhood and adolescent that exposure to IPV led to differing paths for males and females. Males without exposure to IPV had the highest levels of externalized behaviors (e.g., offending or drug use). Males with IPV exposure had the highest level of persistent offending but this was not found for females. Females demonstrated similar externalized behaviors, regardless of exposure. This limited and contradictory research raises the question whether witnessing parental violence has any impact on general violent victimization and offending in adulthood.

A number of studies have confirmed that children are negatively affected by exposure to community violence (Eitle and Turner 2002; see also Johnson et al. 2002, for a review). In particular, there is evidence that exposure to community violence is associated with increased aggressive and violent behavior (Boney-McCoy and Finkelhor 1995; Farrell and Bruce 1997; Overstreet 2000; Tremblay 2000). In a study of urban middle school students Barroso, et al. (2008) found that youth exposed to community violence were at least three times more likely to engage in acts of violence compared to non-exposed youth. The question remains whether exposure to violence in the community has effects not only on subsequent aggressive and violent behavior but also on violent victimization, that persist into middle adulthood.

Based on the evidence from past studies, and insights from strain and social learning theories, we hypothesize that adolescent exposure to violence will be predictive of adult (a) violence victimization, (b) violence perpetration, and (c) arrest. We further expect that of the three outcomes, violence perpetration will be the one most closely associated with adolescent exposure to violence, more so for males than for females, but each of the outcomes in middle adulthood will be associated with at least one of physical abuse by parents, witnessing parental violence, exposure to neighborhood violence, or general violence victimization in adolescence.

ANALYTICAL APPROACH

Once again, the analysis begins with the presentation of the bivariate relationships involving AEV and the adult outcomes, followed by multivariate analyses separately by gender. As was the case with frequency of hard drug use and frequency of marijuana use, frequencies of violence victimization and perpetration tend to be highly skewed. There is strong research evidence that high numeric values for perpetration are less reliable than lower values (Huizinga and Elliott 1986), and while we lack comparable research on victimization, it remains the case that frequency of victimization, like frequency of perpetration, may benefit from the use of the same nonlinear transformation, if only to reduce the skewness in the dependent variable. As with frequency of hard drug and marijuana use, therefore, we use ordinary least squares (OLS) regression, but apply a logarithmic transformation $LnY = \ln(Y + 1)$ to the outcome variables prior to analysis. For arrest, skewness is not an issue, and we use OLS regression without a prior nonlinear transformation in the analysis of frequency of arrest.

BIVARIATE RELATIONSHIPS

Figure 7.1 illustrates the relationships of AEV to general violence victimization, general violence perpetration, and arrest. As in the previous chapters, AEV is coded "no" for respondents who reported neither parental physical

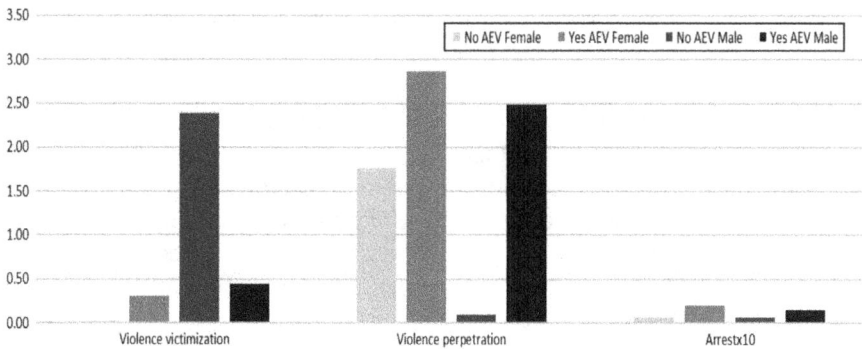

Figure 7.1   AEV and Adult Violence Victimization, Violence Perpetration, and Arrest.
Source: Created by the authors.

abuse nor witnessing parental violence, nor exposure to neighborhood violence, nor adolescent general violence victimization in adolescence, and "yes" for respondents who reported any one or more of those forms of AEV. Again, the figure is split by gender, going (from left to right within each outcome) from females who reported no AEV to females who reported some (yes) AEV, males who reported no AEV, and to males who reported some (yes) AEV. For both females and males, adult violence perpetration and arrest are higher for individuals who have experienced AEV than for those who have not. For females, adult violence victimization is also higher for individuals who have experienced AEV than for those who have not, but for males, unexpectedly, adult violence victimization is *lower* for those who have experienced AEV than for those who have not. This relationship will be further examined in the multivariate results here.

Breaking down these relationships by specific types of AEV as well as gender, bivariate correlations indicate that for females, there is a significant positive relationship of adult general violence victimization with parental physical abuse ($r = .082$, $p = .036$), inconsistent reporting of parental violence ($r = .142$, $p = .000$), and exposure to neighborhood violence ($r = .164$, $p = .000$). For males, adult general violence victimization is not significantly associated with parental physical abuse, consistent reports of witnessing parental violence, or exposure to neighborhood violence. For both females and males, there is a significant positive association of frequency of adult general violence victimization with adolescent general violence victimization ($r = .146$, $p = .000$ for females; $r = .111$, $p = .005$ for males) and perpetration ($r = .083$, $p = .034$ for females; $r = .126$, $p = .001$ for males), and also with minority ethnicity ($r = .137$, $p = .000$ for females; $r = .093$, $p = .018$ for males). For females, there is a significant negative relationship between adult general violence victimization and having a two-parent family structure at the beginning of the study (r = −.090, p = .023), but the relationship does not quite reach the p ≤ .05 cutoff for males (r = −.072, p = .069). For males but not for females, upper/middle parental SES background is significantly negatively associated with adult general violence victimization (r = −.092, p = .024). For both females and males, adult general violence victimization is not significantly associated with lower parental SES or with residence.

Bivariate correlations indicate that for females, adult general violence perpetration is significantly and positively associated with frequency of adolescent general violence victimization (r = .141, p = .000) and perpetration (r = .092, p = .018), but not with parental physical abuse, witnessing parental violence, exposure to neighborhood violence, ethnicity, parental SES, residence, or two-parent family. For males, there is a significant positive relationship of adult general violence perpetration with adolescent general violence victimization (r = .180, p = .000) and perpetration (r = .163, p = .000), and a borderline significant positive relationship of adult general violence perpetration with parental physical abuse in adolescence (r = .077, p = .053), but no significant relationship for males of adult general violence perpetration with witnessing parental violence, exposure to neighborhood violence, ethnicity, parental SES, residence, or being in a two-parent family in adolescence. For males but not for females, adult violence perpetration is positively associated with adolescent general offending (r = .155, p = .000), hard drug use (r = .104, p = .008), and marijuana use (r = .083, p = .036).

For females, adult frequency of arrest is significantly positively related to only three predictors, parental physical abuse (r = .094, p = .024), adolescent frequency of marijuana use (r = .095, p = .022), and minority ethnicity (r = .108, p = .009), and not significantly related to witnessing parental violence, exposure to neighborhood violence, adolescent general violence victimization or perpetration, adolescent frequency of general offending or hard drug use, parental SES, residence, or two-parent family. For males, adult frequency of arrest is significantly positively related to adolescent frequency of general violence victimization (r = .171, p = .000), general violence perpetration (r = .186, p = .000), general offending (r = .138, p = .001), hard drug use (r = .096, p = .027), marijuana use (r = .103, p = .018), and also to minority ethnicity (r = .106, p = .015), and significantly negatively related to upper/middle parental SES (r = −.108, p = .015) and to having been in a two-parent family in adolescence (r = −.155, p = .000). For males, adult frequency of arrest is not significantly related to parental physical abuse, witnessing parental violence, exposure to neighborhood violence, lower parental SES, or residence.

The bivariate correlations support the hypothesis that AEV will be associated with adult violence victimization, violence perpetration, and arrest, for both females and males. General violence victimization appears to be the principal risk factor for adult violence victimization and perpetration, and for arrest, closely followed by parental physical abuse in adolescence. For the more indirect measures of AEV, there is one significant correlation each for inconsistent reporting of witnessing parental violence and for exposure to neighborhood violence, and none for consistent reporting of witnessing parental violence.

MULTIVARIATE ANALYSIS

Tables 7.1–7.3 follow the same format as the tables in the previous chapters, as described in the first two paragraphs in the Multivariate Analysis section in chapter 4. Table 7.1 presents the OLS regression results for frequency of adult violence victimization. For females in table 7.1, frequency of violence victimization in adulthood has significant positive relationships with exposure to neighborhood violence and minority ethnicity. In the bivariate analysis, it also had significant positive correlations with parental physical abuse, inconsistent reports of witnessing parental violence, and frequency of general violence victimization and perpetration, plus a significant negative relationship with two-parent family, but controlling for the other predictors in the multivariate model in table 7.1, those relationships are not statistically significant, suggesting that they are spurious with or mediated by other predictors in the model. The variance explained in adult violence victimization for females is 6.7%.

For males, the relationship of frequency of violence victimization is significant, but unexpectedly negative, with parental physical abuse and with inconsistent reports of witnessing parental violence. This relationship, while unexpected based on our theory and hypotheses, is consistent with the apparent negative relationship between AEV and adult violence victimization for males in figure 7.1. Adult male violence victimization also has a significant negative relationship with upper/middle parental SES, and a significant positive relationship with adolescent general violence victimization. In the bivariate analysis, its relationship with parental physical abuse was not statistically significant at the .05 level, so the negative relationship with violence victimization in the multivariate analysis in table 7.1 suggests a suppressor effect, with the negative effect of parental physical abuse on adult frequency of violence victimization emerging only in the presence of controls for other variables in the model. In the bivariate analysis, frequency of adult violence victimization also had significant positive relationships with adolescent general violence perpetration and minority ethnicity, but controlling for the other predictors in the multivariate model in table 7.1, those relationships are not statistically significant, suggesting that they are spurious with or mediated by other predictors in the model. The variance explained in adult violence victimization for males is 6.0%.

Table 7.1 OLS Regression Results for Logged Frequency of Adult Violence Victimization

Predictors	Coefficients: Female/Male			
	Standardized Coefficient (b*)	Unstandardized Coefficient (b)	Standard Error of b	Statistical Significance (p)
Parental Physical Abuse	−.016/−.106	−.009/−.146	.027/.066	.740/.028
Witnessing Parental Violence (Inconsistent)	.052/−.106	.047/−.166	.040/.073	.237/.023
Witnessing Parental Violence (Consistent)	.036/−.000	.027/−.005	.037/.073	.453/.994
Neighborhood Violence	.119/.013	.097/.019	.037/.070	.008/.790
Adolescent General Violence Victimization	.085/.118	.023/.050	.014/.023	.104/.033
Adolescent General Violence Perpetration	.039/.072	.018/.039	.022/.030	.422/.195
Minority Ethnicity	.132/.052	.103/.070	.038/.069	.007/.308
Upper/Middle Parental SES	−.030/−.118	−.021/−.138	.033/.063	.537/.031
Lower Parental SES	−.042/−.071	−.025/−.072	.029/.055	.404/.193
Urban	.022/−.031	.016/−.039	.034/.061	.345/.522
Rural	.007/−.008	.005/−.010	.034/.061	.873/.869
Two-Parent Family Structure	−.022/−.067	−.017/−.098	.037/.073	.647/.178
Constant	NA/NA	.017/.214	.045/.092	.709/.021

Note: $R^2 = .067$, p = .000, N = 525 for females; $R^2 = .060$, p = .004, N = 474 for males. NA = not applicable.

Table 7.2 presents the OLS regression results for frequency of adult serious violence perpetration. The only significant predictor of adult serious violence perpetration for females is frequency of adolescent general violence victimization, which is positively related with adult serious violence perpetration. In the bivariate analysis, adolescent general violence perpetration was also significantly positively correlated with adult serious violence perpetration, but it has no significant direct effect in table 7.2. One possibility is that the relationship of adolescent general violence perpetration with adult serious violence perpetration is spurious, possibly with adolescent general violence victimization affecting violence perpetration both in adolescence, as suggested in Menard (2002), and in adulthood, as indicated in the present study. The variance explained in adult violence perpetration for females is 7.8%.

For males, adolescent general violence victimization and adolescent general violence perpetration have direct positive effects on adult serious violence perpetration, with adolescent general violence perpetration having the

Table 7.2 OLS Regression Results for Logged Frequency of Adult Violence Perpetration

Predictors	Coefficients: Female/Male			
	Standardized Coefficient (b*)	Unstandardized Coefficient (b)	Standard Error of b	Statistical Significance (p)
Parental Physical Abuse	−.009/−.072	−.002/−.062	.013/.038	.526/.103
Witnessing Parental Violence (Inconsistent)	.027/−.027	.012/−.027	.019/.042	.894/.524
Witnessing Parental Violence (Consistent)	.105/.071	.039/.070	.018/.042	.992/.098
Neighborhood Violence	−.021/−.039	−.008/−.035	.018/.040	.064/.385
Adolescent General Violence Victimization	.090/.149	.012/.039	.007/.013	.007/.003
Adolescent General Violence Perpetration	.147/.345	.033/.117	.011/.017	.274/.000
Minority Ethnicity	−.065/.015	−.025/.013	.019/.040	.152/.744
Upper/Middle Parental SES	.041/.056	.014/.041	.016/.037	.148/.268
Lower Parental SES	.076/.080	.022/.051	.014/.032	.090/.112
Urban	.107/.028	.039/.022	.017/.035	.653/.530
Rural	.104/−.021	.039/−.017	.017/.035	.144/.632
Two-Parent Family Structure	.008/.004	.003/.004	.018/.042	.228/.931
Constant	NA/NA	−.024/−.060	.022/.053	.601/.259

Note: R^2 = .078, p = .000, N = 526 for females; R^2 = .199, p = .000, N = 475 for males. NA = not applicable.

stronger of the two effects. In the bivariate analysis, parental physical abuse was also marginally (p = .053) significantly positively correlated with adult serious violence perpetration for males, but controlling for the other predictors in table 7.2, the direct effect of parental physical abuse is not statistically significant at the .05 level. This suggests that the relationship of parental physical abuse with adult serious violence perpetration is spurious with or mediated by other predictors in the multivariate analysis, and both adolescent general violence victimization and especially adolescent general violence perpetration seem like good candidates for explaining that relationship. In particular, if parental physical abuse results in adolescent general violence perpetration, then adolescent general violence perpetration, and the pattern of continuity of violence perpetration from adolescence to adulthood, could mediate the relationship of parental physical violence perpetration with adult serious violence perpetration. Because adolescent violence offending and victimization, including victimization by parental physical abuse, are measured contemporaneously in the present study, it is not possible to disentangle the potential mediating relationship in the present study. The variance explained in adult violence perpetration for males is 19.9% in table 7.2.

Table 7.3 presents the OLS regression results for frequency of arrest. For females, only one predictor, adolescent marijuana use, which was also significantly correlated with adult arrest, has a significant direct effect, indicating that adolescent frequency of marijuana use is predictive of a higher frequency of arrest. In the bivariate analysis, besides adolescent frequency of marijuana use, frequency of arrest also has significant positive correlations with parental physical abuse and minority ethnicity, but controlling for the other predictors in table 7.3, those variables have no significant direct effect on adult arrests for females, suggesting that their effects may be spurious with or mediated by other predictors in table 7.3. In particular, parental physical abuse may result in adolescent substance use, including marijuana use (with which it is

Table 7.3 OLS Regression Results for Frequency of Adult Arrest

Predictors	Coefficients: Female/Male			
	Standardized coefficient (b*)	Unstandardized Coefficient (b)	Standard Error of b	Statistical Significance (p)
Parental Physical Abuse	.004/−.070	.001/−.090	.013/.062	.932/.145
Witnessing Parental Violence (Inconsistent)	.041/.034	.018/.050	.019/.069	.357/.471
Witnessing Parental Violence (Consistent)	.059/−.041	.022/−.061	.018/.070	.227/.387
Neighborhood Violence	.013/.038	.005/.051	.018/.066	.777/.438
Adolescent General Violence Victimization	.000/.076	.000/.030	.007/.023	.998/.183
Adolescent General Crime Perpetration	−.026/.129	−.002/.034	.005/.017	.670/.046
Adolescent Hard Drug Use	−.076/.023	−.008/.007	.006/.022	.216/.739
Adolescent Marijuana Use	.138/.072	.009/.014	.004/.015	.031/.323
Minority Ethnicity	.072/.049	.027/.062	.019/.065	.159/.344
Upper/Middle Parental SES	−.025/−.097	−.008/−.106	.016/.060	.630/.078
Lower Parental SES	.040/−.029	.011/−.028	.014/.052	.437/.593
Urban	.011/.041	.004/.048	.017/.058	.818/.411
Rural	−.042/.071	−.016/.086	.017/.058	.357/.140
Two-Parent Family Structure	−.004/−.032	−.002/−.044	.018/.069	.934/.522
Constant	NA/NA	−.002/−.033	.023/.091	.933/.714

Note: R^2 = .032, p = .296, N = 514 for females; R^2 = .005, p = .120, N = 461 for males. NA = not applicable.

positively correlated) as a form of self-medication, and marijuana use may then lead to a higher risk of arrest. Again, given the contemporaneous measurement of adolescent marijuana use and parental physical abuse, it is not possible in the present study to conclusively establish the suggested mediating relationship. For females in table 7.3, 3.2% of the variance in frequency of adult arrests is explained.

Adolescent general crime perpetration has a significant positive correlation with adult frequency of arrest for males in the bivariate analysis and a significant positive direct effect on adult frequency of arrest for males in table 7.3, and is the only significant predictor in table 7.3. In the bivariate analysis, adolescent frequencies of general violence victimization, general violence perpetration, general offending, hard drug use, and marijuana use, and also minority ethnicity, all had significant positive correlations with adult frequency of arrest, and upper/middle parental SES and two-parent family had significant negative correlations with frequency of arrest for males. Adolescent frequency of general violence perpetration is one component of adolescent general crime perpetration, and is thus included as part of the direct effect of adolescent frequency of general offending on adult arrests in table 7.3. The other predictors that are significant in the bivariate analysis but not in the multivariate model in table 7.3 may plausibly be suspected of having their effects mediated through their impact on adolescent general crime perpetration, but directly testing that possibility is not feasible, given the contemporaneous measurement of adolescent general crime perpetration and general violence victimization. For the other predictors that have statistically significant correlations with frequency of adult arrests in the bivariate analysis, however, it is clear that the sociodemographic characteristics (minority ethnicity, upper/middle parental SES, two-parent family) are necessarily temporally (and thus causally, if a causal relationship is to be inferred) prior to adolescent general crime perpetration. Despite general crime perpetration being a plausible influence on adult frequency of arrest, the explained variance for adult frequency of arrest for males in table 7.3 is extremely weak, $R^2 = .005$, and not statistically significant, $p = .120$.

DISCUSSION

Franzese et al. (2017) analyzed the relationship of prevalence, rather than frequency, of adult violence victimization and perpetration, using prevalence rather than frequency of parental physical abuse and adolescent general violence victimization as predictors, and also using adolescent prevalence (not frequency) of violence (not general crime) perpetration as a predictor. They included neither adolescent hard drug use nor adolescent marijuana use as predictors, and did not include arrest as an outcome. There are thus sufficient differences between Franzese et al. (2017) and the present analysis to make the comparisons between the two informative.

In the bivariate analysis, parental violence victimization is positively correlated with adult violence victimization and with adult arrests for females, and (marginally) with adult violence perpetration for males. In the multivariate regression results, it is statistically significant as a predictor of adult violence victimization for males, but in the opposite of the expected direction: higher frequency of parental physical abuse is predictive of lower frequency of adult violence victimization for males. One possibility for explaining this anomalous result is that, controlling for the predictors in the model, males react to parental physical abuse in adolescence by taking measures in adulthood that reduce their risk of victimization. Alternatively, this may be nothing more than a statistical artifact, a chance finding that is not replicated in other analyses. One check we can perform is to compare the relationship of frequency of parental physical abuse with frequency of adult violence victimization and perpetration in the present study with the relationship of prevalence of parental physical abuse with prevalence of adult violence victimization and perpetration, for the same sample, in Franzese et al. (2017). In Franzese et al. (2017), prevalence of parental physical abuse was not a significant predictor of adult violence victimization or offending for females or males. We also explored an alternative using imputation of zero for missing data for frequency of parental physical abuse, which increased the effective sample size from 474 to 547, and that resulted in a nonsignificant direct influence of parental physical abuse on adult violence victimization for males. On balance, it seems best to regard the negative direct effect of physical abuse on adult violence victimization for males as, despite its statistical significance, a chance result, a statistical artifact, until and unless the result is replicated in other samples with comparable measures.

Inconsistent reports of witnessing parental violence are positively associated with adult violence victimization for females in the bivariate correlations, but have no significant direct effects on any of the three outcomes for females in the multivariate analysis. For males, inconsistent reports of witnessing parental violence have a marginally (p = .054) significant negative correlation with frequency of adult violence victimization, and also a significant negative direct effect on frequency of adult violence victimization. This significant negative direct effect on adult violence victimization for males was also found in Franzese et al. (2017) for prevalence (instead of frequency) of adult violence victimization for males (and note again that the full set of predictors used in Franzese et al. was somewhat different from the set used in the present analysis). The significant negative direct effect of inconsistent reports of witnessing parental violence on adult violence victimization for males also appears robust to the alternative imputation method used to check the sensitivity of the negative effect of parental physical abuse on adult violence victimization that was described in the previous paragraph. The significant negative association of inconsistent reports of witnessing parental violence thus seems more likely to be real, as opposed to being a statistical artifact produced by chance, than the negative effect of parental physical violence on adult violence victimization examined above. This and other significant relationships involving inconsistent reports of witnessing parental violence across the full range of outcomes in the present study will be considered in more detail chapter 9. Consistent reports of witnessing parental violence are not significantly correlated with, and have no significant direct effects on, adult violence victimization, adult violence perpetration, or adult frequency of arrest for females or for males in either the present study or in Franzese et al. (2017).

Exposure to neighborhood violence has a significant positive bivariate correlation with, and in the multivariate analysis a significant positive direct effect on, the frequency of adult violence victimization for females. Neither its bivariate correlations nor its direct effects on adult frequency of violence victimization for males, or for adult frequency of violence perpetration or adult frequency of arrest for females or males, are statistically significant. Franzese et al. (2017), for females, also found a significant positive direct effect of exposure to neighborhood violence on prevalence of adult violence victimization, and additionally a marginally significant ($p = .055$) positive rather than negative direct effect on the prevalence of adult violence offending. On balance, for females, there appears to be a positive effect of neighborhood exposure to violence on adult frequency and prevalence of violence victimization, but there is more uncertainty about the effect of neighborhood exposure to violence on adult violence perpetration. For males, exposure to neighborhood violence appears to have no impact on the outcomes in this chapter.

The frequency of adolescent general violence victimization has significant positive bivariate correlations with the frequency of adult violence victimization and perpetration for both females and males, and with adult frequency of arrest for males but not females. In the multivariate analyses, it has significant positive direct effects on adult violence victimization for males and adult violence perpetration for both females and males. In Franzese et al. (2017), the prevalence of adolescent general violence victimization had significant positive direct effects on the prevalence of adult violence victimization and perpetration for females but not for males. Whether the impact of adolescent violence victimization has more of an impact on adult violence victimization for females or males thus appears to depend at least in part on whether we use prevalence (two significant direct effects for females but none for males) or frequency (two significant direct effects for males, one for females) for the predictor and the outcomes.

Of the eleven direct effects that are significant at the .05 level, nine represent direct effects that are significant for either females or males but not both on the same outcome variable. Six of the significant effects are only for males, and three are for females, with the remaining two (for the effects of adolescent general violence victimization on adult violence perpetration) significant for both females and males. Using a formal test for differences when at least one of the coefficients for a predictor for a given outcome is statistically significant, gender differences are significant for the effect of inconsistent reports of witnessing parental violence on frequency of adult violent victimization ($z = 2.56$, $p = .010$), frequency of adolescent violence perpetration on frequency of adult violence perpetration ($z = -4.15$, $p = .000$), and frequency of adolescent general crime perpetration on adult frequency of arrest ($z = -2.03$, $p = .042$). In addition, the gender difference for the direct effect of frequency of parental physical abuse on frequency of adult violence victimization is marginally significant ($z = 1.92$, $p = .055$). These results further reinforce the importance of considering gender differences in the impact of adolescent exposure to violence on adult outcomes.

There is one other result that deserves some additional attention. As noted earlier, the variance explained in adult violence perpetration for males is 19.9% (in table 7.1), and this is one of the results that is significantly different for females and males. Compared to the other results in this chapter, this is a relatively high level of explained variance. Looking at the standardized coefficients, the coefficient for the influence of adolescent general violence perpetration on adult violence perpetration for males is $b^* = .345$, more than twice the magnitude of any of the other standardized coefficients in this chapter. This suggests a relatively high degree of continuity in violence perpetration from adolescence to middle adulthood for males. In light of other research on violence victimization, violence offending, and other criminal offending in the life cycle (see, for example, Benson 2013; Piquero et al. 2007), particularly for this sample (Elliott et al. 1989; Menard 2012), including the decline in violence perpetration with age, this continuity most likely takes the form that individuals who perpetrate violence in adulthood are very likely to have done so in adolescence (in other words, little initiation of violence perpetration in adulthood), even though many of those who perpetrated violence in adolescence desisted from violence perpetration as they got older.

CONCLUSIONS

What to make of all this? Overall, the multivariate analysis results offer a mixture of support, nonsupport, and contradiction for the hypothesis that AEV will lead to higher levels of adult violence victimization, adult violence perpetration, and adult arrest. For adult violence victimization, the hypothesis is supported for females by virtue of the significant positive direct effect of adolescent exposure to neighborhood violence. For males, however, there are three significant direct effects of AEV on adult violence victimization, two of them negative, and thus in the opposite of the expected direction. For adult violence perpetration, adolescent general violence victimization has a significant positive direct effect for both females and males, but note the not-quite-significant (p = .064) negative direct effect of adolescent exposure to neighborhood violence for females. For adult arrest, none of the AEV predictors has a significant direct effect.

The results thus offer mixed support for our first hypothesis, that AEV will be positively related to adult violence victimization, adult violence perpetration, and adult arrest. Consistent with our second hypothesis for males but not for females, the strongest direct effect of AEV on the adult outcomes for males is for adult violence perpetration (b* = .149), but the strongest direct effect for females is the effect of exposure to neighborhood violence on adult violence victimization (b* = .119). Finally, for adult violence perpetration, the effect of AEV (more specifically, the direct effect adolescent general violence victimization) is stronger for males (b* = .149) than for females (b* = .090), consistent with our third hypothesis. In summary, the effects of AEV on adult violence victimization, adult violence perpetration, and arrest, and also the support for our three hypotheses, are all best described as mixed. Also, for males but not for females, adolescent violence perpetration has a significant positive direct effect on both adult violence perpetration (both prevalence and frequency) and on frequency of arrest. This suggests continuity in violence perpetration from adolescence to adulthood for males, and also an increased risk of arrest for males who are involved in violence perpetration in adolescence.

Most strikingly, it is adolescent violence victimization that appears to be most important as a predictor for adult violence victimization and perpetration. Adolescent violence victimization has a significant positive direct effect on both adult violence victimization and adult violence perpetration. Its effect on adult violence victimization is slightly different for females and males, with prevalence (whether it occurs) being significant for females but not for males, and frequency (how many times it occurs) being significant for males but not for females. Likewise, the impact of adolescent violence victimization on adult violence perpetration varies slightly by gender, with both prevalence and frequency being significant for females, but frequency and not prevalence being significant for males. To oversimplify only slightly, adult violence victimization and perpetration depend more on *whether* one experiences adolescent violent victimization for females, but on *how many times* one experiences adolescent violence victimization for males. More broadly speaking, it is general exposure to violence, rather than violence centered specifically on the home and community, that is most predictive of adult involvement in general violence as victims or perpetrators. In the next chapter, we examine whether this is the case not only for general violence but also for the more specific outcome of IPV.

Chapter 8

Adolescent Exposure to Violence and Adult Intimate Partner Violence Victimization and Perpetration

As described in the previous chapter and in Menard et al. (2014), the expectation that adolescent exposure to violence (AEV) in the home and community may be associated with subsequent intimate partner violence (IPV) stems from both criminological theory and past research. Agnew's (1985, 1992, 2002) general strain theory predicts that exposure and/or inability to avoid noxious stimuli, including but not limited to AEV, may provoke perpetration of IPV. This may occur to gain revenge, to express frustration, to try to exercise or regain a sense of control over one's circumstances, or, by projecting an image of toughness, to deter further victimization (Baron 2009; Hay and Evans 2006; Rebellon and Van Gundy 2005). What is not clear from the theory is whether we should expect correlations between AEV and later violence only in the short term, or whether the correlations should persist later in life; and also whether exposure to violence of a particular form in the home or community (e.g., IPV) should be associated with the same forms of violence in those same specific contexts (again, e.g., IPV), or should be associated with violence more generally (perpetration of violence other than IPV). As indicated in the previous chapter, the modes of adaptation in Merton's (1938) anomie theory, including the extension of anomie theory by Cloward and Ohlin (1960), that should lead to violence perpetration may include either or both of innovation and rebellion.

As in the previous chapter, while general strain theory makes predictions about perpetration in response to AEV, social learning theory (Akers 1985; Bandura 1977) predicts that exposure to violence will affect both perpetration and victimization, a prediction consistent with the intergenerational cycle of violence perspective and research (e.g., Straus et al. 1980; Widom 1989b). According to social learning theory, violent behavior is learned just like any other behavior, through a process of imitation, modeling, and reinforcement.

Children who witness their parents using violence (against one another or against the children) may interpret aggressive behavior as an appropriate response to conflict and may extend this interpretation to view aggressive behavior as socially acceptable, leading them to more readily take on the roles of either or both, victim or perpetrator. Both general strain and social learning theories would predict a link of exposure to violence in the home and community with subsequent IPV, general strain by regarding exposure to violence as a noxious stimulus, and social learning theory by regarding exposure to violence as a source of modeling and imitation.

Costa et al. (2015) found that physical abuse in adolescence was predictive of IPV in adulthood. Wolfe et al. (2001), using a community sample of adolescents, found child maltreatment to be predictive of IPV perpetration for both males and females, and of dating violence perpetration for males, as well as of violence more generally for females. Using data from the National Longitudinal Study of Adolescent Health, Fang and Corso (2007) found that child maltreatment was a significant risk factor for future perpetration of youth violence and young adult IPV, but less of an effect was shown to exist for future IPV or more general violence victimization. Fagan (2005) used data from the National Youth Survey (NYS) and found a weak relationship between adolescent physical abuse and minor partner violence in early adulthood, a relationship which appeared to decline over time. Fagan's study did not control for other potential explanatory variables, such as exposure to parental violence or exposure to violence in the community. Mihalic and Elliott (1997), in contrast, found no impact of physical abuse on young adult IPV in the NYS when controlling for witnessing parental violence and other predictors, although physical abuse did have a significant bivariate correlation with adult IPV. With respect to more general violence victimization in adolescence, Menard (2002) used a measure of general violence victimization that included but was not limited to parental physical abuse, and found that adolescent violence victimization in the NYS was a significant predictor of adult IPV victimization and offending in early adulthood.

A meta-analysis of sixty-six qualified studies found child maltreatment was related to adult male IPV victimization and perpetration (Godbout et al. 2019). This review also found that either being physically abused or witnessing IPV had an association (albeit small) with physical IPV for men. Another meta-analysis of male survivors of child maltreatment and IPV concluded that although numerous valid studies have been conducted, findings differ greatly among them regarding the impact of child maltreatment on adult IPV (Godbout et al. 2017). Altogether, these mixed results raise two questions: first, whether the impact of physical abuse, if any, is short term, not persisting into middle adulthood, or longer term, possibly continuing into the middle adult years; and second, whether the impact of physical abuse is gender-specific, as suggested in the results from Wolfe et al. (2001).

Among the studies that have examined the impact of witnessing parental violence on subsequent partner violence, Bevan and Higgins (2002) found witnessing family violence to be a significant predictor of subsequent psychological spouse abuse but not physical spouse abuse in adulthood. Similar findings suggesting that witnessing parental violence is not a significant predictor of future IPV are provided by Alexander et al. (1991) using a college student sample, Simons et al. (1998) examining dating violence in a sample of adolescent boys, Capaldi and Clark (1998) in a young adult sample, and Ernst et al. (2007) in a sample of emergency room patients. In contrast, Bensley et al. (2003) examined various types of child maltreatment and found witnessing parental violence to be the strongest single predictor of adult IPV victimization for a female sample. Ehrensaft et al. (2003) utilized data from a 20-year prospective study to examine the intergenerational transmission of violence and examined child physical abuse, child sexual abuse, and exposure to parental violence as predictors. With all three types of maltreatment in the model, only witnessing parental violence was found to be a significant predictor of both IPV perpetration and victimization in adulthood.

Iverson et al. (2011) collected data from a sample of robbery victims and found that both men and women who witnessed parental violence as a child had 2.4 times the odds of being in an adult relationship characterized by IPV. Ernst et al. (2009) sampled respondents from an emergency room environment and found that perpetrators of IPV were significantly more likely to report witnessing parental violence as a child but were not more likely to be victims. Mihalic and Elliott (1997), using an American national sample, found that witnessing parental violence had only an indirect effect, if any, on adult IPV perpetration and victimization, a result similar to that of Fergusson et al. (2006) for a New Zealand sample. Taken together these studies raise the question of whether witnessing parental violence is or is not predictive of adult IPV at all, as well as whether any effects persist into middle adulthood.

What limited research exists specifically on the relationship between exposure to violence in the community and IPV tends to be consistent with the predictions from strain and social learning theories, but still leaves some questions to be answered. As noted by Benson et al. (2003), community violence is often correlated with rates of domestic violence. Raghavan et al. (2006), using a sample of low-income women, found that exposure to violence in the community was significantly related to IPV. Malik et al. (1997) found high school students' exposure to weapons and violent injury in the community to be predictive not only of community violence perpetration and victimization but also to dating violence perpetration and victimization. This leaves open the question whether these results on short-term consequences of exposure to community violence can be extended to long-term adult IPV.

Based on a combination of general strain and anomie theory, plus social learning theory, plus past empirical results, we hypothesize that AEV, in at least one of its forms (physical abuse, witnessing parental violence, neighborhood violence, general violence victimization) will be positively associated with adult IPV including (a) general IPV victimization, (b) serious IPV victimization, (c) general IPV perpetration, and (d) serious IPV perpetration. We further hypothesize, based on general strain theory (which specifies differences in responses to strain by females and males) and past research, that the impact of AEV on adult IPV perpetration (as an externalizing behavior) will be more pronounced for males than for females. Finally, based on past results, we hypothesize that the impacts of direct physical victimization (parental abuse, general violence victimization) will be more pronounced than the effects of indirect victimization (witnessing parental violence, exposure to neighborhood violence). It is in the area of adult IPV that the distinctions between responses of females and males, and the impacts of direct as opposed to indirect exposure to violence, seem to be most clearly suggested by theory and past research.

ANALYTICAL APPROACH

The present analysis differs from the results presented in Menard et al. (2014) primarily in the use of frequency rather than prevalence of parental physical abuse, adolescent violence victimization, and adolescent violence perpetration as predictors. The outcome variables are the Conflict Tactics Scale (CTS) scores for general and serious IPV victimization and perpetration, as described in chapter 2. As in the previous chapters, the analysis begins with a brief presentation of the significant bivariate relationships of the adult partner violence outcomes to AEV and sociodemographic characteristics. For the multivariate analysis of the relationship of AEV to adult IPV perpetration and victimization, as in Menard et al. (2014), we use the Heckman two-step model (Breen 1996), to account for the fact that in order to have partner violence, one must have a partner, and past research (Cherlin et al. 2004; Covey et al. 2013) indicates that there may be self-selection into or out of marital or cohabiting relationships based on, among other things, AEV and past IPV. In the NYSFS data, respondents who reported being neither married nor cohabiting were not asked the questions about partner violence.

The first part of the Heckman two-step analysis, the selection model, is the same for all of the dependent variables, and models the selection into being married or cohabiting at waves 10–11. The second part, the prediction model, is unique to each of the dependent variables, and models the impact of the predictors on the outcomes for those who are in the at-risk population. The prediction model adjusts for the likelihood of being or not being in the at-risk group when calculating the effects of the predictors on the outcomes. In order to estimate the model, it is necessary that there be at least one variable that predicts selection but not the outcome. After examination of the relationships of the control variables with the outcomes, ethnicity (minority) and residence (urban and rural, with suburban as the reference category) were chosen for inclusion in the selection but not the prediction models, as was the case in Menard et al. (2014).

BIVARIATE RELATIONSHIPS

Figure 8.1 illustrates the relationships of AEV to the four CTS outcome variables. As in the previous chapters, AEV is coded "no" for respondents who reported neither parental physical abuse, nor witnessing parental violence, nor exposure to neighborhood violence, nor general violence victimization in adolescence, and "yes" for respondents who reported any one or more of those forms of AEV. Again, the figure is split by gender, going (from left to right within each outcome) from females who reported no AEV, to females who reported some (yes) AEV, to males who reported no AEV, to males who reported some (yes) AEV. For both females and males, CTS general and serious IPV victimization and CTS general and serious IPV perpetration appear to be higher for individuals who have experienced AEV than for individuals who have not.

Breaking down these relationships by specific types of AEV as well as gender, bivariate correlations indicate that for both females and males, general IPV victimization is significantly and positively associated with

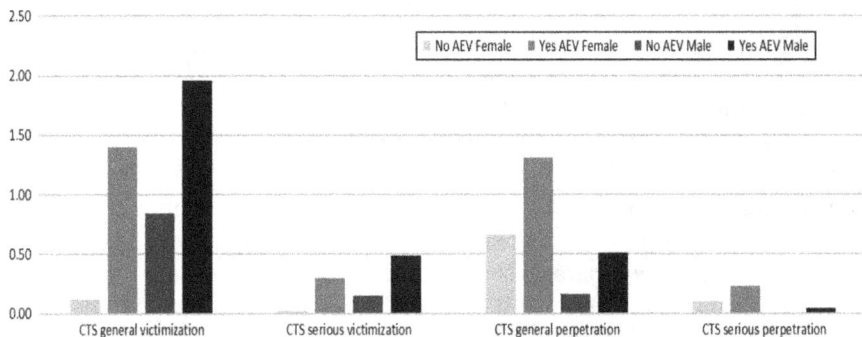

Figure 8.1   AEV and Adult Intimate Partner Violence. *Source:* Created by the authors.

parental physical abuse (r = .153, p = .001 for females; r = .150, p = .003 for males), and also with adolescent frequency of general violence victimization (r = .195, p = .000 for females; r = .161, p = .002 for males) and perpetration (r = .159, p = .001 for females; r = .239, p = .000 for males). For females but not for males, it is also significantly positively associated with inconsistent reports of witnessing parental violence (r = .120, p = .013). For both females and males, general IPV victimization is not significantly related to minority ethnicity (although it comes close for females at r = .090, p = .060), parental SES, or residence. For females but not for males, it is significantly negatively related to two-parent family structure in adolescence (r = −.149, p = .002).

There is a significant positive association of serious IPV victimization with parental physical abuse (r = .170, p = .000) and inconsistent reports of parental violence (r = .121, p = .012) for females but not for males. For both females and males, there is a significant positive association of serious IPV victimization with adolescent general violence victimization (r = .140, p = .004 for females; r = .164, p = .001 for males) and perpetration (r = .128, p = .008 for females; r = .242, p = .000 for males). Serious IPV victimization is not significantly associated with consistent reports of witnessing parental violence or with exposure to neighborhood violence for females or for males, or with parental physical abuse or inconsistent reports of witnessing parental violence for males. For females but not for males, serious IPV victimization is significantly positively associated with minority ethnicity (r = .126, p = .008) and significantly negatively associated with having been in a two-parent family in adolescence (r = −.179, p = .000). It is not significantly associated for females or males with parental SES or with residence.

General IPV perpetration is significantly positively related to adolescent general violence victimization (r = .150, p = .002) and perpetration (r = .156, p = .001), and significantly negatively related to being in a two-parent family in adolescence (r = −.131, p = .007), for females. There is no significant association of general IPV perpetration with parental physical abuse, witnessing parental violence, or exposure to neighborhood violence for females, nor with ethnicity (although, as with general IPV perpetration, the relationship is close to meeting the p ≤ .05 criterion at r = .089, p = .066), parental SES, or residence. For males, there is a significant positive relationship of general IPV perpetration in adulthood with parental physical abuse (r = .210, p = .000) and with adolescent general violence victimization (r = .105, p = .039) and perpetration (r = .123, p = .015), but no significant relationship with witnessing parental violence, exposure to neighborhood violence, ethnicity, parental SES, residence, or two-parent family structure at the beginning of the study.

For females, adult serious IPV perpetration is significantly positively related with parental physical abuse (r = .157, p = .001) and inconsistent reports of witnessing parental violence (r = .113, p = .020), but not significantly related with consistent reports of witnessing parental violence or with exposure to neighborhood violence. It is significantly positively related to adolescent frequency of general violence victimization (r = .130, p = .007) and perpetration (r = .170, p = .000), and to minority ethnicity (r = .144, p = .003), and significantly negatively related to having been in a two-parent family in adolescence (r = −.178, p = .000). It is not significantly related to parental SES or residence for females. For males, *none* of the correlations indicates a significant relationship of adult serious IPV perpetration with *any* of the predictors considered here.

The hypothesis that AEV is predictive of higher levels of adult IPV is supported for all but one of the gender-specific outcomes (serious IPV perpetration for males). The strengths of the correlations, and the number of significant correlations for females and males respectively, however, do not appear to support the second hypothesis, that the impact of AEV on adult partner violence will be more pronounced for males than for females. The third hypothesis, that the impacts of direct physical victimization will be more pronounced than the effects of more indirect forms of AEV, is supported, with adolescent violence victimization significant for seven of the eight gender-specific outcomes, parental physical abuse significant for five of the eight, and inconsistent reports of witnessing parental violence significant for three, all three of which are for females.

MULTIVARIATE ANALYSIS

Tables 8.1–8.5 follow the same format as the tables in the previous chapters, as described in the first two paragraphs in the Multivariate Analysis section in chapter 4. Table 8.1 presents the selection component of the Heckman two-step model for females and males, respectively. The Heckman two-step model involves two components, the selection model, which models the likelihood that a respondent is in the at-risk group (here, married or cohabiting) for the outcomes (CTS general and serious IPV victimization and perpetration), is the same for all of the outcomes, but is not assumed to be the same for females and males. The selection model is a logit model for which the outcome is being currently married or cohabiting (as opposed to never married or formerly married), and in that sense is different from and complements the models for adult marital status in chapter 4, this time comparing being married with both (combined) never married and formerly married. In table 8.1, parental physical abuse has a negative direct effect on being married for females. This indicates that females who have experienced parental physical

Table 8.1 Selection Model for Heckman Two-Step Analysis of CTS Intimate Partner Violence (IPV)

Predictors	Coefficients: Female/Male			
	Odds ratio	Unstandardized Coefficient (b)	Standard Error of b	Statistical Significance (p)
Parental Physical Abuse	.804/.944	−.218/−.058	.109/.148	.046/.697
Witnessing Parental Violence (Inconsistent)	1.340/1.906	.293/.645	.180/.181	.104/.000
Witnessing Parental Violence (Consistent)	1.042/.878	.041/−.130	.150/.159	.782/.412
Neighborhood Violence	.759/.898	−.276/−.108	.145/.151	.057/.475
Adolescent General Violence Victimization	1.055/.966	.054/−.035	.060/.051	.368/.492
Adolescent Serious Violence Perpetration	.857/.965	−.154/−.036	.094/.067	.102/.593
Minority Ethnicity	.849/.532	−.164/−.631	.157/.150	.294/.000
Upper/Middle Parental SES	.946/1.071	−.056/.069	.140/.139	.686/.618
Lower Parental SES	.913/.936	−.091/−.066	.124/.120	.463/.583
Urban	.780/1.009	−.249/.009	.139/.137	.072/.948
Rural	1.232/1.184	.209/.169	.151/.134	.166/.206
Two-Parent Family Structure	1.117/1.237	.111/.210	.141/.156	.432/.177
Constant	1.420/.995	.351/−.005	.173/.194	.043/.981

Note: R^2 = .055, p = .000, N = 631 for females; R^2 = .057, p = .000, N = 650 for males.

abuse are less likely than females who have not been physically abused by their parents to be in the at-risk pool for IPV. Also in table 8.1, inconsistent reporting of parental violence has a positive effect, and minority ethnicity has a negative effect, on being currently married for males. Of the three significant coefficients in the two tables, only one, the effect of minority ethnicity on being currently married or cohabiting, is statistically significantly different for females and males ($z = 2.15$, $p = .032$). The primary interest in the selection models is not substantive, however, but simply as a way of adjusting the estimates in the models for CTS general and serious IPV victimization and perpetration to account for the fact that some individuals may not experience partner violence because they have self-selected themselves (or otherwise been selected) out of the risk group.

Table 8.2   Heckman Two-Step Regression Results for CTS General IPV Victimization

Predictors	Coefficients: Female/Male			
	Standardized Coefficient (b*)	Unstandardized Coefficient (b)	Standard Error of b	Statistical Significance (p)
Parental Physical Abuse	−.055/.094	−.494/1.515	.561/.986	.378/.124
Witnessing Parental Violence (Inconsistent)	.025/.019	.321/.328	.761/1.220	.673/.788
Witnessing Parental Violence (Consistent)	.039/.109	.449/2.191	.637/1.225	.481/.074
Neighborhood Violence	.012/.008	.151/.143	.836/1.101	.857/.897
Adolescent General Violence Victimization	.126/.076	.514/.384	.256/.333	.045/.249
Adolescent Serious Violence Perpetration	.054/.183	.435/1.252	.519/.460	.405/.006
Upper/Middle Parental SES	.005/.072	.047/.946	.559/.891	.933/.288
Lower Parental SES	.059/.084	.505/1.002	.506/.803	.318/.213
Two-Parent Family Structure	−.045/.031	−.507/.598	.685/1.207	.459/.620
Constant	NA/NA	.760/1.570	1.730/2.512	.660/.532

Note: R^2 = .036, p = .000, N = 393 for females; R^2 = .077, p = .000, N = 333 for males. NA = not applicable.

Table 8.2 presents the prediction model for general CTS IPV victimization for females and males. In the bivariate analysis, parental physical abuse, inconsistent reports of witnessing parental violence, adolescent general violence victimization, adolescent general violence perpetration, and two-parent family were significantly correlated with adult general IPV victimization for females, but controlling for the other predictors in the multivariate analysis in table 8.2, only adolescent general violence victimization emerges as significantly and positively related to adult general IPV victimization. This suggests that the relationships of the predictors other than adolescent general violence victimization are either spurious with or mediated by other predictors in the model, most likely mediated by adolescent violence victimization. The explained variance for female general IPV victimization is low, only 3.6%.

In the bivariate analysis, parental physical abuse, adolescent general violence victimization, and adolescent general violence perpetration were significantly correlated with adult general IPV victimization for males, but in table 8.2, only adolescent serious violence perpetration has a significant direct effect on adult general IPV victimization, with perpetration of violence in adolescence being predictive of more general IPV victimization in adulthood. This suggests that the relationships of the predictors other than adolescent general violence perpetration are either spurious with or mediated by other predictors in the model, most likely mediated by adolescent violence perpetration. For males, the model explains 7.7% of the variance in adult general IPV victimization, not very high, but a little more than twice the explained variance for females.

Table 8.3 presents the results of the Heckman two-step prediction model for serious IPV victimization for females and males. In the bivariate analysis, serious IPV victimization for females had significant correlations with parental physical abuse, inconsistent reports of witnessing parental violence, adolescent general violence victimization, adolescent general violence perpetration, minority ethnicity, and two-parent family. In the multivariate analysis in table 8.3, controlling for the other predictors in the model, only two-parent family structure has a significant direct effect on serious IPV victimization, with being in a two-parent family at the beginning of the study being predictive of lower serious IPV victimization in adulthood. This suggests that the other relationships are mediated by or spurious with other predictors in the model. In this instance it is possible that they are mediated by (for ethnicity) or spurious with (for the other variables) two-parent family, implying that two-parent family structure may perhaps be affected by minority ethnicity, and may affect parental physical abuse, witnessing parental violence, general violence victimization, and general violence perpetration in adolescence, as well as serious IPV victimization in adulthood, for females. This possibility is speculative, however, and because of the contemporaneous measurement of the predictors in adolescence, it cannot be resolved with the present data. As with general IPV victimization, explained variance is low, 3.2% for serious IPV victimization for females in table 8.3.

In the bivariate analysis, serious IPV victimization for males in middle adulthood was significantly correlated only with general violence victimization and perpetration in adolescence. In table 8.3, only general violence perpetration has a direct effect on serious IPV victimization for males, paralleling the result for general IPV victimization in table 8.2, and suggesting that any impact of adolescent general violence victimization may be mediated through an effect of adolescent general violence victimization on general violence perpetration. Explained variance in table 8.3 is 6.6%, again a little more than twice the explained variance found for females for the same outcome.

In the bivariate analysis, adult CTS general IPV perpetration for females in middle adulthood was significantly positively correlated with adolescent

Table 8.3   Heckman Two-Step Regression Results for CTS Serious IPV Victimization

Predictors	Coefficients: Female/Male			
	Standardized Coefficient (b*)	Unstandardized Coefficient (b)	Standard Error of b	Statistical Significance (p)
Parental Physical Abuse	−.070/−.004	−.194/−.021	.175/.315	.266/.947
Witnessing Parental Violence (Inconsistent)	.014/.012	.056/.066	.237/.390	.813/.865
Witnessing Parental Violence (Consistent)	.012/.088	.041/.565	.198/.392	.837/.150
Neighborhood Violence	−.049/.013	−.197/.072	.260/.352	.449/.838
Adolescent General Violence Victimization	.059/.088	.074/.141	.080/.107	.354/.185
Adolescent Serious Violence Perpetration	.077/.211	.193/.462	.161/.147	.231/.002
Upper/Middle Parental SES	.025/.041	.097/.171	.174/.284	.577/.548
Lower Parental SES	.037/.075	.111/.284	.158/.257	.480/.268
Two-Parent Family Structure	−.119/.014	−.421/.087	.213/.386	.048/.821
Constant	NA/NA	.535/.469	.538/.804	.321/.560

Note: R^2 = .032, p = .000, N = 393 for females; R^2 = .066, p = .000, N = 333 for males. NA = not applicable.

general violence victimization and perpetration and with minority ethnicity. In table 8.4, for females, none of the predictors is significant at the .05 level, but adolescent general violence victimization comes close at p = .058. Explained variance remains similar to the two previous models for females at 3.7%. For males in the bivariate analysis, adult general IPV perpetration was significantly and positively correlated with parental physical abuse, and with adolescent general violence victimization and perpetration. In table 8.4, only parental physical abuse has a significant direct effect on adult general IPV perpetration for males, with parental physical abuse being predictive of higher levels of general IPV perpetration. This suggests that any effects of adolescent general violence victimization or perpetration may be mediated by, or more likely spurious with, parental physical abuse. There is also a near-significant effect of lower parental SES also being predictive of higher levels of general IPV perpetration for males in middle adulthood.

Looking at bivariate relationships for females, adult serious IPV perpetration was significantly and positively correlated with parental physical abuse, inconsistent reports of witnessing parental violence, adolescent general

Table 8.4   Heckman Two-Step Regression Results for CTS General IPV Perpetration

Predictors	Coefficients: Female/Male			
	Standardized Coefficient (b*)	Unstandardized Coefficient (b)	Standard Error of b	Statistical Significance (p)
Parental Physical Abuse	−.066/.264	−.500/1.491	.470/.337	.288/.000
Witnessing Parental Violence (Inconsistent)	.002/−.109	.017/−.662	.636/.415	.978/.111
Witnessing Parental Violence (Consistent)	−.045/−.079	−.432/−.561	.533/.421	.417/.183
Neighborhood Violence	−.069/.050	−.744/.314	.699/.378	.287/.406
Adolescent General Violence Victimization	.119/.055	.407/.098	.214/.114	.058/.391
Adolescent Serious Violence Perpetration	.048/−.028	.327/−.067	.434/.157	.452/.669
Upper/Middle Parental SES	.020/−.004	.163/−.017	.468/.303	.728/.956
Lower Parental SES	.070/.125	.503/.520	.424/.274	.235/.058
Two-Parent Family Structure	.093/−.068	.888/−.459	.573/.414	.122/.268
Constant	NA/NA	1.193/1.137	1.448/.862	.410/.187

Note: R^2 = .037, p = .000, N = 393 for females; R^2 = .083, p = .000, N = 333 for males. NA = not applicable.

violence victimization and perpetration, and minority ethnicity, and negatively correlated with two-parent family structure. In the multivariate analysis in table 8.5, controlling for the other predictors in the model, only two-parent family structure has a significant direct effect on serious IPV perpetration for females, with two-parent family structure at the beginning of the study being predictive of lower levels of serious IPV perpetration in adulthood. Here as with serious IPV victimization for females, effects of other variables that were significantly correlated with adult serious IPV perpetration may be mediated by or spurious with two-parent family structure for females. Explained variance for females in table 8.5 is 4.9%. For males, none of the bivariate correlations with serious IPV perpetration is significant at the .05 level, and none of the direct effects on serious IPV perpetration in the multivariate model in table 8.5 is statistically significant. Close to the .05 cutoff, however, is the positive direct effect of parental physical abuse on adult serious IPV perpetration. Explained variance for males is an extremely weak, but statistically significant, 1.4%.

Table 8.5   Heckman Two-Step Regression Results for CTS Serious IPV Perpetration

Predictors	Coefficients: Female/Male			
	Standardized Coefficient (b*)	Unstandardized Coefficient (b)	Standard Error of b	Statistical Significance (p)
Parental Physical Abuse	−.103/.124	−.168/.088	.102/.046	.098/.057
Witnessing Parental Violence (Inconsistent)	.015/−.098	.035/−.075	.138/.057	.801/.191
Witnessing Parental Violence (Consistent)	−.012/.002	−.024/.002	.115/.057	.836/.976
Neighborhood Violence	−.105/.079	−.247/.063	.151/.052	.102/.218
Adolescent General Violence Victimization	.074/−.004	.055/−.001	.046/.016	.236/.942
Adolescent Serious Violence Perpetration	.061/−.030	.090/−.009	.094/.022	.339/.676
Upper/Middle Parental SES	.024/−.048	.042/−.028	.101/.042	.681/.508
Lower Parental SES	.067/.068	.104/.036	.092/.038	.259/.338
Two-Parent Family Structure	−.143/−.073	−.295/−.062	.124/.056	.017/.274
Constant	NA/NA	.217/.232	.313/.117	.488/.049

Note: R^2 = .049, p = .000, N = 393 for females; R^2 = .014, p = .032, N = 333 for males. NA = not applicable.

DISCUSSION

The principal difference between the analyses here compared with those in Menard et al. (2014) is the use of frequency (in the present study) as opposed to prevalence (in Menard et al. 2014) measures for parental physical abuse, adolescent general violence victimization, and adolescent general violence perpetration, so the results across that and the present study could be expected to be generally similar. In the bivariate analysis, parental physical abuse was significantly positively correlated with general IPV victimization for females and males, with serious IPV victimization for females, with general IPV perpetration for males, and with serious IPV perpetration for females. It also had a significant negative direct effect on being currently married or cohabiting in the selection component of the Heckman two-step model for females. In the prediction component of the Heckman two-step model, it was not significant in predicting general or serious IPV victimization, or serious IPV perpetration, for females or males, although its positive effect on serious IPV perpetration for males (b* = .124, p = .057) is close enough that it should not be completely disregarded as nonsignificant. The one direct effect of parental physical abuse that was statistically significant in the prediction model was the positive direct effect on general IPV perpetration for males. Menard et al. (2014) similarly found that parental physical abuse had a significant direct effect on only CTS general IPV perpetration and not the other three CTS outcome measures for males.

For males more than for females, then, the results for parental physical abuse are at least somewhat consistent with the cycle of violence (Straus et al. 1980; Widom 1989b) and social learning theory (Akers 1985; Bandura 1977) perspectives on the intergenerational transmission of domestic violence. The results should not, however, be interpreted as indicating that parental physical abuse has no effects for females. Instead, although parental physical abuse is not predictive of CTS IPV victimization or offending for females, here and in Menard et al. (2014) it is significantly predictive for females of not currently being married or cohabiting, and thus, given the screen for marriage or cohabitation before administering the CTS questions in the NYSFS, not in the risk set for IPV victimization and offending in the data used in the present study.

Inconsistent reports of witnessing parental violence are positively correlated with general and serious IPV victimization and with serious IPV perpetration for females but not for males in the bivariate relationships. Inconsistent reports of witnessing parental violence have a direct and perhaps unexpectedly positive effect on being currently married or cohabiting for males but not for females in the selection model. In the multivariate prediction models, inconsistent reports of witnessing parental violence had no direct effects on any of the CTS outcome variables. Menard et al. (2014) similarly found a significant positive direct effect of inconsistent reports of witnessing parental violence on being married or cohabiting in the selection model for males, but no significant direct effects on any of the CTS outcomes in the prediction models. Consistent reports of witnessing parental violence were not significantly correlated in the bivariate analysis with any of the CTS outcomes, and had no significant direct effects in the prediction models, and also had no significant effects in the selection models. Menard et al. (2014) similarly found no significant effects of consistent reports of witnessing parental violence in the selection or prediction models for females or males.

In the bivariate analysis, exposure to neighborhood violence has no significant bivariate correlations with any of the CTS outcome measures. It has no significant direct effect on being married or cohabiting in the selection model (although the negative effect on being married or cohabiting for females at $p = .057$ comes close), and it has no significant direct effects on any of the CTS outcomes in the multivariate prediction models. Menard et al. (2014) also found no significant direct effects of exposure to neighborhood violence in the prediction or selection models, although there as here there was a marginal (p = .063) negative effect on being married or cohabiting in the selection model.

In the bivariate analysis, adolescent frequency of general violence victimization is significantly and positively correlated with all four CTS measures for females, and with all except adult serious IPV perpetration for males, but it has no significant direct effect on being married or cohabiting in the selection model for females or males. It does have a significant positive direct effect on general but not serious IPV victimization for females. Its effects on general and serious IPV perpetration are not statistically significant at the .05 level, but its positive effect on general IPV perpetration for females (b* = .119, p = .058) comes close. Menard et al. (2014) found no significant direct effect of adolescent general violence victimization on being married or cohabiting in the selection model, but a significant direct effect on general CTS IPV victimization, and in a slight contrast to the results in the present chapter, also for CTS general IPV perpetration (p = .046), for females. Unlike the results in the present chapter, Menard et al. (2014) did not find a significant effect of adolescent general violence perpetration on CTS general IPV victimization for males, and this difference is probably attributable to the use of prevalence (in Menard, et al. 2014) as opposed to frequency (in the present chapter) of adolescent general violence perpetration.

Of the eleven statistically significant direct effects in tables 8.2 to 8.5, in no instance does the same predictor have a statistically significant effect on the same outcome for both females and males. Of the eleven gender comparisons for those coefficients, two are statistically significant at the .05 level: the effect of minority ethnicity on being married or cohabiting in the selection model (z = 2.15, p = .012), and the effect of parental abuse on general IPV perpetration in the prediction model (z = −3.56, p = .000). In addition, the marginally significant and opposite signed effects of parental physical abuse on serious IPV perpetration for females (b* = −.103, p = .098) and males (b* = .124, p = .057) are also statistically significantly different (z = −2.29, p = .022). One particular relationship worth noting is that the difference in the effect of two-parent family structure is not statistically significantly different for females and males, but the fact that it is significantly negatively related to serious IPV victimization and perpetration for females and not for males in tables 8.3 and 8.5 suggests that it may be worthwhile to explore further whether being in a two-parent family during adolescence may be a protective factor against serious IPV victimization and perpetration for those females who are in the at-risk set of being married or cohabiting in adulthood.

CONCLUSIONS

One general conclusion that can be drawn from this analysis is that the cycle of violence is real for males. For males but not females, the direct effect of parental physical abuse on general IPV perpetration is statistically significant whether it is prevalence or frequency of parental abuse that is used as the predictor, and the direct effect of parental physical abuse on serious IPV perpetration is marginally significant, $.05 < p < .10$, whether prevalence ($p = .088$ in Menard et al. 2014, who did not provide standardized coefficients) or frequency ($b^* = .124$, $p = .057$) is used. These results are consistent with our first hypothesis, that AEV will affect adult IPV, and with our second hypothesis, that the impact of AEV on adult IPV will be greater for males than for females (even though this second hypothesis did not appear to be supported in the bivariate analysis); with the cycle of violence perspective; with social learning theory; and with prior research indicating that males are more likely than females to respond to strain with externalizing behavior, such as violence, rather than internalizing behavior, such as anxiety or depression. Not consistent with our first or third hypothesis, however, is the absence of any direct effects of AEV on adult CTS general or serious IPV victimization for males. Note, however, that adolescent violence *perpetration* does have a significant direct effect on adult CTS general and serious IPV victimization for males. Still consistent with our first hypothesis (albeit in what seems like an indirect way), for females but not for males, as indicated the selection model, parental physical abuse does have an impact on females; but rather than being predictive of higher levels of IPV victimization or perpetration for females, it is instead predictive of selection out of being involved (married or cohabiting) in the intimate partner relationship in which they would be at risk of IPV victimization or perpetration.

A second general conclusion, consistent with our third hypotheses, is that when the outcome in question is adult IPV victimization or offending, more indirect AEV in the form of witnessing parental violence or exposure to violence in the neighborhood does not matter as much as more direct exposure to violence in the form of direct violence victimization by parents or others. Although not a form of AEV in the sense of being victimized, a history of perpetration of more serious forms of violence for males is also predictive of general and serious IPV victimization in adulthood. In short, it is general violence victimization that matters for females, general violence perpetration that matters for males, and although it operates differently for females and males, parental physical abuse that matters for both, in their effects on adult IPV victimization and perpetration.

Comparing these results with the results in the previous chapter, it was adolescent violence perpetration that mattered for males but not females in both chapters, as a predictor of adult general and IPV and arrest. In contrast, for both females and males, it was parental physical abuse that mattered for general violence and arrest in the previous chapter, but adolescent violence victimization that mattered for IPV in the present chapter. For IPV in the present chapter, but not for general violence in the previous chapter, parental physical abuse matters in different ways for females and males, but in ways that are consistent with the predictions derived from strain and social learning theories. These partially contrasting results reinforce the point that specific types of AEV as predictors may have either similar or different importance as predictors of different adult outcomes.

Chapter 9

Conclusion and Implications for Theory, Practice, and Future Research

Chapter 1 presented the social and historical context of the present study; reviewed definitions of child maltreatment and abuse, adverse childhood experiences, and adolescent exposure to violence (AEV); and presented the theories that were used in guiding the present study in terms of generating expectations and the interpretation of the results. Chapter 2 described the sample used in the present study, including operational definitions and descriptive statistics for the variables used in the study. Chapter 3 indicated how the predictors and outcomes in the study were distributed by the sociodemographic control variables used in the study (gender, ethnicity, parental socioeconomic status [SES], adult residence, and family structure at the time of the initial interview), plus the intercorrelations of selected outcomes in adulthood. Chapters 4–8 presented detailed analyses of the impacts of the different dimensions of AEV (parental physical abuse, inconsistent and consistent reports of witnessing inter-parental violence, exposure to neighborhood violence, and general violence victimization) on, respectively, adult social statuses, mental health, illicit and problem substance use, general violence victimization and perpetration plus arrests, and IPV victimization and perpetration. Metaphorically, chapters 4–8 represent a close, detailed look at the "trees" represented by the different groups of outcomes.

The present chapter begins with, to continue the metaphor, an attempt to look at the "forest" of results. Instead of focusing in detail on one outcome at a time, we try to provide a shallower but broader view of all of the outcomes at once. We do so with two questions in mind: first, which are the most important of the AEV predictors for all of the outcomes combined, and second, for which of the adult outcomes is each of the AEV predictors most important? In examining these two questions, we consider not only significant direct effects but also significant bivariate correlations. Where only the latter exist, we consider what best explains the attenuation of the bivariate relationships in the multivariate analysis in the present study. In this context, we begin with a consideration of the continuity of statuses and behaviors from adolescence to adulthood. Next, we consider the impacts of each of the predictors across the full range of outcomes in the present study. Following this review of the substantive results, we consider their implications for intervention policies and programs, theory, and future research on the relationship of AEV to adult outcomes.

For those relationships characterized by significant bivariate correlations but nonsignificant direct effects in the multivariate model, the question arises why this pattern occurs. One possibility is a mediated relationship, in which the influence of the predictor on the outcome is mediated by another variable in the model. In other words, the variable with the positive correlation but no direct effect has an indirect effect, by affecting a third variable, when that third variable has a direct (or possibly indirect) effect on the outcome. A second possibility is that the relationship is spurious, that the predictor and outcome are correlated because both are influenced by another variable in the model. A third possibility is that the sample size is adequate (has sufficient statistical power) to establish the significance of the bivariate association, but not adequate to establish the significance of the direct effect in the multivariate analysis. Examination of the significance of the influences of other predictors in the multivariate models can help us identify possible mediating variables or spurious relationships. Unless we are willing to make assumptions that go beyond the information that is actually provided by the data, however, it is not possible within the structure of the present data to perform a formal analysis of mediation or spuriousness because the temporal, and hence causal, ordering of predictors in the model relative to one another (as opposed to their ordering relative to the outcomes) is often ambiguous. For example, we cannot tell for certain whether the family structure at the beginning of the study (two-parent or other) was in place prior to or subsequent to the onset of parental physical abuse. As a result, we cannot tell whether physical abuse is a potential mediator of the relationship between two-parent family status and adult marital status. To be a mediating variable, physical abuse would need to occur temporally subsequent, not prior, to two-parent family structure. The suggestions that follow in this chapter regarding possible mediated or spurious relationships are thus speculative, suggested by but by no means conclusively established in the present data.

PATTERNS OF CONTINUITY FROM
ADOLESCENCE TO ADULTHOOD

Table 9.1 summarizes the relationships of each of the adult outcomes to its closest cognate behavior or status in adolescence, the variable that was used as the primary control in assessing the impact of AEV on the adult outcome. In table 9.1, and also in table 9.2 to follow, the designation "table/figure" is used because entries have been formatted to present a visual indication of the relative impacts of the different predictors. Relationships for which neither the direct effect nor the bivariate correlation is statistically significant are represented with "ns" (for "nonsignificant") which, at a length of only two characters, is the shortest entry in the last column of the table. Relationships involving a significant bivariate correlation but not a significant direct effect are represented with an entry that includes the sign of the relationship plus "corr" (for "correlation") which, at five characters, is intermediate in length. Significant direct effects are represented with the appropriately signed standardized coefficient, best for comparison of the strength of effects across differently scaled predictors (Menard 2011), plus in parentheses the statistical significance (p) of the relationship, based on the unstandardized coefficient (the most appropriate basis for assessing statistical significance; again, see Menard 2011). The selection of this presentation format is less about trying to be precise about the strength and significance of the relationship, which is already available in the previous chapters, than with having an entry that at twelve characters in length is over twice the length of the entry for a relationship involving only a significant bivariate correlation. In viewing tables 9.1 and 9.2, think of the length of the table entry in the last column as being akin to the height of the metaphorical tree in the forest, and the table as a whole as a map of the metaphorical forest of relationships in the present study. Asterisked (*) entries in the table indicate relationships for which the formal test described in earlier chapters indicates a statistically significant gender difference in the relationship.

Table 9.1 shows the extent of continuity from adolescence to adulthood of the adult relationships with their adolescent precursors. The relationships for social statuses specifically involve *intergenerational* continuity. For the adult social statuses except for marital status, the adolescent precursor is parental SES in adolescence, measured (as described in chapter 2) using the Hollingshead index of social position, which is based on the education and the occupational status of the parents. For adult marital status, the adolescent precursor is being in a two-parent family at the beginning of the study.

Bearing in mind that for parental SES, the two dummy variables (upper and lower parental SES) represent a single conceptual variable, there is strong evidence, in the form of direct effects, for intergenerational continuity from the SES of the parents to the educational attainment, income, and net worth of their offspring. Parental SES does not, however, appear to be a good predictor of adult employment status. In addition to the results for continuity, minority ethnicity is also predictive of less desirable social status outcomes, as shown in chapter 4.

There is weaker, largely correlational, evidence for intergenerational continuity in marital stability (two-parent family in adolescence, expected to be

Table 9.1 Continuity of Adult Outcomes with Corresponding Adolescent Statuses and Behaviors

Outcome	Gender	Precursor	Continuity
Social Status			
Educational Attainment	Female	Upper parental SES	+.278 (.000)
		Lower parental SES	−.158 (.000)
	Male	Upper parental SES	+.244 (.000)
		Lower parental SES	−.187 (.000)
Employment	Female	Upper parental SES	ns
		Lower parental SES	ns
	Male	Upper parental SES	+corr
		Lower parental SES	ns
Income	Female	Upper parental SES	+.099 (.030)
		Lower parental SES	−.107 (.016)
	Male	Upper parental SES	+.175 (.000)
		Lower parental SES	−.128 (.009)
Net Worth	Female	Upper parental SES	-corr
		Lower parental SES	−.151 (.001)
	Male	Upper parental SES	+.113 (.025)
		Lower parental SES	-corr
Never Married	Female	Two-parent family	-corr
	Male	Two-parent family	-corr
Previously Married	Female	Two-parent family	ns
	Male	Two-parent family	−.089 (.036)
Mental Health (MH)			
Mental Health Problems	Female	Parent report of MH problems	+corr
		Self report of MH problems	+.160 (.002)
	Male	Parent report of MH problems	+corr
		Self report of MH problems	+.169 (.003)
General Mental Health Service Use	Female	Parent report of MH problems	+corr
		Self report of MH problems	+corr
	Male	Parent report of MH problems	ns
		Self report of MH problems	+.113 (.025)
Professional Mental Health Service Use	Female	Parent report of MH problems	+corr
		Self report of MH problems	+.103 (.032)
	Male	Parent report of MH problems	ns
		Self report of MH problems	+.140 (.006)
Life Satisfaction	Female	Parent report of MH problems	−.092 (.032)
		Self report of MH problems	-corr
	Male	Parent report of MH problems	−.128 (.004)
		Self report of MH problems	−.108 (.017)
Substance Abuse			
Hard Drug Use Frequency	Female	Hard drug use frequency	+corr
	Male	Hard drug use frequency	+.131 (.048)
Marijuana Use Frequency	Female	Marijuana use frequency	+.181 (.002)
	Male	Marijuana use frequency	+.215 (.001)

(Continued)

Table 9.1   Continuity of Adult Outcomes with Corresponding Adolescent Statuses and Behaviors (Continued)

Outcome	Gender	Precursor	Continuity
Problem Hard Drug Use	Female	Problem drug use	+corr*
	Male	Problem drug use	+.213 (.000)*
Problem Marijuana Use	Female	Problem drug use	+corr*
	Male	Problem drug use	+.226 (.000)*
Problem Alcohol Use	Female	Problem alcohol use	+corr
	Male	Problem alcohol use	+.150 (.007)
General Violence and Arrest			
Violence Victimization	Female	Violence victimization	+corr
	Male	Violence victimization	+.118 (.033)
Violence Perpetration	Female	Violence perpetration	ns*
	Male	Violence perpetration	+.345 (.000)*
Arrest	Female	General offending	ns*
		Hard drug use frequency	ns
		Marijuana use frequency	+.138 (.030)
	Male	General offending	+.129 (.046)*
		Hard drug use frequency	+corr
		Marijuana use frequency	+corr
Intimate Partner Violence (IPV)			
Conflict Tactics Scale General IPV Victimization	Female	Violence victimization	+.126 (.045)
	Male	Violence victimization	+corr
Conflict Tactics Scale Serious IPV Victimization	Female	Violence victimization	+corr
	Male	Violence victimization	+corr
Conflict Tactics Scale General IPV Perpetration	Female	Violence perpetration	+corr
	Male	Violence perpetration	+corr
Conflict Tactics Scale Serious IPV Perpetration	Female	Violence perpetration	+corr
	Male	Violence perpetration	ns

*Gender difference statistically significant at p ≤ .05.
Note: ns = no significant correlation or direct effect; corr = significant correlation but no significant direct effect; for predictors with significant direct effects, the standardized coefficient is presented with, in parentheses, the statistical significance of the unstandardized coefficient. Italics indicate relationships that have the opposite of the expected sign.

on the results in chapter 7, exposure to neighborhood violence emerges as a possible mediator of the relationship of adolescent to adult violence victimization, and adolescent violence victimization is a possible mediator for the relationship of adolescent to adult violence perpetration. There is some evidence for continuity from adolescent offending (marijuana use for females, general offending for males) to adult arrest.

When we turn to intimate partner violence (IPV), the only relationship that is nonsignificant in both the bivariate and multivariate analysis is between

Table 9.2 Relationships of AEV with Adult Outcomes: The "Forest"

Dependent Variable in Adulthood	Gender	Parental Physical Abuse	Inconsistent Reports of Witnessing Inter-parental violence	Consistent Reports of Witnessing Inter-Parental Violence	Exposure to Neighborhood Violence	General Violence Victimization
Social status						
Educational Attainment	F	-corr*	ns	-corr	ns	-.089 (.033)
	M	-.107 (.008)*	ns	-corr	ns	-corr
Employment	F	-.108 (.012)	ns	ns	-.099 (.036)	ns
	M	ns	ns	ns	-.073 (.042)	ns
Income	F	-corr	ns	-corr	ns	ns
	M	-.096 (.020)	ns	-corr	ns	-.087 (.047)
Net Worth	F	-.116 (.028)	ns	-.095 (.038)	-corr	-corr
	M	-corr	ns	-corr	ns	-.093 (.033)
Never Married	F	ns	ns	ns	+corr	ns
	M	+.122 (.008)	ns	ns	+corr	ns
Previously Married	F	+corr	ns	ns	ns	+corr
	M	+.140 (.000)	ns	ns	ns	+.112 (.015)
Mental Health (MH)						
MH Problems	F	+corr	ns	+corr	ns	+.112 (.042)
	M	ns	ns	ns	ns	+.127 (.042)
General MH Service Use	F	+corr	ns	+.114 (.016)	+.097 (.030)*	+corr
	M	ns	ns	ns	ns*	+corr
Professional MH Service Use	F	ns	ns	+.108 (.023)	ns	+corr
	M	ns	ns	ns	-.095 (.049)	+corr
Life Satisfaction	F	-.090 (.048)	ns	-corr	-.090 (.032)	-.136 (.003)
	M	-corr	ns	-corr	-corr	-corr
Substance Abuse						

Hard Drug Use Frequency	F	+.115 (.019)	ns	+.137 (.004)	ns	+corr
	M	+corr	ns	+corr	+.120 (.012)	+corr
Marijuana Use Frequency	F	+corr	+corr	+corr	ns	+.137 (.004)
	M	+corr	ns	+corr	ns	+corr
Problem Hard Drug Use	F	+corr	ns	ns	ns	+.190 (.000)*
	M	+corr	ns	ns	ns	+corr*
Problem Marijuana Use	F	ns	+corr	ns	ns	+.107 (.037)*
	M	ns	+.119 (.011)	ns	ns	ns*
Problem Alcohol Use	F	ns	ns	ns	ns	+.109 (.037)
	M	ns	ns	ns	ns	+corr
General Violence and Arrest						
Violence Victimization	F	+corr	+corr*	ns	+.119 (.008)	+corr
	M	-.106 (.028)	-.106 (.023)*	ns	ns	+.118 (.033)
Violence Perpetration	F	ns	ns	ns	ns	+.090 (.007)
	M	+corr	ns	ns	ns	+.149 (.003)
Arrest	F	+corr	ns	ns	ns	ns
	M	ns	ns	ns	ns	+corr
Intimate Partner Violence (IPV)						
General IPV Victimization	F	+corr	+corr	ns	ns	+.126 (.045)
	M	+corr	ns	ns	ns	+corr
Serious IPV Victimization	F	+corr	+corr	ns	ns	+corr
	M	ns	ns	ns	ns	+corr
General IPV Perpetration	F	ns	ns	ns	ns	+corr
	M	+.264 (.000)	ns	ns	ns	+corr
Serious IPV Perpetration	F	+corr*	+corr	ns	ns	+corr
	M	[+.124 (.057)]*	ns	ns	ns	ns

*Gender difference statistically significant at p ≤ .05.

Note: ns = no significant correlation or direct effect; corr = significant correlation but no significant direct effect; for predictors with significant direct effects, the standardized coefficient is presented with, in parentheses, the statistical significance of the unstandardized coefficient. Italics indicate relationships that have the opposite of the expected sign.

negatively associated with being never married or formerly married in adulthood). One possible reason for the absence of a significant direct effect from adolescent family structure to adult marital status may be that the dynamic nature of parental marital or cohabiting status is not adequately captured by a single-time snapshot of family structure. Alternatively, it may be that the intergenerational transmission of marital status is simply weaker than that of other socioeconomic statuses. Speculatively, based on the results in tables 4.12 and 4.13, it is possible that for males the relationship is mediated by parental physical abuse and adolescent general violence victimization. For both females and males, urban-suburban-rural residence in adulthood is another candidate for a mediating variable. Besides the results for continuity, two-parent family structure in adolescence is generally predictive of more desirable adult social status outcomes.

Continuity in the remaining outcome measures represents not intergenerational, but rather *life course* continuity, in either states (e.g., having mental health problems) or behaviors (e.g., illicit and problem drug use). Beginning with mental health, both parental reports and, for males, self-reports of adolescent mental health problems are predictive of lower adult life satisfaction. For both females and males, there is strong evidence of continuity from self-reported adolescent mental health problems to adult mental health problems, and to general and professional mental health service use. The presence of significant correlations but not significant direct effects between one but not both of parental and self-reported problems in adolescence and adult mental health problems and mental health service use may reflect a situation in which both parental reports and self-reports are capturing much the same information, but one (usually self-report) is doing so better than the other.

Except for marijuana use, for which there is a direct effect from adolescent to adult frequency of use, illicit and problem substance use in adolescence is correlated with, but has no direct effect on, the corresponding type of illicit or problem drug use in adulthood for females. Based on the results in chapter 6, this suggests that the relationship of adolescent to adult substance abuse for females may be indirect, possibly mediated by physical abuse and witnessing parental violence for frequency of hard drug use, and by adolescent general violence victimization for problem hard drug, marijuana, and alcohol use. This pattern would be consistent with self-medication in response to AEV, particularly direct physical victimization. For males, however, all five types of substance abuse in adulthood have direct positive effects from their precursors in adolescence, consistent evidence of adolescence to middle adulthood continuity in illicit and problem substance use for males.

Similarly, there is strong evidence of life course continuity in violence victimization and perpetration for males but not for females. For females, based adolescent violence perpetration and adult serious Conflict Tactics Scale (CTS) IPV perpetration for males; and the only statistically significant direct effect is for adolescent general violence victimization on adult general CTS IPV victimization for females. All of the other relationships are characterized by positive correlations but no significant direct effects between adult CTS IPV victimization and perpetration and their adolescent precursors. This suggests broadly that the relationship of adolescent violence victimization and perpetration to adult IPV victimization and perpetration may be either spurious, both effects of common causes, or indirect, mediated by other variables in the model.

The results in chapter 8 suggest several potential mediators or variables that would explain spurious relationships among the predictors included in the models. For females, both the relationship between adolescent general violence victimization and adult serious IPV victimization, and the relationship between adolescent violence perpetration and adult serious IPV perpetration, may be spurious, with two-parent family status in adolescence influencing them both. Also for females, the relationship of adolescent general violence perpetration with adult general IPV perpetration may be mediated by adolescent general violence victimization, which has a marginally significant relationship ($b^* = .119$, $p = .058$) with adult general IPV perpetration. For males, it appears that the relationship of adolescent general violence victimization with both general and serious adult IPV victimization may be mediated by adolescent violence perpetration; and the relationship of adolescent violence perpetration with both general and serious IPV perpetration in adulthood may be mediated by parental physical abuse. These suggested patterns of spuriousness and mediation are all based on the existence of significant direct effects of the potential mediating variables in the tables in chapter 8. An interesting feature of these suggested mediators is that they involve (1) perpetration for relationships involving IPV victimization, and (2) victimization for relationships involving IPV perpetration, in a sort of violence-begets-violence pattern. It is worth reiterating here that all of the suggested mediating relationships are speculative, and would benefit from examination using different data from the data used in the present study.

Generally speaking, the evidence for continuity from adolescence to adulthood is most consistent for those states and behaviors that are most similar in adolescence and adulthood, such as parental SES and adult educational attainment, or adolescent and adult general violence victimization and perpetration; and less so for measures which are less similar across adolescence and adulthood, such as parental SES with adult employment status, or adolescent general violence victimization and perpetration with adult IPV victimization and perpetration. There are significant gender differences, some of which persist even using a conservative test for differences, as indicated by asterisked entries for two of the five substance abuse outcomes and two of the three general violence and arrest outcomes. Females and males are more similar in their patterns of continuity for social statuses, mental health, and IPV. While the possibility of gender differences for the latter three outcomes should not be dismissed based on the results of the present study, neither should the possibility that whether gender differences exist may depend on the outcome being examined.

PATTERNS OF IMPACTS OF AEV ON ADULT OUTCOMES: FOCUSING ON PREDICTORS

As described in chapter 1, our primary concern is to examine the impact of AEV on a variety of adult outcomes. Chapters 4–8 viewed that question primarily from the perspective of a focus on the outcomes, or to describe it another way, the rows in table 9.2. In this section, we focus on the columns, the predictors, asking the question, for which of the outcomes is each of the different forms of AEV most important? Table 9.2 presents the relationships of the adult outcomes to the different forms of AEV as predictors. Table 9.2 follows the same format as table 9.1, with the shortest entries in the last column for relationships that are significant for neither direct effects nor bivariate correlations, and the longest entries (signed coefficient plus statistical significance) for significant direct effects. For both general and IPV victimization, some of the relationships in table 9.2 duplicate entries in table 9.1, because adolescent violence victimization was used as the adolescent precursor for both general and intimate partner victimization in adulthood. Also in table 9.2, we have included both a significant direct effect of parental physical abuse on adult general IPV perpetration, and a marginally significant ($p = .057$) direct effect of parental physical abuse on adult serious IPV perpetration, for males. The latter effect was included in consideration of the magnitude of its effect (standardized coefficient = .124), its near-significance using the .05 cutoff, and the fact that it is statistically significantly stronger than the direct effect of parental physical abuse on adult serious IPV perpetration for females.

Beginning with the measures of more vicarious or indirect AEV, exposure to neighborhood violence has a total of only six direct effects, one of them, the negative direct effect of neighborhood violence on adult professional mental health service use for males, in the opposite of the expected direction. For both females and males, it has a direct negative effect on adult employment status, possibly reflecting a persistent impact of growing up in a disorganized neighborhood on adult employment opportunities.

Note that neighborhood violence has been used as one component of a more general index of neighborhood social disorganization in past studies using the National Youth Survey data (for example in Menard 1995, 1997). Exposure to neighborhood violence also has a direct negative effect for females, and a negative bivariate correlation for males, with adult life satisfaction; a direct positive effect for females and no significant relationship for males with adult general mental health service use and adult general violence victimization; and a direct positive effect for males and no significant effect for females on adult hard drug use frequency. Besides these direct effects, it has a negative correlation with net worth for females and positive correlations for both females and males with never having been married in adulthood. The remaining relationships involving exposure to neighborhood violence are nonsignificant. In general, the effects of neighborhood exposure to violence are most apparent for adult social status and mental health, but overall it appears to have very limited impact on the adult outcomes in the present study.

Inconsistent reporting of witnessing inter-parental violence has two significant direct effects, one in the expected direction for male adult problem marijuana use and one in the opposite of the expected direction for male adult general violence victimization. Besides these direct effects, there are only five significant correlations, all for females, with adult marijuana use, problem marijuana use, general IPV victimization, serious IPV victimization, and serious IPV perpetration. Consistent witnessing has four direct effects, all for females: a negative direct effect on adult net worth, positive direct effects on adult general and professional mental health service use, and a positive direct effect on adult hard drug use frequency. Also for females, it has a positive correlation with adult mental health problems. For males, it has a significant negative correlation with adult net worth and a significant positive correlation with hard drug use frequency, paralleling the relationships for females; and for both females and males, it has significant negative correlations with adult educational attainment, income, and life satisfaction, and significant positive correlations with marijuana use frequency. It is not significantly related to adult problem substance use, to adult arrest, or to general or serious IPV victimization or perpetration in adulthood. Only once do inconsistent and consistent witnessing have the same significant relationship with any outcome, a positive correlation with adult frequency of marijuana use.

There are three conclusions that can be drawn from this pattern of relationships involving inconsistent and consistent witnessing. First, the difference between inconsistent and consistent witnessing matters. Failing to separate the two, for example by using a single data point for long-term retrospective reporting of witnessing inter-parental violence, may dilute the effect that might be observed if only consistent reports, or better still prospective reports, were used. Second, it appears to be inconsistent rather than consistent witnessing that is associated with higher levels of adult violence, most particularly adult general violence and CTS general and serious victimization, specifically for females. Consistent witnessing is associated more with adult social statuses, mental health, and frequency of illicit drug use. Third, neither consistent nor inconsistent witnessing appears to have much in the way of direct effects on adult outcomes.

Moving to more direct forms of AEV, the effects of parental physical abuse are most evident for adult social statuses, and less so for the other adult outcomes. It has a negative direct for males on adult educational attainment and income, positive direct effects on being never married or previously married (as opposed to being currently married), and a negative correlation with adult net worth. For females, it has negative direct effects on adult employment and net worth, a positive correlation with having been previously married (as opposed to being currently married), and negative correlations with educational attainment and income. For each of the other sets of outcomes, it has a single significant direct effect (two for IPV if we include the marginally significant effect of parental physical abuse on serious IPV perpetration for males), and one, its direct effect on adult violence victimization for males, is in the opposite of the expected direction.

Besides its direct effects, parental physical abuse also has significant correlations involving substance abuse and violence for both females and males: with frequency of hard drug use, frequency of marijuana use, problem hard drug use, and general IPV violence victimization. For females, it also has significant correlations with serious IPV victimization and perpetration, general violence victimization, and arrest, and for males a significant correlation with adult general violence perpetration. It appears to have less of an impact on adult problem marijuana or alcohol use, and on adult mental health problems and mental health service use. The effects of parental physical abuse thus occur across the range of adult outcomes, but other than adult social statuses, its relationships with the adult outcomes appear to be largely either spurious or indirect.

For adolescent general violence victimization, even more than for parental physical abuse, the effects are pervasive and substantial across the full range of adult outcomes considered here. The relationship of adolescent violence victimization is nonsignificant for both females and males for employment, for females but not for males for income and arrest, and for males but not for females for problem marijuana use and serious IPV perpetration in adulthood. For adult marital status, although it is nonsignificant for never having been married, it has a significant direct positive effect for males and a positive correlation for females with being previously married. For every other outcome, for both females and males, it has at least a significant correlation (a total of

20) or a significant direct effect (15), all in the expected direction. Its impacts are weakest on adult IPV, arrest, hard drug use, general and professional mental health service, and employment. For these outcomes, there are no significant direct effects except for general IPV victimization for females. For adult social statuses and substance abuse, its impact is more direct for females than for males, while its impacts are more similar across genders for mental health, violence victimization, and violence perpetration.

Moreover, there appears to be some complementarity between the effects of adolescent general violence victimization and parental physical abuse. There are eighteen instances in which one but not the other has a significant direct effect on one of the outcomes. Counting marriage (both never married plus formerly married) as a single variable, there are only three outcomes for which neither parental physical abuse nor general violence victimization in adolescence has at least one significant correlation or direct effect between them: adult employment for males, problem marijuana use for males, and general IPV perpetration for females, with the rest being nearly evenly split between outcomes with at least one significant correlation but no direct effects (18), and outcomes with at least one direct effect (21).

In summary, it appears that the direct experience of violent victimization, whether parental abuse or more general violence victimization, is the best predictor of adverse adult outcomes. Exposure to neighborhood violence has impacts primarily on adult employment and mental health measures. Inconsistent reports of witnessing parental violence are inconsistent and largely insignificant in their effects on adult outcomes. Consistent reports of witnessing parental violence show some evidence of having effects on socio-economic status, mental health, and frequency of substance use, but not on problem substance use, violence victimization, or violence perpetration. It is parental physical abuse, particularly for adult social statuses, and adolescent general violence victimization that have consistently significant relationships, either direct effects or bivariate correlations, across all of the adult outcomes considered in this study. These results suggest that, aside from reducing AEV itself, efforts to reduce the negative consequences of AEV may have the greatest potential for a significant favorable impact if they focus on direct rather than indirect exposure to violence in adolescence.

POLICY AND PROGRAM IMPLICATIONS: GENERAL CONSIDERATIONS AND SELECTED PROGRAMS

Finkelhor et al. (2014) estimated that of children 5–17 years old in the United States, nearly two-thirds (65%) have been exposed to a violence prevention program, over half (55%) within the past year, based on data from the National Survey of Children's Exposure to Violence II (NatSCEV II). NatSCEV II is the successor to the original NatSCEV study described in chapter 1, and has used data collected from a national sample of 4,503 children ranging in age from 1 month to 17 years old, using primarily telephone interviewing (random digit dialing), supplemented by a mobile phone sample and an address-based sample. In NatSCEV II, respondents 10 years and older, or the primary caretaker for children 5–9 years old, were asked whether they had ever been exposed to violence prevention programs in the school or community, and if so, both what type of program and also whether the program contained certain features characteristic of higher quality programs. Regarding type of program, 55% reported being exposed to a bullying prevention program, 43% to violence avoidance, 32% to dating violence prevention, 27% to gang avoidance, and 21% to sexual assault prevention. Based on Finkelhor et al.'s criteria for high-quality programs, however, only 16% were exposed to a high-quality program, at least in the most recent program to which they were exposed. Finkelhor et al. (2014) also note prior research by the U.S. Department of Education that in the early 2000s, violence prevention curricula were present in 71% of high schools, 75% of middle schools, and 56% of elementary schools, but that those data lacked information about program effectiveness.

From the last decade of the twentieth century to the beginning of the third decade of the twenty-first, there has been an increased concern with whether, and if so under what circumstances, programs designed to prevent violence victimization and perpetration were effective in doing so. During this period, the state of prevention science has increasingly moved from single studies and "systematic" reviews, the latter with no formal criteria for assessing which studies provided the best information about the effectiveness of the programs they reviewed, to a much stronger emphasis on randomized control trials (RCTs) and meta-analysis to assess program effectiveness. Prominent among the former is the Blueprints for Violence Prevention Program at the University of Colorado, Boulder, renamed and expanded in scope as the Blueprints for Healthy Youth Development and Crime Prevention (see Mihalic et al. 2004 regarding the original Blueprints program, plus the continually updated website at https://www.blueprintsprograms.org for the more recent information). For a program to be included as a "model" program, it must provide (1) evidence of a favorable effect on the targeted outcome, (2) that is sustained over time, (3) based on strong research evidence, preferably experimental or at least strong quasi-experimental design, with (4) multiple site replication of the favorable effects. The Blueprints program also identifies as "promising" those programs which show evidence of favorable effects for which the evidence is not as strong as required for classification as a "model" program.

The second approach, meta-analysis, has been pioneered by Lipsey (see, for example, Lipsey 1992, 2009). Meta-analysis relies on statistical techniques to estimate the size of the effects of a program based on multiple studies, with a consideration of the quality of the research in deciding which studies to include in the analysis and how much weight to place on the results. Meta-analysis has in practice tended to identify more programs as being successful, than the strong experimental criteria used in the Blueprints program (see, for example, Greenwood and Turner 2012). Meta-analytic reviews could in principle focus on specific programs, as does the Blueprints program, but often focus instead on more general types of programs. For example, Blueprints assesses the Nurse-Family Partnership (NFP) intervention separately from all other home visitation and parent training programs, while Mikton and Butchart (2009) and Chen and Chan (2015) include NFP as one of several home visitation or parent training interventions, and evaluate those interventions collectively, rather than separately by specific program (although they do both single out NFP as a program with exceptional evidence of success in reducing child abuse and maltreatment).

Interventions are sometimes divided into three classifications (e.g., Chen and Chan 2015; Mihalic et al. 2004; Mikton and Butchart 2009): (1) primary/universal interventions, applied to the general population to prevent behavior such as child abuse or violence perpetration before it occurs; (2) secondary/selective interventions, still trying to prevent behavior before it occurs, but specifically targeted to individuals selected because they are believed to be at higher risk of that behavior than others in the general population; and (3) tertiary/indicated interventions, applied after the behavior has already occurred, in order to prevent recurrence of the behavior. With successful primary or secondary interventions, adverse effects of child abuse or violence perpetration are avoided by preventing the behavior that would have caused them. With tertiary prevention, it is necessary to consider whether preventing recurrence is sufficient, or alternatively whether prevention of the adverse effects of the victimization or perpetration requires components to mitigate the effects of the behavior that has already occurred.

For our present purposes, the most important distinction is between preventing onset of the behavior (primary and secondary prevention) and preventing recurrence of the behavior (tertiary prevention). In light of the findings of the present study, we need to consider (1) prevention of physical abuse and, separately, (2) prevention of violence victimization more generally, as the two forms of prevention most likely to result in reductions of adverse consequences; and (3) in addition, components of tertiary interventions that can reduce the consequences of physical abuse and violence victimization, once they have already been experienced. Given our results, interventions that reduce more indirect exposure to violence would also be desirable, but secondary in priority to reducing direct victimization.

Selected Family-Based Interventions

Mikton and Butchart (2009) in their "review of reviews" of primary and secondary interventions to prevent child maltreatment considered seven types of programs: home visitation (typically a secondary intervention for at-risk families delivered to parents and children in the home context), parent education (distinguished from home visitation by typically being a primary intervention occurring outside the home, and delivered to groups rather than individual parents), child sex abuse prevention, abusive head trauma prevention, multi-component interventions, media-based interventions, and support and mutual aid groups. Four types of programs showed "promise" in preventing actual child maltreatment (home visitation, parent education, abusive head trauma prevention, and multi-component interventions), while three (home visitation, parent education, and child sexual abuse prevention) showed evidence of reducing risk factors (but in the case of child sexual abuse prevention, not actual abuse) for child maltreatment. They singled out David Olds' NFP program as the only home visitation program with clear evidence of effectiveness in preventing child abuse and maltreatment, citing Olds et al. (1997), who found a 48% reduction in actual abuse in a 15-year follow-up to the original intervention. For parent education and abusive head trauma prevention, they characterize the evidence as insufficient, and they characterize the evidence for multi-component programs as a mix of insufficient, mixed, and promising results, for the reduction of child maltreatment.

Mikton and Butchart also note that a single program may account for the characterization of one type of intervention as being promising, as is the case with the NFP for home visitation programs, and suggest that methodological problems with reviews of programs allow no better than tentative conclusions about their effectiveness. Chen and Chan (2015), in a later review, citing methodological limitations in previous reviews, reviewed only randomized controlled trials (RCTs) that focused on child maltreatment, included some form of home visitation or parent training component in the treatment but not the control group, and provided sufficient data to calculate effect sizes. They combined nurse visitation and parent training programs into a single category, parenting programs, and examined primary, secondary, and tertiary prevention of effects of parenting programs.

They concluded that parenting programs reduced both substantiated child maltreatment, based on official records of child maltreatment, and also self-reported child maltreatment, and that both home visitation and parent education programs were effective as primary, secondary, and tertiary interventions to prevent child maltreatment.

Included among the programs reviewed by Chen and Chan (2015) was the NFP, which has also been cited for its reduction in child abuse and neglect in other reviews of family interventions (e.g., Gonzalez and MacMillan 2008; Mihalic et al. 2004; Schindler and Black 2015; Welsh and Zane 2019), which note not only its favorable impact on reducing child maltreatment, but also its impact on reducing antisocial and aggressive behavior, delinquency and crime, substance use, and mental health problems for children and/or their parents (e.g., Olds et al. 1986, 1997). The NFP has shown these favorable results particularly for at-risk families (secondary prevention), and there is evidence that the favorable results for prevention of violence and other problem behaviors (as opposed to child maltreatment) may dissipate by the end of adolescence (Eckenrode et al. 2010), and possibly earlier (Kitzman et al. 2010) in some implementations. Based on its sustained effects from infancy to at least early, and possibly late, adolescence on reducing problem behaviors, NFP has been one of the programs identified as a model program (or more recently, "model-plus" program, based on the extensive and well-replicated evidence of its effectiveness) by the Blueprints for Violence Prevention program (Mihalic et al. 2004; and see also the Blueprints website at https://www.blueprintsprograms.org). Additionally, the federal Title IV-E Prevention Services Clearing House (FFPSA) (2019c) has assessed and found NFP to be a well-supported (effective) program.

Another intervention identified by the Blueprints program as being effective in reducing child maltreatment is GenerationPMTO (originally Parent Management Training—Oregon Model), a tertiary intervention designed for parents with children who exhibit antisocial behavior. GenerationPMTO is delivered in a variety of settings (group or individual, in homes, schools, community centers, clinics, and homeless shelters) to teach parenting management skills to parents of children 3–16 years old (see, e.g., Patterson 2005; Patterson et al. 1982). Welsh and Zane (2019), however, based on evidence from meta-analysis, make the mixed assessment that the effects of the Oregon parent management training model have been nonsignificant (hence not supportive) to moderate (hence supportive) of the effectiveness of the program in preventing violence and other problem behaviors. Gonzalez and MacMillan (2008) identify both NFP and the Early Start program in New Zealand as promising interventions to reduce child maltreatment. Like NFP, Early Start is a secondary intervention targeting at-risk families.

Several other family-based interventions are identified by the Blueprints program as model programs for reducing violence, delinquency, crime, and related problem behaviors. These include Functional Family Therapy (FFT), a tertiary intervention to reduce illicit drug use, other illegal behaviors, and conduct problems; Treatment Foster Care Oregon (TFCO), a secondary or tertiary intervention to reduce violence perpetration, illicit drug use, alcohol and tobacco use, teen pregnancy, delinquency and crime, and also to improve school attendance and reduce truancy, for at-risk children in foster care placement; and multisystemic therapy (MST), a tertiary intervention to reduce violence, illicit drug use, other forms of crime and delinquency, and mental health problems. MST includes not only the family but also the school and neighborhood as intervention contexts. MST and FFT are individualized tertiary interventions, appropriate for children who might otherwise be at risk for external placement for problem behavior, or who are retained within the home other reasons. These interventions may be of particular interest in light of the Family First Prevention Services Act (FFPSA), with its emphasis on keeping children in placements with family members and avoiding foster placement (Lindell et al. 2020). Under FFPSA, the FFPSA (2019a, b) has assessed MST and FFT and concluded both were effective and well-supported by evidence. Alternatively, TFCO offers an intervention which may help mitigate the strains and potential deleterious consequences when, even with the predisposition to keep children within family placements, children do need to be placed into foster care.

Selected Interventions Based in the School and Community

School-based interventions classified by Blueprints as model programs include Project Towards No Drug Abuse (here abbreviated PTNDA), Life Skills Training (LST), Positive Action, and by virtue of its inclusion of the school as a context for intervention, the aforementioned MST. All three of the programs as well as MST show evidence of reducing violence perpetration (specifically bullying and antisocial/aggressive behavior in the case of Positive Action) and illicit drug use (and for all except MST, alcohol, and tobacco use). PTNDA, LST, and Positive Action also show evidence of reducing risky sexual behaviors, and PTNDA also shows evidence of reducing violence victimization. LST and Positive Action reduce general delinquency and crime, and LST improves emotional regulation. Positive Action shows improvements in mental health, physical health, prosocial behavior, school attendance, and academic performance. In addition to these programs, Ttofi and Farrington (2011) offer a meta-analytic review of school-based anti-bullying programs, and more general reviews of the effectiveness of school-based programs may be found in Kim et al. (2015) and Zych and Farrington (2019).

Table 9.3 presents a summary of the Blueprints for Healthy Youth Development and Crime Prevention model (and model-plus) programs discussed thus far. As can be seen in the table, these programs with strong evidence of effectiveness include programs for child maltreatment prevention and prevention of violence victimization, the two targets that emerge as most important for intervention in the present study. Several of the programs also reduce violence perpetration, desirable in its own right, but also an outcome likely to result in reductions in violence victimization. NFP, GenerationPMTO, MST, and Positive Action address mental health problems, with the prospect of breaking the link between AEV and adult mental health problems. Several of the interventions operate to reduce alcohol and tobacco use, potential gateways to more serious drug use (Elliott et al. 1989), and, most importantly both in its own right and for its influence on adult illicit and problem drug use, illicit drug use among adolescents. Treatment Foster Care, NFP, and Positive Action address school attendance, and the latter two also have beneficial effects on academic performance. These are highlighted (*italicized*) in the table because they are less frequently the focus when considering the effects of AEV, and also because, just as alcohol and tobacco may be gateways to more serious drug use, academic performance may, in a more positive way, be a gateway to academic achievement (how far one goes in school) and, through that, to other desirable social statuses.

Numerous other interventions to reduce child maltreatment have been suggested, among them cognitive behavioral therapy (CBT) and restorative justice, both tertiary interventions. As described, by Zara (2019), models of CBT include aggression replacement training, moral reconation (reboot the ego) therapy, reasoning and rehabilitation, relapse prevention therapy, and thinking for change, all of which recognize that there may be multiple influences on criminal behavior, and focus on assisting individuals in changing their cognitive approach, and as a result their behavioral approach, to stimuli that would result in problematic behavioral outcomes. As Zara notes, however, there is generally mixed evidence regarding the effectiveness of CBT programs for both children and adults. Similarly, the Title IV-E Prevention Services, Clearing House (2019d) has identified one variant of CBT, Trauma-Focused Cognitive Behavioral Therapy, as promising but in need of further research. As noted by Godbout et al. (2019), in some cases single-trauma CBT techniques may be insufficient to address multiple traumatizing events and high-risk environments associated specifically with child maltreatment (see also Briere and Scott 2015). As the present study has indicated, there is a complexity to exposure to violence that suggests that any therapeutic intervention, including but not limited to CBT, must be targeted

Table 9.3 Selected Blueprints Model and Model-plus Programs and Their Demonstrated Favorable Outcomes

Program: Setting	Victimization	Violence	Substance Abuse	Mental Health	Other (Education italicized)
Nurse-Family Partnership (NFP): Family (Home Visitation)	Child Maltreatment	Antisocial/ Aggressive Behavior	Illicit Drug Use, Alcohol, Tobacco	Anxiety, Depression, Conduct Problems, Emotional Regulation, Externalizing, Other Mh	Delinquency, Crime, Parent Relationships, Gestation And Birth, Teen Pregnancy, Physical Health, Communication/ Language Development, Sexual Risk Behaviors, Employment, Cognitive Development, *Academic Performance, High School Graduation/Dropout*
GenerationPMTO: Family (Parent Training, Community Based)	Child Maltreatment	Antisocial/ Aggressive Behavior		Anxiety, Conduct Problems, Emotional Regulation, Internalizing, Externalizing, Other Mh	Delinquency, Crime, Prosocial Behavior
Project Towards No Drug Abuse: School	Violent Victimization	Violence Perpetration	Illicit Drug Use, Alcohol, Tobacco		Sexual Risk Behaviors

Program	Substance Use	Mental Health	Violence/Aggression	Delinquency/Crime
Functional Family Therapy (FFT): Family	Illicit Drug Use			Delinquency, Crime, Gang Involvement, Conduct Problems
Life Skills Training (LST): School	Illicit Drug Use, Alcohol, Tobacco		Violence Perpetration	Delinquency, Crime, Sexual Behaviors, Emotional Regulation
Multisystemic Therapy (MST): Home, School, and Neighborhood	Illicit Drug Use	Conduct problems, Externalizing, Internalizing, Other MH	Violence Perpetration	Delinquency, Crime, Parent Relationships, Prosocial Behavior, Prosocial Peers
Treatment Foster Care Oregon: Family	Illicit Drug Use, Alcohol, Tobacco		Violence Perpetration	Delinquency, Crime, Teen Pregnancy, *School Attendance/Truancy*
Positive Action: School	Illicit Drug Use, Alcohol, Tobacco	Anxiety, Depression, Conduct problems, Emotional regulation, Internalizing, Other MH	Bullying, Antisocial/Aggressive Behavior	Delinquency, Crime, Sexual Risk Behaviors, Physical Health, Prosocial Behavior, Academic Performance, *School Attendance/Truancy*

Note: MH = mental health.

to the individual and the types of exposure, in some cases multiple and/or prolonged exposure.

While CBT is an individual-level intervention, restorative justice is a broadly-based justice system intervention (Bazemore 2012). As described by Bazemore, restorative justice programs have shown some evidence of reducing aggression, recidivism, and post-traumatic stress, as well as increasing victim satisfaction with the justice process, but as Bazemore cautions, the findings across different studies are mixed. While CBT and restorative justice are worth further exploration, in particular to resolve the reasons for their mixed findings with respect to effectiveness, the state of prevention science appears to have progressed to a point where there are well-supported evidence-based programs available to address primary, secondary, and tertiary interventions to reduce both AEV and its consequences.

THEORETICAL IMPLICATIONS

As we described in chapter 1, our study of the relationship of AEV with adult outcomes has been informed primarily by a combination of two variants of strain theory, the individual level anomie theory of Merton (1938) and Cloward (1959) and the general strain theory of Agnew (1992), plus, particularly for violence victimization and perpetration, the social learning theory of Akers (1985). The present research should not be regarded as a formal test of any of those theories, which have been tested and supported elsewhere; see for example Menard (1995, 1997) for anomie theory, Agnew (2012) for general strain theory, and Akers and Sellers (2012) for social learning theory. The points to be made about these theories based on the present research are how well they help us not only to predict but also to understand the effects of AEV on adult outcomes, including gender differences in the relative effects of different predictors on different outcomes.

In particular, anomie theory alerts us to the point that the same stimulus, whether direct physical victimization or more indirect exposure to violence, may produce different outcomes. This is consistent with the findings particularly regarding the pervasive impacts of general violence victimization and parental physical abuse across a range of outcomes including adult social statuses, mental health, substance abuse, and violence victimization and perpetration. General strain theory alerts us to the point that there may be gender differences in the impacts of AEV on different outcomes. This is most readily apparent in the gender differences for adult mental health and substance abuse, for both of which AEV had more direct impacts for females than for males, and for adult violence, for which AEV had more direct effects for males than for females.

For social learning theory, the interpretation of the results of the present study is more complicated. First, while anomie and general strain theories are directly applicable to all of the adult outcomes, variants of social learning theory, in particular the cycle of violence variant (Widom 1989b), is most applicable to adult violence victimization and especially to adult violence perpetration. Second, there is overlap between social learning and strain theories. For example, from the perspective of Akers (1985), differential association is one component of social learning theory; but it is also one component of Cloward's (1959) version of individual-level anomie theory. This makes it difficult to completely separate strain and social learning theories to compare their effects.

If we look only at direct effects on adult outcomes in table 9.2, of twelve possible effects (general violence victimization and offending, general and serious IPV victimization and offending, separately for females and males) that would be relevant for learning theory, there are only four direct effects for general violence victimization; two or (counting p = .057 as significant) three, one in the opposite of the expected direction, for parental physical abuse; one, in the opposite of the expected direction, for inconsistent witnessing; none for consistent witnessing; and one for exposure to neighborhood violence. Including significant correlations does not change the count for consistent witnessing or neighborhood violence, and increases the count for inconsistent witnessing by three, but increases the number of relationships consistent with the theory to nine of twelve for parental physical abuse and eleven of twelve for adolescent general violence victimization. The results that include correlations are consistent with results from past studies involving simpler models or only bivariate relationships. The reduction of the significant bivariate correlations to nonsignificant multivariate direct effects suggests that the relationship of adolescent violence victimization hypothesized by learning theories is either spurious (in which case learning theories are not supported) or indirect, via other variables in the analysis (in which case learning theory receives at least some support). The present data do not allow us to conclusively decide between these two possibilities. To the extent that learning theory is supported, it is more for the direct experience of being victimized than for the more vicarious or indirect experiences of witnessing or otherwise being exposed to violence in the family or neighborhood.

As we indicated in chapter 1, we are not trying to test the most comprehensive models of strain or learning theories for the adult outcomes. Our focus is on the predictors, rather than the outcomes. In order to see whether each type of AEV plausibly affects each of the adult outcomes, we do control for the adolescent precursors, characteristics (for socioeconomic statuses and mental health) or behaviors (for substance use, violence victimization, and violence perpetration) that, of the variables available in the data set, most closely parallel each adult outcome. In none of these models can we claim to have included all possible relevant predictors. For illicit substance use and other illegal behavior in particular, we have not included such theoretically relevant variables as exposure to delinquent or criminal friends, belief that it is wrong to violate the law, or adolescent problem behaviors other than those that most closely parallel the adult outcomes in which we are interested, variables that past research using the NYS/NYSFS (e.g., Elliott et al. 1989) suggests would be relevant to a more complete model for these outcomes. The first reason for this is our focus on effects rather than causes. A second reason is the practical impossibility, even if there were no constraints on the available data, of including all possible hypothesized influences on each of the adult outcomes. It is entirely possible that there would be fewer direct effects and more indirect effects of AEV were each of the models expanded to include additional predictors. What we have done with the less complete, more focused models in the present study is identify those types of AEV that seem to have the most evidence supporting their utility as predictors, and possibly as targets for intervention, separately for females and males, for each of the diverse sets of adult outcomes suggested by the theories that have informed this study.

The results of the present study are broadly supportive of a combined anomie, general strain, and social learning perspective that suggests that AEV should result in a range of undesirable outcomes in adulthood, with differences by gender in the extent to which different aspects of AEV affect different adult outcomes. In terms of a life course developmental perspective, the results support a concern with the timing of exposure to violence, identifying adolescence as a period in which exposure to violence may have long-term effects that persist through middle adulthood. There are additional issues not addressed in the present research which it would be useful to examine in future research.

IMPLICATIONS FOR FUTURE RESEARCH

As indicated in the previous section, it was not possible to include all of the predictors that might influence each of the adult outcomes, sometimes for reasons of availability of data in the present study, and sometimes for reasons of maintaining the focus on the predictors, rather than the outcomes. One possibility for future research would be to examine the impacts of AEV in the context of expanded models for each of the outcomes. For example, a more expanded model of adult income or net worth might include such predictors as educational achievement and employment history, while an expanded model for illicit drug use or violence perpetration might include involvement with delinquent or criminal friends and belief that it is wrong to violate the law as predictors. Of interest would be whether the expanded model included variables which mediated some or all of the apparent direct effects of AEV on adult outcomes that were found in the present study.

To adequately examine possible indirect or mediating effects, one would need longitudinal data, and ideally longitudinal data collected annually, rather than at the wide measurement intervals that characterize the later waves of the National Youth Survey Family Study (NYSFS). The NYSFS is adequate for establishing the existence of relationships that persist over long intervals, but for a proper analysis of mediating effects, the length of the measurement interval becomes more important to more precisely measure the strength of indirect effects. It would also be important to collect prospective data on each of the variables of interest. The longer term retrospective reports of witnessing inter-parental violence proved to be somewhat unreliable, with some respondents reporting that they had witnessed their parents hurting one another, only to report three or more years later that they had not, in effect recanting their previous report of witnessing parental violence. This finding, plus the different results for inconsistent and consistent reports of witnessing parental violence, reinforce the need for prospective data.

The set of predictors used as indicators of AEV in the present study was limited, consisting largely of single-item measures (a single question each about parental physical abuse, witnessing parental violence, and neighborhood violence). Missing from the measures are indicators of parental neglect of children and adolescents, which should be considered for future studies. Part of the reason for their omission from the present study is that the NYSFS was not specifically designed to study the impact of AEV on adult outcomes, but rather to study the causes of adolescent delinquency and drug use. It would be desirable to have multiple-item indicators for these predictors, as we have for adolescent violence victimization, in order to be able to better assess the reliability of the variables and to reduce random measurement error. This is not as much an issue with the adult outcome measures, some of which are inherently single-item variables (highest grade completed, income, net worth), and others of which are in the present study, and ideally should be in future research, multiple-item indicators (violence victimization and perpetration, mental health problems, problem substance use).

A great deal of work has been done on accumulating evidence of program effectiveness during the first two decades of the twenty-first century. Even so, as several of the reviews cited in this chapter indicate, there is still much to be done. First on the list is assessment of the impact of programs to prevent child abuse and maltreatment, adolescent violence victimization, and other forms of AEV, by actually measuring the outcome of interest, rather than just risk factors for that outcome. Reviews repeatedly noted the absence of direct outcome measures in all but a few studies of program impact. Expanding on the present study and the point made in the previous paragraph, it would be most helpful in general population sample survey research to ask, as in NatSCEV II, whether they had ever, and whether they had within the past year, been exposed to violence prevention programs, either as children or as adults (as in some of the family-based programs), and if so to which specific programs. This would give us a better idea of the extent of exposure to intervention programs, and perhaps more importantly allow the use of program exposure or participation as a potential mediating variable in studies of the impact of AEV on adult outcomes.

CONCLUSION

AEV is intrinsically problematic because of its direct impact on adolescent health and safety. It is also problematic because its effects may be enduring, reaching into adulthood, either directly or, particularly via continuity of short-term behavioral effects in adolescence into the adult years, indirectly. AEV has multiple enduring effects, and those effects differ by gender in terms of both which predictors are most important, and which outcomes are most affected for females and males. AEV is not limited to the home and community, and it is in fact the broader experience of general violence victimization in adolescence, rather than specifically abuse within the home, that appears in the present study to have the most pervasive effects on adverse adult outcomes. There are at present a relatively limited number of programs with sufficient evidence of effectiveness in preventing or reducing either the onset or the continuation of AEV, and also of mitigating its consequences on adverse outcomes, but these programs provide a good basis for intervention policy and practice. Still, more research is needed to better assess the effectiveness of other programs that, although the evidence is insufficient at present, may be effective in reducing AEV and breaking the links between AEV and adverse adult outcomes.

References

Acosta, O. M., K. E. Albus, M. W. Reynolds, D. Spriggs, and M. Weist. 2001. Assessing the status of research on violence-related problems among youth. *Journal of Clinical and Adolescent Psychology* 30:152–160.

Agnew, R. 1985. A revised strain theory of delinquency. *Social Forces* 64:151–167.

———. 1992. Foundation for a general strain theory of crime and delinquency. *Criminology* 30:47–83.

———. 2002. Experienced, vicarious, and anticipated strain: An exploratory study on physical victimization and delinquency. *Justice Quarterly* 19:603–632.

———. 2006. General strain theory: Current status and directions for future research. In *Taking stock: The status of criminological theory*, ed. F. T. Cullen, J. P. Wright, and K. R. Blevins, 101–123. New Brunswick, NJ: Transaction Publishers.

———. 2012. Strain and delinquency. In *The Oxford handbook of juvenile crime and juvenile justice*, ed. B. C. Feld and D. M. Bishop, 289–306. Oxford, UK: Oxford University Press.

Akers, R. L. 1985. *Deviant behavior: A social learning approach*, 3rd edition. Belmont, CA: Wadsworth.

Akers, R. L., and G. F. Jensen. 2006. The empirical status of social learning theory of crime and deviance: The past, present, and future. In *Taking stock: The status of criminological theory*, ed. F. T. Cullen, J. P. Wright, and K. R. Blevins, 37–76. New Brunswick, NJ: Transaction Publishers.

Akers, R. L., and C. S. Sellers. 2012. Social learning theory. In *The Oxford handbook of juvenile crime and juvenile justice*, ed. B. C. Feld and D. M. Bishop, 307–335. Oxford, UK: Oxford University Press.

Alexander, P. C., S. Moore, and E. R. Alexander, III. 1991. What is transmitted in the intergenerational transmission of violence? *Journal of Marriage and the Family* 53:657–667.

Altonji, J. G., and R. M. Blank. 2005. Race and gender in the labor market. In *Handbook of labor economics*, ed. O. Ashenfelter and D. Card, volume 3c, 3143–3259. Amsterdam: Elsevier North Holland.

Altonji, J. G., U. Doraszelski, and L. Segal. 2000. Black/white differences in wealth. *Economic Perspectives, Federal Reserve Bank of Chicago* 24:38–50.

American Psychiatric Association. 1980. *DSM-III: Diagnostic and statistical manual of mental disorders*, 3rd edition. Washington, DC: American Psychiatric Association.

Anda, R. F., V. J. Felitti, J. D. Bremner, J. D. Walker, C. Whitfield, B. D. Perry, S. R. Dube, and W. H. Giles. 2006. The enduring effects of abuse and related adverse experiences in childhood: A convergence of evidence from neurobiology and epidemiology. *European Archives of General Psychiatry and Clinical Neuroscience* 256:174–186.

Archer, J. 2000. Sex differences in aggression between heterosexual partners: A meta-analytic review. *Psychological Bulletin* 126:651–680.

Baglivio, M. T. K. T. Wolff, N. Epps, and R. Nelson. 2017. Predicting adverse childhood experiences: The importance of neighborhood context in youth trauma among delinquent youth. *Crime and Delinquency* 63:166–188.

Ball, J. C. 1967. The reliability and validity of interview data obtained from 59 narcotic drug addicts. *American Journal of Sociology* 72:650–654.

Baltes, P. B., S. W. Cornelius, and J. R. Nesselroade. 1979. Cohort effects in developmental psychology. In *Longitudinal research in the study of behavior and development*, ed. J. R. Nesselroade and P. B. Baltes, 61–87. New York, NY: Academic Press.

Bandura, A. 1977. *Social learning theory*. Upper Saddle River, NJ: Prentice Hall.

Barnea, Z., G. Rahav, and M. Teichman. 1987. The reliability and consistency of self-reports on substance use in a longitudinal study. *British Journal of Addiction* 82:891–898.

Baron, S. W. 2009. Street youths' violent responses to violent personal, vicarious, and anticipated strain. *Journal of Criminal Justice* 37:442–451.

Barroso, C. S., R. J. Peters, S. Kelder, J. Conroy, N. Murray, and P. Orpinas. 2008. Youth exposure to community violence: Association with aggression, victimization, and risk behaviors. *Journal of Aggression, Maltreatment, and Trauma* 17:141–155.

Bastian, L. D. 1993. Criminal victimization 1992: A National Crime Victimization Survey report. *Bureau of Justice Statistics Bulletin*. Washington, DC: U.S. Department of Justice.

Bazemore, G. 2012. Restoration, shame, and the future of restorative practice in U. S. juvenile justice. In *The Oxford handbook of juvenile crime and juvenile justice*, ed. B. C. Feld and D. M. Bishop, 695–722. New York, NY: Oxford University Press.

Beardslee, J., J. Schulenberg, and S. Simonton. 2020. The long-term associations between direct and threatened physical violence in adolescence and symptoms of substance use disorders during the mid-30s. *Journal of Studies on Alcohol and Drugs* 8:125–134.

Bell, C. C., and E. J. Jenkins. 1993. Community violence and children on Chicago's Southside. *Psychiatry* 56:46–54.

Bell, K. L., J. P. Allen, S. T. Hauser, and T. G. O'Connor. 1996. Family factors and young adult transitions: Educational attainment and occupational prestige. In *Transitions through adolescence: Interpersonal domains and context*, ed. J. A. Graber, J. Brooks-Gunn, and A. C. Petersen, 345–366. Mahwah, NJ: Lawrence Erlbaum.

Bellis, M. A., K. Hughes, K. Ford, G. R. Rodriguez, D. Sethi and J. Passmore. 2019. Life course health consequences and associated annual costs of adverse childhood experiences across Europe and North America: A systematic review and meta-analysis. *The Lancet* 4:517–528.

Bensley, L., J. Van Eenwyk, and K. Wynkoop-Simmons. 2003. Childhood family violence history and women's risk for intimate partner violence and poor health. *American Journal of Preventative Medicine* 25:38–44.

Benson, M. L. 2013. *Crime in the life course: An introduction*, 2nd edition. New York, NY: Routledge.

Benson, M. L., G. Fox, A. DeMaris, and J. Van Wyk. 2003. Neighborhood disadvantage, individual economic distress and violence against women in intimate relationships. *Journal of Quantitative Criminology* 19:207–235.

Bevan, E., and D. J. Higgins. 2002. Is domestic violence learned? The contribution of five forms of child maltreatment to men's violence and adjustment. *Journal of Family Violence* 17:223–245.

Beyer, K., A. B. Wallis, and L. K. Hamberger. 2013. Neighborhood environment and intimate partner violence: A systematic review. *Trauma Violence Abuse* 16:16–47.

Bishop, D. M., and M. J. Leiber, 2012. Racial and ethnic differences in delinquency and justice system responses. In *The Oxford handbook of juvenile crime and juvenile justice*, ed. B. C. Feld and D. M. Bishop, 445–484. Oxford, UK: Oxford University Press.

Blau, F. D., and J. W. Graham. 1990. Black-white differences in wealth and asset composition. *The Quarterly Journal of Economics* 105:321–339.

Blau, F. D., and L. M. Kahn. 2017. The gender wage gap: Extent, trends, and explanations. *Journal of Economic Literature* 55:789–865.

Boney-McCoy, S., and D. Finkelhor. 1995. Psychological sequelae of violent victimization in a national youth sample. *Journal of Consulting and Clinical Psychology* 63:726–736.

Bonjean, C. M., R. J. Hill, and S. D. McLemore. 1967. *Sociological measurement: An inventory of scales and indices*. San Francisco, CA: Chandler.

Bosick, S. J. 2009. Operationalizing crime over the life course. *Crime and Delinquency* 55:472–496.

Bowker, L. H., M. Arbitell, and J. R. McFerron. 1988. On the relationship between wife beating and child abuse. In *Feminist perspectives on wife abuse*, ed. K. Yllö and M. Bograd, 158–175. Newbury Park, CA: Sage.

Boynton-Jarrett, R., L. M. Ryan, L. F. Berkman, and R. J. Wright. 2008. Cumulative violence exposure and self-rated health: Longitudinal study of adolescents in the United States. *Pediatrics* 122:961–970.

Brame, R., and R. Paternoster. 2003. Missing data problems in criminological research: Two case studies. *Journal of Quantitative Criminology* 19:55–78.

Brame, R., R. Paternoster, P. Mazerolle, and A. Piquero. 1998. Testing for the equality of maximum-likelihood regression coefficients between two independent equations. *Journal of Quantitative Criminology* 14:245–261.

Breen, R. 1996. *Regression models: Censored, sample selected, or truncated data.* Thousand Oaks, CA: Sage.

Breen, R., and J. H. Goldthorpe. 1997. Explaining educational differentials: Towards a formal rational action theory. *Rationality and Society* 9:275–305.

Briere, J., and C. Scott. 2015. Complex trauma in adolescents and adults: Effects and treatment. *Psychiatric Clinics of North America* 38:515–527.

Broidy, L. M. 2001. A test of general strain theory. *Criminology* 39:9–35.

Broidy, L. M. and R. Agnew. 1997. Gender and crime: A general strain perspective. *Journal of Research in Crime and Delinquency* 34:275–306.

Buka, S. L., T. L. Stichick, I. Birdthistle, and F. J. Earls. 2010. Youth exposure to violence: Prevalence, risks, and consequences. *American Journal of Orthopsychiatry* 71:298–310.

Bunting, L., G. Davidson, C. McCartan, J. Hanratty, P. Bywaters, W. Mason, and N. Steils. 2018. The association between child maltreatment and adult poverty: A systematic review of longitudinal research. *Child Abuse and Neglect* 77:121–133.

Bureau of Justice Statistics. 1988. *Report to the nation on crime and justice*, 2nd edition. Washington, DC: U.S. Department of Justice.

Cahalan, D. 1970. *Problem drinkers.* San Francisco: Jossey-Bass.

Capaldi, D. M., and S. Clark. 1998. Prospective family predictors of aggression toward female partners for at-risk young men. *Developmental Psychology* 34:175–188.

Carrion, V. G., C. F. Weems, and A. L. Reiss. 2007. Stress predicts brain changes in children: A pilot longitudinal study on youth stress, posttraumatic stress disorder, and the hippocampus. *Pediatrics* 119:510–516.

Caspi, A., B. R. E. Wright, T. E., Moffitt, and P. A. Silva. 1998. Early failure in the labor market: Childhood and adolescent predictors of unemployment in the transition to adulthood. *American Sociological Review* 63:424–451.

Catalano, R. F., and J. D. Hawkins. 1996. The social development model: A theory of anti-social behavior. In *Delinquency and crime: Current theories*, ed. J. D. Hawkins, 149–197. New York, NY: Cambridge University Press.

Centers for Disease Control and Prevention. 2014. Cost of child abuse and neglect rival other major public health problems. https://www.cdc.gov/violenceprevention/childmaltreatment/economiccost.html

Centers for Disease Control and Prevention 2019a. Preventing Youth Violence. https://www.cdc.gov/violenceprevention/youthviolence/fastfact.html.

Centers for Disease Control and Prevention 2019b. Preventing Child Abuse & Neglect. https://www.cdc.gov/violenceprevention/childabuseandneglect/fastfact.html.

Chapman, H., and S. M. Gillespie. 2019. The revised Conflict Tactics Scales (CTS2): A review of the properties, reliability, and validity of the CTS2 as a measure of partner abuse in community and clinical samples. *Aggression and Violent Behavior* 44:27–35.

Chen, M., and K. L. Chan. 2015. Effects of parenting programs on child maltreatment prevention: A meta-analysis. *Trauma, Violence, and Abuse* 17:88–104.

Chen, P. Y., and P. M. Popovich. 2002. *Correlation: Parametric and nonparametric measures.* Thousand Oaks, CA: Sage.

Chen, W-Y. 2010. Exposure to community violence and adolescents' internalizing behaviors among African American and Asian American adolescents. *Journal of Youth and Adolescence* 39:403–487.

Cherlin, A. J., L. M. Burton, T. R. Hurt, and D. M. Purvin. 2004. The influence of physical and sexual abuse on marriage and cohabitation. *American Sociological Review* 69:768–789.

Child Welfare Information Gateway. 2020. *Child abuse and neglect fatalities 2017: Statistics and interventions.* Washington, DC: Children's Bureau. https://www.chi ldwelfare.gov/pubPDFs/fatality.pdf.

Christopher, K., P. England, T. M. Smeeding, and K. R. Phillips. 2002. The gender gap in poverty in modern nations: Single motherhood, the market, and the state. *Sociological Perspectives* 45:219–242.

Cicchetti, D., and F. A. Rogosch. 1997. The role of self-organization in the promotion of resilience in maltreated children. *Development and Psychopathology* 8:597–600.

Clark, J. P., and L. L. Tifft. 1966. Polygraph and interview validation of self-reported deviant behavior. *American Sociological Review* 31:826–834.

Cloward, R. A. 1959. Illegitimate means, anomie, and deviant behavior. *American Sociological Review* 24:164–176.

Cloward, R. A., and L. E. Ohlin. 1960. *Delinquency and opportunity: A theory of delinquent gangs.* New York, NY: Free Press.

Cohen, J., P. Cohen, S. G. West, and L. S. Aiken. 2003. *Applied multiple regression/correlation analysis for the behavioral sciences,* 3rd edition. Mahwah, NJ: Lawrence Erlbaum Associates.

Cohen, S., and D. Janicki-Deverts. 2012. Who's stressed? Distributions of psychological stress in the United States in probability samples from 1983, 2006, and 2009. *Journal of Applied Social Psychology* 42:1320–1334.

Costa, B. M., C. E. Kaestle, A. Walker, A. Curtis, A. Day, J. W. Toumbourou, and P. Miller. 2015. Longitudinal predictors of domestic violence perpetration and victimization: A systematic review. *Aggression and Violent Behavior* 24:261–272.

Covey, H. C., L. M. Grubb, R. J. Franzese, and S. Menard. 2017. Adolescent exposure to violence and adult anxiety, depression, and PTSD. *Criminal Justice Review* 45:185–201.

Covey, H. C., S. Menard, and R. J. Franzese. 2013. Effects of adolescent physical abuse, exposure to neighborhood violence, and witnessing parental violence on adult socioeconomic status. *Child Maltreatment* 18:85–97.

Crittenden, P. M. 1992. Children's strategies for coping with adverse home environments: An interpretation using attachment theory. *Child Abuse and Neglect* 16:329–343.

Cummings, J. G., D. J. Pepler, and T. E. Moore. 1999. Behavior problems in children exposed to wife abuse: Gender differences. *Journal of Family Violence* 14:133–156.

Currie, J., and E. Tekin. 2012. Understanding the cycle of childhood maltreatment and future crime. *Journal of Human Resources* 47:509–549.

Currie, J., and C. S. Widom. 2010. Long-term consequences of child abuse and neglect on adult economic well-being. *Child Maltreatment* 15:111–120.

D'Alessio, S. J., and L. Stolzenberg. 2003. Race and the probability of arrest. *Social Forces* 81:1381–1397.

Daly, K. 1998. Gender, crime, and criminology. In *The handbook of crime and justice*, ed. M. Tonry, 85–108. Oxford, UK: Oxford University Press.

Daylor, J. M., D. V. Blalock, T. Davis, W. X. Klauberg, J. Stuewig, and J. P. Tangney. 2019. Who tells the truth? Former inmates' self-reported arrests vs. official records. *Journal of Criminal Justice*, online first, doi.org/10.1016/j.jcrimjus.2019.04.002.

de Leeuw, E., and W. de Heer. 2002. Trends in household survey nonresponse: A longitudinal and international comparison. In *Survey nonresponse*, ed. R. M. Groves, D. A. Dillman, J. L. Eltinge, and R. J. A. Little, 41–54. New York, NY: John Wiley & Sons.

de Leeuw, E. D., and J. van der Zouwen. 1988. Data quality in face to face interviews: A comparative meta-analysis. In *Telephone survey methodology*, ed. R. M. Groves, P. P. Biemer, L. Lyberg, J. T. Massey, W. L, Nicholls II, and J. Waksberg, 257–282. New York, NY: Russell Sage Foundation.

Dembo, R., W. Wothke, W. Seeberger, M. Shemwell, K. Pacheco, M. Rollie, J. Schmeidler, S. Livingston, and A. Hartsfield. 2002. Testing a longitudinal model of the relationships among high risk youths' drug sales, drug use, and participation in index crimes. *Journal of Child and Adolescent Substance Abuse* 11:36–61.

Dentler, R. A., and L. J. Monroe. 1961. Social correlates of early adolescent theft. *American Sociological Review* 26:733–743.

Dubow, E. G., P. Boxer, and L. R. Huesmann. 2009. Long-term effects of parents' education on children's educational and occupational success: Mediation by family interactions, child aggression, and teenage aspirations. *Merrill Palmer Quarterly* 55:224–249.

Dunn, E. C., S. E. Gilman, J. B. Willett, W. B. Slopen, and B. E. Molnar. 2012. The impact of exposure to interpersonal violence on gender differences in adolescent-onset major depression: Results from the national comorbidity survey replication. *Depression and Anxiety* 29:392–399.

Durant, R. H., A. Getts, C. Cadenhead, S. J. Emans, and E. R. Woods. 1995. Exposure to violence and victimization and depression, hopelessness, and purpose in life among adolescents living in and around public housing. *Journal of Development and Behavioral Pediatrics* 16:233–237.

Eckenrode, J., M. Campa, D. W. Luckey, C. R. Henderson, R. Cole, H. Kitzman, E. Anson, K. Sidora-Arcoleo, J. Powers, and D. Olds. 2010. Long-term effects of prenatal and infancy nurse home visitation on the life course of youths: 19-year follow-up of a randomized trial. *Archives of Pediatrics and Adolescent Medicine* 164:9–15.

Edleson, J. L. 1999. Children's witnessing adult domestic violence. *Journal of Interpersonal Violence* 14:839–870.

Edwards, K. 2014. Intimate partner violence and the rural-urban-suburban divide: Myth or reality? A critical review of the literature. *Trauma, Violence, and Abuse* 16:359–373.

Egeland, B. 1993. A history of abuse is a major risk factor for abusing the next generation. In *Current controversies on family violence*, ed. R. J. Gelles, and D. R. Loseke, 197–208. Newbury Park, CA: Sage.

Egeland, B., D. Jacobvitz, and A. Sroufe. 1988. Breaking the cycle of abuse. *Child Development* 59:1080–1088.

Ehrensaft, M. K., P. Cohen, J. Brown, E. Smailes, H. Chen, and J. G. Johnson. 2003. Intergenerational transmission of partner violence: A 20-year prospective study. *Journal of Consulting and Clinical Psychology* 71:741–752.

Eigenberg, H. M. 1980. The National Crime Survey and rape: The case of the missing question. *Justice Quarterly* 7:655–671.

Eitle, D., and R. J. Turner. 2002. Exposure to community violence and young adult crime: The effects of witnessing violence, traumatic victimization, and other stressful life events. *Journal of Research in Crime and Delinquency* 39:214–237.

Elder, G. H., L. K. George, and M. J. Shanahan. 1996. Psychological stress: Over the Life Course. In *Psychological stress: Perspectives on structure, theory, life course, and methods*, ed. H. Kaplan, 247–292. Orlando, FL: Academic Press.

Elliott, D. S. 1995. *Lies, damn lies, and arrest statistics: The Sutherland award presentation.* Boulder, CO: Center for the Study and Prevention of Violence.

Elliott, D. S., S. S. Ageton, D. Huizinga, B. A. Knowles, and R. J. Canter. 1983. *The prevalence and incidence of delinquent behavior: 1976–1980.* Boulder, CO: Behavioral Research Institute.

Elliott, D. S., and D. Huizinga. 1989. Improving self-reported measures of delinquency. In *Cross-National Research in Self-Reported Crime and Delinquency*, ed. M. W. Klein, 155–186. Dordrecht: Kluwer.

Elliott, D. S., D. Huizinga, and S. S. Ageton. 1985. *Explaining delinquency and drug use.* Newbury Park, CA: Sage.

Elliott, D. S., D. Huizinga, and S. Menard. 1989. *Multiple problem youth: Delinquency, substance use, and mental health problems.* New York, NY: Springer-Verlag.

Elliott, D. S., S. Menard, B. Rankin, A. Elliott, W. J. Wilson, and D. Huizinga. 2006. *Good kids from bad neighborhoods: Successful development in social context.* Cambridge, UK: Cambridge University Press.

Ellis, L., K. Beaver, and J. Wright. 2009. *Handbook of crime correlates.* San Diego, CA: Academic Press.

Elman, C., and A. M. O'Rand. 2004. The race is to the swift: Socioeconomic origins, adult education, and wage attainment. *American Journal of Sociology* 110:123–160.

Ernst, A. A., S. J. Weiss, C. Del Castillo, J. Aagaard, E. Marvez-Valls, J. D'Angelo, . . . and B. Coffman. 2007. Witnessing intimate partner violence as a child does not increase the likelihood of becoming an adult intimate partner violence victim. *Academic Emergency Medicine* 14:411–418.

Ernst, A. A., S. J. Weiss, J. Hall, R. Clark, B. Coffman, L. Goldstein, K. Hobley, Todd Dettmer, C. Lehrman, M. Merhege, B. Corum, T. Rihani, and M. Valdez. 2009. Adult intimate partner violence perpetrators are significantly more likely to have witnessed intimate partner violence as a child than nonperpetrators. *The American Journal of Emergency Medicine* 27:641–650.

Everson, M. D., J. B. Smith, J. M. Hussey, D. English, A. J. Litrownik, H. Dubowitz, R. Thompson, E. D. Knight, and D. K. Runyan. 2008. Concordance between adolescent reports of childhood abuse and child protective service determinations in an at-risk sample of young adolescents. *Child Maltreatment* 13:14–26.

Fagan, A. 2005. The relationship between adolescent physical abuse and criminal offending: Support for an enduring and generalized cycle of violence. *Journal of Family Violence* 20:279–290.

Fang, X., D. S. Brown, C. S. Florence, and J. A. Mercy. 2012. The economic burden of child maltreatment in the United States and implications for prevention. *Child Abuse and Neglect* 36:156–165.

Fang, X., and P. Corso. 2007. Child maltreatment, youth violence, and intimate partner violence. *American Journal of Preventative Medicine* 33:281–290.

Farrell, A. D., and S. E. Bruce. 1997. Impact of exposure to community violence on violent behavior and emotional distress among urban adolescents. *Journal of Clinical Child Psychology* 26:2–14.

Farrington, D. P. 1973. Self reports of deviant behavior: Predictive and stable? *Journal of Criminal Law, Criminology, and Police Science* 64:99–110.

———. 2012. Predictors of violent young offenders. In *The Oxford handbook of juvenile crime and juvenile justice*, ed. B. C. Feld and D. M. Bishop, 146–171. Oxford, UK: Oxford University Press.

Farrington, D. P., R. Loeber, M. Stouthamer-Loeber, W. B. Van Kammen, and L. Schmidt. 1996. Self-reported delinquency and a combined delinquency seriousness scale based on boys, mothers, and teachers: Concurrent and predictive validity for African-Americans and Caucasians. *Criminology* 34:493–517.

Federal Bureau of Investigation. 2019. *Crime in the United States 2017.* https://ucr.fbi .gov/crime-in-the-u.s/2017/crime-in-the-u.s.-2017/tables/table-31.

Feighner, J. P., E. Robins, S. B. Guze, R. A. Woodruff, G. Winokur, and R. Munoz. 1972. Diagnostic criteria for use in psychiatric research. *Archives of General Psychiatry* 26:57–63.

Felitti, V. J., D. Nordenberg, D. F. Williamson, A. M. Spitz, V. Edwards, M. P. Koss, and J. S. Marks. 1998. Relationship of childhood abuse and household dysfunction to many of the leading causes of death in adults. *American Journal of Preventive Medicine* 14:245–258.

Fendrich, M., and Y. Xu. 1994. The validity of drug use reports from juvenile arrestees. *International Journal of the Addictions* 29:971–985.

Fergusson, D. M., J. M. Boden, and L. J. Horwood. 2006. Examining the intergenerational transmission of violence in a New Zealand birth cohort. *Child Abuse and Neglect* 30:89–108.

Fergusson, D. M., and M. T. Lynskey. 1997. Physical punishment/maltreatment during childhood and adjustment in young adulthood. *Child Abuse and Neglect* 21:617–630.

Field, C. A., and R. Caetano. 2005. Intimate partner violence in the U.S. general population: Progress and future directions. *Journal of Interpersonal Violence* 20:463–469.

Finkelhor, D., R. K. Ormrod, and C. W. Turner. 2007. Poly-victimization: A neglected component in child victimization. *Child Abuse and Neglect* 31:7–26.

Finkelhor, D., R. Ormrod, H. Turner, and S. L. Hamby. 2005. The victimization of children and youth: A comprehensive, national survey. *Child Maltreatment* 10:5–25.

Finkelhor, D., H. Turner, S. Hamby, and R. Ormrod. 2011. Polyvictimization: Children's exposure to multiple types of violence, crime, and abuse. *Juvenile Justice Bulletin*. Washington, DC: U.S. Department of Justice.

Finkelhor, D., H. Turner, R. Ormrod, and S. L. Hamby. 2009. Violence, abuse, and crime exposure in a national sample of children and youth. *Pediatrics* 124:1411–1423.

Finkelhor, D., H. Turner, A. Shattuck, S. Hamby, and K. Kracke. 2015. Children's exposure to crime, violence, and abuse: An update. Washington, DC: Office of Juvenile Justice and Delinquency Prevention and Centers for Disease Control.

Finkelhor, D., J. Vanderminden, H. Turner, A. Shattuck, and S. Hamby. 2014. Youth exposure to violence prevention programs in a national sample. *Child Abuse and Neglect* 38:677–686.

Fitzpatrick, K. M. 1993. Exposure to violence and presence of depression among low-income, African-American youth. *Journal of Consulting and Clinical Psychology* 61:528–531.

Fitzpatrick, K. M., and J. P. Boldizar. 1993. The prevalence and consequences of exposure to violence among African American youth. *Journal of the American Academy of Child and Adolescent Psychiatry* 32:424–430.

Foster, J. D., G. P. Kupermine, and A. W. Price. 2004. Gender differences in post-traumatic stress and related symptoms among inner-city minority youth exposed to community violence. *Journal of Youth and Adolescence* 33:59–69.

Fowler, P. J., C. J. Tompsett, J. M. Braciszewski, A. J. Jacques-Tiuva, and B. B. Baltes. 2009. Community violence: A meta-analysis on the effect of exposure and mental health outcomes of children and adolescents. *Development and Psychology* 21:227–259.

Franzese, R. J., H. C. Covey, A. S. Tucker, L. McCoy, and S. Menard. 2014. Adolescent exposure to violence and adult physical and mental health problems. *Child Abuse and Neglect* 38:1955–1965.

Franzese, R. J., S. Menard, A. J. Weiss, and H. C. Covey. 2017. Adolescent exposure to violence and adult violent victimization and offending. *Criminal Justice Review* 42:42–57.

Fuller-Thomson, E., J. L. Roane, and S. Brennenstuhl. 2016. Three types of adverse childhood experiences, and alcohol and drug dependence among adults: An investigation using population-based data. *Substance Use and Misuse* 51:1451–1461.

Garbarino, J., and A. Crouter. 1978. Defining the community context for parent-child relations: The correlates of child maltreatment. *Child Development* 49:604–616.

Gewirtz, A. H., and J. L. Edleson. 2007. Young children's exposure to intimate part-ner violence: Towards a development risk and resilience framework for research and intervention. *Journal of Family Violence* 22:151–163.

Gittleman, M., and E. N. Wolff. 2004. Racial differences in patterns of wealth accumulation. *Journal of Human Resources* 39:193–227.

Godbout, N., M-P. Vaillancourt-Mortel, N. Bigras, J. Briere, M. Hébert, M. Runtz, and S. Sabourin. 2019. Intimate partner violence in male survivors of child maltreatment: A meta-analysis. *Trauma, Violence, and Abuse* 20:99–113.

Gold, M. 1966. Undetected delinquent behavior. *Journal of Research in Crime and Delinquency* 3:27–46.

———. 1970. *Delinquent behavior in an American city.* Belmont, CA: Brooks/Cole.

Gonzalez, A., and H. L. MacMillan. 2008. Preventing child maltreatment: An evidence-based update. *Symposium: Violence Against Children and Women* 54:280–286.

Goodman, L. A., K. M. Thompson, K. Weinfurt, S. Corl, P. Acker, K. T. Mueser, and S. D. Rosenberg. 1999. Reliability of reports of violent victimization and post-traumatic stress disorder among men and women with serious mental illness. *Journal of Traumatic Stress* 12:587–599.

Gorman-Smith, D., and P. Tolan. 1998. The role of exposure to community violence and developmental problems among inner-city youth. *Development and Psychopathology* 10:101–116.

Graber, J. A., J. Brooks-Gunn, and A. C. Petersen. 1996. Adolescent transitions in context. In *Transitions through adolescence: Interpersonal domains and context,* ed. J. A. Graber, J. Brooks-Gunn, and A. C. Petersen, 369–383. Mahwah, NJ: Lawrence Erlbaum.

Greenwood, P., and S. Turner. 2012. Probation and other noninstitutional treatment: The evidence is in. In *The Oxford handbook of juvenile crime and juvenile justice,* ed. B. C. Feld and D. M. Bishop, 723–747. New York, NY: Oxford University Press.

Groves, R. M., F. Fowler, Jr., M. P. Couper, J. M. Lepkowski, E. Singer, and R. Tourangeau. 2004. *Survey methodology.* New York, NY: Wiley.

Guterman, N. B., and M. Cameron. 1997. Assessing the impact of community violence on children and youths. *Social Work* 42:495–505.

Guterman, N. B., H. C. Hahm, and M. Cameron. 2002. Adolescent victimization and subsequent use of mental health counseling services. *Journal of Adolescent Health* 30:336–345.

Hamby, S., D. Finkelhor, H. Turner, and R. Ormrod. 2011. Children's exposure to intimate partner violence and other family violence. *Juvenile Justice Bulletin.* Washington, DC: National Survey of Children's Exposure to Violence, Office of Juvenile Justice and Delinquency Prevention and Centers for Disease Control.

Hardt, J., and M. Rutter. 2004. Validity of adult retrospective reports of adverse childhood experiences: Review of the evidence. *Journal of Child Psychology and Psychiatry* 45:260–273.

Hardt, R. H., and S. Peterson-Hardt. 1977. On determining the quality of the delinquency self-report method. *Journal of Research in Crime and Delinquency* 14:247–261.

Harrison, L. 1995. The validity of self-reported data on drug use. *Journal of Drug Issues* 35:91–111.

Harrison, L., S. S. Martin, T. Enev, and D. Harrington. 2007. *Comparing drug testing and self-report of drug use among youths and young adults in the general population*. Rockville, MD: Substance Abuse and Mental Health Services Administration, Office of Applied Studies.

Harrison, P. A., J. A. Fulkerson, and T. J. Beebe. 1997. Multiple substance use among adolescent physical and sexual abuse victims. *Child Abuse and Neglect* 21:529–539.

Hay, C., and M. M. Evans. 2006. Violent victimization and involvement in delinquency: Examining predictions from General Strain Theory. *Journal of Criminal Justice* 34:261–274.

Heinze, J. E., S. A. Stoddard, S. M. Aiyer, A. B. Eisman, and M. A. Zimmerman. 2017. Exposure to violence during adolescence as a predictor of perceived stress trajectories in emerging adulthood. *Journal of Applied Developmental Psychology* 49:31–38.

Helfer, R. E., and C. H. Kempe, eds. 1968. *The battered child*. Chicago: University of Chicago Press.

Henggler, S. W. 2015. Effective family-based treatments for adolescents with serious antisocial behavior. In *The development of criminal and antisocial behavior: Theory, research, and practical applications*, ed. J. Morizot and I. Kazemian, 461–475. New York, NY: Springer.

Herrenkohl, T. I., B. Huang, E. A. Tajima, and S. D. Whitney. 2003. Examining the link between child abuse and youth violence. *Journal of Interpersonal Violence* 18:1189–1208.

Herrenkohl, T. I., C. Sousa, E. A. Tajima, R. C., Herrenkohl, and C. A. Moylan. 2008. Intersection of child abuse and children's exposure to domestic violence. *Trauma, Violence, and Abuse* 9:84–89.

Herrera, V. M., and L. A. McCloskey. 2001. Gender differences in the risk for delinquency among youth exposed to family violence. *Child Abuse and Neglect* 25:1037–1051.

Hesselbrock, V., J. Stabenau, M. Hesselbrock, P. Mirkin, and R. Mey. 1982. A comparison of two interview schedules. *Archives of General Psychiatry* 29:674–677.

Heyman, R. E., and A. M. S. Slep. 2002. Do child abuse and interparental violence lead to adulthood family violence? *Journal of Marriage and the Family* 64:864–870.

Hindelang, M. J., T. Hirschi, and J. G. Weis. 1981. *Measuring delinquency*. Beverly Hills, CA: Sage.

Hirschi, T. 1969. *Causes of Delinquency*. Berkeley, CA: University of California Press.

Huizinga, D., and D. S. Elliott. 1986. Reassessing the reliability and validity of self-report delinquency measures. *Journal of Quantitative Criminology* 2:293–327.

Ireland, T. O., C. A. Smith, and T. P. Thornberry. 2002. Developmental issues in the impact of child maltreatment on later delinquency and drug use. *Criminology* 40:359–399.

Irwin, K., and M. Chesney-Lind. 2008. Girls violence: Beyond dangerous masculinity. *Sociology Compass* 2/3:837–855.

Iverson, K. M., S. Jimenez, K. M. Harrington, and P. A. Resick. 2011. The contribution of childhood family violence on later intimate partner violence among robbery victims. *Violence and Victims* 26:73–87.

Jackson, P. G. 1990. Sources of data. In *Measurement issues in criminology*, ed. K. L. Kempf, 21–50. New York, NY: Springer-Verlag.

Jaffe, P., D. A. Wilson, and L. Zak. 1986. Similarities in behavioral and social maladjustment among child victims and witnesses to family violence. *American Journal of Orthopsychiatry* 56:142–146.

Jang, S. J. 1999. Different definitions, different modeling decisions, and different interpretations: A rejoinder to Lauritsen. *Criminology* 37:695–703.

Jessor, R., and S. L. Jessor. 1977. *Problem behavior and psychsocial development: A longitudinal study of youth.* New York, NY: Academic Press.

Johnson, R. M., J. B. Kotch, D. J. Catellier, J. R. Winson, V. Dufort, W. Hunter, and L. Amaya-Jackson. 2002. Adverse behavioral and emotional outcomes from child abuse and witnessed violence. *Child Maltreatment* 7:179–186.

Jones-Webb, R, and M. Wall. 2008. Neighborhood racial/ethnic concentration, social disadvantage, and homicide risk: An ecological analysis of 10 U.S. cities. *Journal of Urban Health* 85:662–676.

Kaminar, D., A. Hardy, K. Heath, J. Mosdell, and U. Bawa. 2013. Gender patterns in the contribution of different types of violence to posttraumatic stress symptoms among South African urban youth. *Child Abuse and Neglect* 37:320–330.

Karl, A., M. Schaefer, L. S. Malta, D. Dorfel, N. Rohleder, and A. Werner. 2006. A meta-analysis of structural brain abnormalities in PTSD. *Neuroscience and Biobehavioral Reviews* 30:1004–1031.

Kempe, C. H., F. N. Silverman, B. F. Steele, W. Droegemueller, and H. K. Silver. 1962. The battered-child syndrome. *Journal of the American Medical Association* 181:17–24.

Kendall-Tackett, K. 2013. *Treating the lifetime health effects of childhood victimization*, 2nd edition. Kingston, NJ: Civic Research Institute.

Kerig, P. K., and S. P. Becker. 2015. Early abuse and neglect as risk factors for the development of criminal and antisocial behavior. In *The development of criminal and antisocial behavior*, ed. J. Morizot and L. Kazemian, 181–199. New York, NY: Springer.

Kessler, R. C., S. Avenevoli, E. J. Costello, J. G. Green, M. J. Gruber, S. Heeringa, K. R. Merikangas, B. E. Pennell, N. A. Sampson, and A. M. Zaslavsky. 2009. Design and field procedures in the U.S. National Comorbidity Survey Replication Adolescent Supplement (NCS-A). *International Journal of Methods in Psychiatric Research* 18:69–83.

Kessler, R. C., P. Berglund, O. Demler, R. Jin, K. R. Merikangas, and E. E. Walters. 2005. Lifetime prevalence and age-of-onset distributions of DSM-IV disorders in the National Comorbidity Survey Replication. *Archives of General Psychiatry* 62:593–602.

Kilpatrick, D. G., K. J. Ruggiero, R. Acierno, B. E. Saunders, H. S. Resnick, and C. L. Best. 2003. Violence and risk of PTSD, major depression, substance abuse/dependence, and comorbidity: Results from the National Survey of Adolescents. *Journal of Consulting and Clinical Psychology* 71:692–700.

Kim, B. K. E., A. B. Gilman, and J. D. Hawkins. 2015. School- and community-based preventive interventions during adolescence: Preventing delinquency through science-guided collective action. In *The development of criminal and antisocial behavior: Theory, research, and practical applications*, ed. J. Morizot and L. Kazemian, 447–460. New York, NY: Springer.

Kitzman, H. J., D. L. Olds, R. E. Cole, C. A. Hanks, E. A. Anson, K. J. Arcoleo, D. W. Luckey, M. D. Knudtson, C. R. Henderson, Jr., and J. R. Holmberg. 2010. Enduring effects of prenatal and infancy home visiting by nurses on children: Follow-up of a randomized trial among children at age 12 years. *Archives of Pediatrics and Adolescent Medicine* 164:412–418.

Kitzmann, K. M., N. K. Gaylord, A. R. Holt, and E. D. Kenny. 2003. Child witnesses to domestic violence: A meta-analytic review. *Journal of Counseling and Clinical Psychology* 71:339–352.

Knight, G., M. Little, S. Losoya, and E. Mulvey. 2004. The self-report of offending among serious juvenile offenders: Cross-gender, cross-ethnic/race measurement equivalence. *Youth Violence and Juvenile Justice* 2:273–295.

Kolbo, J. R., E. H. Blakely, and D. Engleman. 1996. Children who witness domestic violence: A review of empirical literature. *Journal of Interpersonal Violence* 11:281–293.

Kruttschnitt, C., J. D. McLeod, and M. Dornfield. 1994. The economic environment of child abuse. *Social Problems* 41:299–315.

Kuh, D., and M. Maclean. 1990. Women's childhood experience of parental separation and their subsequent health and socioeconomic status in adulthood. *Journal of Biosocial Science* 22:131–135.

Lackey, C. 2003. Violent family heritage, the transition to adulthood, and later partner violence. *Journal of Family Issues* 24:74–98.

Lansford, J. E., S. Miller-Johnson, L. J. Berlin, K. A. Dodge, J. E. Bates, and G. S. Pettit. 2007. Early physical abuse and later violent delinquency: A prospective longitudinal study. *Child Maltreatment* 12:233–245.

Ledgerwood, D. M., B. A. Goldberger, N. K. Risk, C. E. Lewis, and R. K. Price. 2008. Comparison between self-report and hair analysis of illicit drug use in a community sample of middle-age men. *Addictive Behaviors* 33:1131–1139.

Leiber, M. J., and J. H. Peck. 2015. Race, ethnicity, immigration, and crime. In *The development of criminal and antisocial behavior: Theory, research and practical applications*, ed. J. Morizot and L. Kazemian, 331–347. New York, NY: Springer.

Lemmon, J. H. 2006. The effects of maltreatment recurrence and child welfare services on dimensions of delinquency. *Criminal Justice Review* 31:5–32.

Lemmon, J. H., and P. J. Verrecchia. 2009. A world of risk: Victimized children in the juvenile justice system-an ecological explanation, a holistic solution. In *Controversies in juvenile justice and delinquency*, 2nd edition, ed. P. J. Benekos and A. V. Merlo, 131–171. Newark, NJ: LexisNexis.

Liebetrau, A. M. 1983. *Measures of association*. Thousand Oaks, CA: Sage.

Lindell, K. U., C. K. Sorenson, and S. V. Mangold. 2020. The Family First Prevention Services Act: A new era of child welfare reform. *Public Health Reports* 135:282–286.

Lipsey, M. W. 2009. The primary factors that characterize effective interventions with juvenile offenders: A meta-analytic review. *Victims and Offenders* 4:124–147.

Lipsey, M. W., and D. B. Wilson. 1993. The efficacy of psychological, educational, and behavioral treatment: Confirmation from meta-analysis. *American
Psychologist* 48:1181–1209.

Liu, Y., J. B. Croft, D. P. Chapman, G. S. Perry, K. J. Greenlund, G. Zhao, and V.
J. Edwards. 2013. Relationship between adverse childhood experiences and unem-
ployment among adults from five US states. *Social Psychiatry and Psychiatric
Epidemiology* 48:357–369.

Luster, T., S. A. Small, and R. Lower. 2002. The correlates of abuse and witnessing
abuse among adolescents. *Journal of Interpersonal Violence* 17:1323–1340.

Lynch, M. 2003. Consequences of children's exposure to community violence.
Clinical Child and Family Psychology Review 6:265–274.

Macmillan, R. 2000. Adolescent victimization and income deficits in adulthood: Rethinking the costs of criminal violence from a life-course perspective.
Criminology 38:553–587.

Macmillan, R., and J. Hagan. 2004. Violence in the transition to adulthood:
Adolescent victimization, education, and socioeconomic attainment in later life.
Journal of Research on Adolescence 14:127–158.

Malik, S., S. B. Sorenson, and C. S. Aneshensel. 1997. Community and dating violence among adolescents: Perpetration and victimization. *Journal of Adolescent
Health* 21:291–302.

Margolin, G., and E. B. Gordis. 2000. The effects of family and community violence
on children. *Annual Review of Psychology* 51:445–479.

Margolin G., K. A. Vickerman, P. H. Oliver, and E. B. Gordis. 2010. Violence
exposure in multiple interpersonal domains: Cumulative and differential effects.
Journal of Adolescent Health 47:198–205.

Martinez, P., and J. E. Richters. 1993. The NIMH community violence project:
Children as victims of and witnesses to violence. *Psychiatry* 56:7–21.

Maxfield, M. G., B. L. Weiler, and C. S. Widom. 2000. Comparing self-reports and
official records of arrests. *Journal of Quantitative Criminology* 16:87–110.

Menard, S. 1995. A developmental test of Mertonian anomie theory. *Journal of
Research in Crime and Delinquency* 32:136–174.

———. 1997. A developmental test of Cloward's differential opportunity theory.
In *The Future of Anomie Theory*, ed. N. Passas and R. Agnew, 142–186. Boston:
Northeastern University Press.

———. 2000. The "normality" of repeat victimization from adolescence through
early adulthood. *Justice Quarterly* 17:543–574.

———. 2002. Short- and long-term consequences of adolescent victimization. *Youth
Violence Research Bulletin.* Washington, DC: Office of Juvenile Justice and
Delinquency Prevention.

———. 2010. *Logistic regression: From introductory to advanced concepts and
applications.* Los Angeles, CA: Sage.

———. 2011. Standards for standardized logistic regression coefficients. *Social
Forces* 89:1409–1428.

———. 2012. Age, criminal victimization, and offending: Changing relationships
from adolescence to middle adulthood. *Victims and Offenders* 7:227–254.

Menard, S., L. C. Bowman-Bowen, and Y. Lu. 2016. Self-reported crime and delinquency. In *The handbook of measurement issues in criminology and criminal justice*, ed. B. M. Huebner and T. S. Bynum, 475–495. Hoboken, NJ: Wiley-Blackwell.

Menard, S., H. C. Covey, and R. J. Franzese. 2015. Adolescent exposure to violence and adult illicit drug use. *Child Abuse and Neglect* 42:30–39.

Menard, S., and D. S. Elliott. 1990. Longitudinal and cross-sectional data collection and analysis in the study of crime and delinquency. *Justice Quarterly* 7:11–55.

———. 1993. Data set comparability and short-term trends in crime and delinquency. *Journal of Criminal Justice* 21:433–445.

Menard, S., and S. Mihalic. 2001. The tripartite conceptual framework in adolescence and adulthood: Evidence from a national sample. *Journal of Drug Issues* 31:905–940.

Menard, S., S. Mihalic, and D. Huizinga. 2001. Drugs and crime revisited. *Justice Quarterly* 18:269–299.

Menard, S., A. J. Weiss, R. J. Franzese, and H. C. Covey. 2014. Types of adolescent exposure to violence as predictors of adult intimate partner violence. *Child Abuse and Neglect* 38:627–639.

Merikangas, K. R., J. He, M. Burstein, S. A. Swanson, S. Avenevoli, L. Cui, C. Benjet, K. Georgiades, and J. Swendsen. 2010. Lifetime prevalence of mental disorders in U.S. Adolescents: Results from the National Comorbidity Study-Adolescent Supplement (NCS-A). *Journal of the American Academy of Child and Adolescent Psychiatry* 49:980–909.

Merikangas, K. R., E. F. Nakamura, and R. C. Kessler. 2009. Epidemiology of mental disorders in children and adolescents. *Dialogues in Clinical Neuroscience* 11:7–20.

Merrick, M. T., K. A. Ports, D. C. Ford, T. O. Afifi, E. T. Gershoff, and A. Grogan-Kaylor. 2017. Unpacking the impact of adverse childhood experiences on adult mental health. *Child Abuse and Neglect* 69:10–19.

Merton, R. K. 1938. Social structure and anomie. *American Sociological Review* 3:72–682.

———. 1968. *Social theory and social structure*, enlarged edition. New York, NY: Free Press.

Metzler, M., M. T. Merrick, J. Kelevens, K. A. Ports, and D. C. Ford. 2017. Adverse childhood experiences and life opportunities: Shifting the narrative. *Children and Youth Services Review* 72:141–149.

Mieczkowski, T. 1990. The accuracy of self-reported drug use: An evaluation and analysis of new data. In *Drugs, Crime, and the Criminal Justice System*, ed. R. Weisheit, 275–302. Cincinnati: Anderson.

Mieczkowski, T., H. J. Landress, R. Newel, and S. D. Coletti, S. D. 1993. Testing hair for illicit drug use. *National Institute of Justice Research in Brief*. Washington, DC: U.S. Department of Justice.

Mihalic, S. W., and D. S. Elliott. 1997a. A social learning theory model of marital violence. *Journal of Family Violence* 12:21–48.

———. 1997b. If violence is domestic, does it really count? *Journal of Family Violence* 12:293–311.

Mihalic, S. W., A. Fagan, K. Irwin, D. Ballard, and D. Elliott. 2004. *Blueprints for violence prevention*. Washington, DC: Office of Juvenile Justice and Delinquency Prevention.

Mikton, C., and A. Butchard. 2009. Child maltreatment prevention: A systematic review of reviews. *Bulletin of the World Health Organization* 87:353–361.

Miller, J., and C. W. Mullins. 2006. The status of feminist theories in criminology. In *Taking stock: The status of criminological theory*, ed. F. T. Cullen, J. P. Wright, and K. R. Blevins, 217–249. New Brunswick, NJ: Transaction Publishers.

Mills, R., J. Scott, R. Alati, M. O'Callaghan, J. M. Najman, and L. Strathearn. 2013. Child maltreatment and adolescent mental health problems in a large birth cohort. *Child Abuse and Neglect* 37:292–302.

Moffitt, T. E., and P. A. Silva. 1988. Self-reported delinquency: Results from an instrument for New Zealand. *Australian and New Zealand Journal of Criminology* 21:227–240.

Mohammed, E. T., E. R. Shapiro, J. D. Wainwright, and A. S. Carter. 2015. Impacts of family and community violence exposure on child coping and mental health. *Journal of Abnormal Child Psychology* 43:203–215.

Monnat, S. M., and R. F. Chandler. 2015. Long-term physical health consequences of adverse childhood experiences. *The Sociological Quarterly* 56:723–752.

Morgan, R. E., and J. L. Truman. 2018. *Criminal victimization, 2017*. Washington, DC: U.S. Department of Justice.

Morris, R. R. 1965. Attitudes toward delinquency by delinquents, non-delinquents, and their friends. *British Journal of Criminology* 5:249–265.

Morse, B. J. 1995. Beyond the conflict tactics scale: Assessing gender differences in partner violence. *Violence and Victims* 10:257–272.

Mueser, K. T., L. B. Goodman, and S. L. Trumbetta. 1998. Trauma and posttraumatic stress disorder in severe mental illness. *Journal of Consulting and Clinical Psychology* 66:493–499.

Olds, D. L., J. Eckenrode, C. R. Henderson, H. Kitzman, J. Powers, R. Cole, K. Sidora, P. Morris, L. M. Pettitt, and D. W. Luckey. 1997. Long-term effects of home visitation on maternal life course and child abuse and neglect: Fifteen-year follow-up of a randomized trial. *Journal of the American Medical Association* 278:637–643.

Olds, D. L., C. R. Henderson, L. Chamberlain, and R. Tatelbaum. 1986. Preventing child abuse and neglect: A randomized trial of nurse home visitation. *Pediatrics* 78:65–78.

Overstreet, S. 2000. Exposure to community violence: Defining the problem and understanding the consequences. *Journal of Child and Family Studies* 9:7–25.

Pardini, D. A., R. Waller, and S. Hawes. 2015. Familial influences on the development of serious conduct problems and delinquency. In *The development of criminal and antisocial behavior: Theory, research and practical applications*, ed. J. Morizot and L. Kazemian, 201–220. New York, NY: Springer.

Paternoster, R., R. Brame, P. Mazerolle, and A. Piquero, A. 1998. Using the correct statistical test for the equality of regression coefficients. *Criminology* 36:859–866.

Patterson, G. R. 2005. The next generation of PMTO models. *The Behavior Therapist* 28:25–32.

Patterson, G. R, P. Chamberlain, and J. B. Reid. 1982. A comparative evaluation of parent training procedures. *Behavior Therapy* 13:638–651.

Perez, C. M., and C. S. Widom. 1994. Childhood victimization and long-term intellectual and academic outcomes. *Child Abuse and Neglect* 18:617–633.

Perry, B. D. 2001. The neurodevelopmental impact of violence in childhood. In *Textbook of child and adolescent forensic psychiatry*, ed. D. Schetky and E. P. Benedict, 221–238. Washington, DC: American Psychiatric Press.

Pinchevsky, G. M., E. M. Wright, and A. A. Fagan. 2013. Gender differences in the effects of exposure to violence on adolescent substance use. *Violence and Victims* 28:122–144.

Piquero, A. R., D. P. Farrington, and A. Blumstein. 2007. *Key issues in criminal career research: New analyses of the Cambridge study in delinquent development.* Cambridge, UK: Cambridge University Press.

Pollock, W., and S. Menard. 2014. "It was a bum rap": Self-reports of being erroneously arrested in a national sample. *Criminal Justice Review* 39:325–338.

Pollock, W., S. Menard, D. S. Elliott, and D. H. Huizinga. 2015. It's official: Predictors of self-reported vs. officially recorded arrests. *Journal of Criminal Justice* 43:69–79.

Pollock, W., S. Menard, and M. C. Hill. 2016. Revisiting "Measuring the Problem": Separate examination of police contact in serious and nonserious offenders. *Criminal Justice Review* 41:294–317.

Pollock, W., W. Oliver, and S. Menard. 2012. Measuring the problem: A national examination of disproportionate police contact in the United States. *Criminal Justice Review* 37:153–173.

Raghavan, C., A. Mennerich, E. Sexton, and S. James. 2006. Community violence and its direct, indirect, and mediating effects on intimate partner violence. *Violence Against Women* 12:1132–1149.

Rebellon, C. J., and K. Van Gundy. 2005. Can control theory explain the link between parental physical abuse and delinquency? A longitudinal analysis. *Journal of Research in Crime and Delinquency* 42:247–274.

Rennison, C. M., W. S. DeKeseredy, and M. Dragiewicz. 2013. Intimate relationship status variations in violence against women: Urban, suburban, and rural differences. *Violence Against Women* 19:1312–1330.

Reynolds, A. J., S.-R. Ou, and J. W. Topitzes. 2004. Paths of effects of early childhood intervention on educational attainment and delinquency: A confirmatory analysis of the Chicago child-parent centers. *Child Development* 75:1299–1328.

Robins, L. N., J. E. Helzer, J. Croughan, J. B. W. Williams, and R. L. Spitzer. 1981. The NIMH Diagnostic Interview Schedule: Its history, characteristics, and validity. *Archives of General Psychiatry* 38:381–389.

Robins, L. N., J. E. Helzer, K. Ratcliff, and W. Seyfried. 1982. Validity of the Diagnostic Interview Schedule, Version II, DSM-III diagnoses. *Psychological Medicine* 12:855–870.

Rosenblum, G. D., and M. Lewis. 2003. Emotional development in adolescence. In *Blackwell handbook of adolescence*, ed. G. R. Adams and M. D. Berzonsky, 269–289. Oxford, UK: Blackwell Publishing.

Ruback, R. B., and M. P. Thompson. 2001. *Social and psychological consequences of violent victimization*. Thousand Oaks, CA: Sage.

Ruel, E., and R. M. Hauser. 2013. Explaining the gender wealth gap. *Demography* 50:1155–1176.

Rutter, M., B. Maughan, A. Pickles, and E. Simonoff. 1998. Retrospective recall recalled. In *Methods and models for studying the individual*, ed. R. B. Cairns, L. R. Bergman, and J. Kagan, 219–242. Thousand Oaks, CA: Sage.

Ryan, J. P., A. B. Williams, and M. E. Courtney. 2013. Adolescent neglect, juvenile delinquency, and the risk of recidivism. *Journal of Youth and Adolescence* 42:454–465.

Scarpa, A. 2001. Community violence exposure in a young adult sample: Lifetime prevalence and socioemotional effects. *Journal of Interpersonal Violence* 16:36–53.

Schindler, H. S., and C. F. D. Black. 2015. Early prevention of criminal and antisocial behavior: A review of interventions in infancy and childhood. In *The development of criminal and antisocial behavior: Theory, research, and practical applications*, ed. J. Morizot and L. Kazemian, 433–446. New York, NY: Springer.

Schneider, A. L. 1981. Differences between survey and police information about crime. In *The National Crime Survey: Working papers, Volume I: Current and historical perspectives*, ed. R. G. Lehnen and W. G. Skogan, 29–46. Washington, DC: U.S. Government Printing Office.

Schurer, S., and K. Trajkovski. 2018. *Understanding the mechanisms through which adverse childhood experiences affect lifetime economic outcomes*. Bonn, Germany: IZA Institute of Labor Economics.

Shaffer, A., L. Huston, and B. Egeland. 2008. Identification of child maltreatment using prospective and self-reported methodologies: A comparison of maltreatment incidence and relation to later psychopathology. *Child Abuse and Neglect* 32:682–692.

Shakoor, B., and D. Chalmers. 1991. Co-victimization of African American children who witness violence and the theoretical implications of its effect on their cognitive, emotional, and behavioral development. *Journal of the National Medical Association* 83:233–238.

Shapiro, S., E. A. Skinner, L. G. Kessler, M. Von Korff, P. S. German, G. L. Tischler, P. J., Leaf, L. Benham, I. Cottler, and D. A. Regier. 1984. Utilization of health and mental health services. *Archives of General Psychiatry* 41:971–982.

Sickmund, M., and C. Puzzanchera. 2014. *Juvenile offenders and victims: 2014 national report*. Pittsburg, PA: National Center for Juvenile Justice.

Siegel, J. A., and L. M. Williams. 2003. The relationship between child sexual abuse and female delinquency and crime: A prospective study. *Journal of Research in Crime and Delinquency* 40:71–94.

Silva, M., A. Loureiro, and G. Cardoso. 2016. Social determinants of mental health: A review of the evidence. *The European Journal of Psychiatry* 30:1–15. http://scielo.isciii.es/scielo.php?pid=S0213-61632016000400004&script=sci_arttext&tlng=en, ISSN 0123-6163.

Simmons, S. B., K. E. Knight, and S. Menard. 2015. Consequences of intimate partner violence on substance use and depression for women and men. *Journal of Family Violence* 30:351–361.

———. 2018. Long-term consequences of intimate partner abuse on physical health, emotional well-being, and problem behaviors. *Journal of Interpersonal Violence* 33:539–570.

Simons, R. L., C. Johnson, R. D. Conger, and Elder, G. H., Jr. 1998. A test of latent trait versus life course perspectives on the stability of adolescent antisocial behavior. *Criminology* 36:217–244.

Simons, R. L., L. G. Simons, and D. Hancock. 2012. Linking family processes and adolescent delinquency: Issues, theories, and research findings. In *The Oxford handbook of juvenile crime and juvenile justice*, ed. B. C. Feld and D. M. Bishop, 175–202. Oxford, UK: Oxford University Press.

Singer, M. I., T. M. Anglin, L. Y. Song, and T. Lunghofer. 1995. Adolescents' exposure to violence and associated symptoms of psychological trauma. *Journal of the American Medical Association* 273:477–482.

Skogan, W. G. 1976. The victims of crime. Some national survey results. In *Criminal behavior and social systems*, 2nd edition, ed. A. L. Guenther, 131–148. Chicago: Rand McNally.

———. 1981. *Issues in the measurement of victimization*. Washington, DC: U. S. Government Printing Office.

Snyder, H. N., and M. Sickmund. 2006. *Juvenile offenders and victims: 2006 National Report*. Washington, DC: U.S. Department of Justice, Office of Justice Programs, Office of Juvenile Justice and Delinquency Prevention.

Solon, G. 1992. Intergenerational income mobility in the United States. *American Economic Review* 82:393–408.

Sousa, C., T. I. Herrenkohl, C. A. Moylan, E. A. Tajima, J. B. Klika, R. C., Herrenkohl, and M. J. Russo. 2011. Longitudinal study of the effects of child abuse and children's exposure to domestic violence, parent child attachments, and anti-social behavior in adolescence. *Journal of Interpersonal Violence* 26:111–136.

Spitzer, R. L., J. Endicott, and E. Robins. 1978. Research diagnostic criteria. *Archives of General Psychiatry* 35:773–782.

Steffensmeier, D., H. Zhong, J. Ackerman, J. Schwartz, and S. Agha. 2006. Gender gap for violent crimes, 1980 to 2003. *Feminist Criminology* 1:72–98.

Stevens, N. R., J. Gerhart, R. E. Goldsmith, N. M. Heath, S. A. Chesney, and S. E. Hobfoll. 2013. Emotion regulation difficulties, low social support, and interpersonal violence mediate the link between childhood abuse and posttraumatic stress symptoms. *Behavior Therapy* 44:152–161.

Stewart, A., M. Livingston, and S. Dennison. 2008. Transitions and turning points: Examining the links between child maltreatment and juvenile offending. *Child Abuse and Neglect* 32:51–66.

Stockman, J. K., H. Hayashi, and J. C. Campbell. 2015. Intimate partner violence and its health impact on ethnic minority women. *Journal of Women's Health* 24:62–79.

Straus, M. A., and R. J. Gelles. 1990. *Physical violence in American families*. New Brunswick, NJ: Transaction Publishers.

Straus, M. A., R. J. Gelles, and S. K. Steinmetz. 1980. *Behind closed doors: Violence in the American family*. Piscataway, NJ: Transaction Publishers.

Straus, M. A., S. L. Hamby, S. Boney-McCoy, and D. B. Sugarman. 1996. The revised conflict tactics scales (CTS2): Development and preliminary psychometric data. *Journal of Family Issues* 17:283–316.

Straus, M. A., and E. L. Mickey. 2012. Reliability, validity, and prevalence of partner violence measured by the conflict tactics scales in male-dominant nations. *Aggression and Violent Behavior* 17:463–474.

Swahn, M. H., D. J. Whitaker, C. B. Pippen, R. T. Leeb, L. A. Teplin, K. M. Abram, and G. M. McClelland. 2006. Concordance between self-reported maltreatment and court records of abuse or neglect among high-risk youths. *American Journal of Public Health* 96:1849–1853.

Tajima, E. A. 2004. Correlates of the co-occurrence of wife abuse and child abuse among a representative sample. *Journal of Family Violence* 19:399–410.

Tapia, M. 2010. Untangling race and class effects on juvenile arrests. *Journal of Criminal Justice* 38:255–265.

Teicher, M. H., S. L. Andersen, A. Polcari, C. M. Anderson, C. P. Navalta, and D. M. Kim. 2003. The neurobiological consequences of early stress and childhood maltreatment. *Neuroscience and Biobehavioral Reviews* 27:33–44.

Teicher, M. H. and J. A. Samson. 2016. Annual research review: Enduring neurobiological effects of childhood abuse and neglect. *Journal of Child Psychology and Psychiatry* 57:241–266.

Thornberry, T. P., T. O. Ireland, and C. A. Smith. 2001. The importance of timing: The varying impact of childhood and adolescent maltreatment on multiple problem outcomes. *Development and Psychopathology* 13:957–979.

Thornberry, T. P., and M. Krohn. 2003. Comparison of self-report and official data for measuring crime. In *Measurement problems in criminal justice research: Workshop summary*, ed. J. V. Pepper and C. V. Petrie, 43–94. Washington, DC: National Academies Press.

Title IV-E Prevention Services, Clearing House. 2019a. Functional Family Therapy. https://preventionservices.abtsites.com/programs/108/show

Title IV-E Prevention Services, Clearing House. 2019b. Multisystemic Therapy—MST. https://preventionservices.abtsites.com/programs/107/show

Title IV-E Prevention Services, Clearing House. 2019c. Nurse Family Partnership. https://preventionservices.abtsites.com/programs/110/show

Title IV-E Prevention Services, Clearing House. 2019d. Trauma-focused Cognitive Behavioral Therapy. https://preventionservices.abtsites.com/programs/106/show

Tjaden, P., and N. Thoennes. 2000. Prevalence and consequences of male-to-female and female-to-male intimate partner violence as measured by the National Violence Against Women Survey. *Violence Against Women* 6:142–161.

Topitzes, J., D. J. Pate, N. D. Berman, and C. Medina-Kirchner. 2016. Adverse childhood experiences, health, and employment: A study of men seeking job services. *Child Abuse and Neglect* 61:23–34.

Tremblay, R. 2000. The development of aggressive behavior during childhood: What have we learned in the past century? *International Journal of Behavior Development* 24:129–141.

Ttofi, M. M., and D. P. Farrington. 2011. Effectiveness of school-based programs to reduce bullying: A systematic and meta-analytic review. *Journal of Experimental Criminology* 7:27–56.

Turner, H. A., D. Finkelhor, and R. Ormrod. 2006. The effect of lifetime victimization on the mental health of children and adolescents. *Social Science and Medicine* 62:13–27.

———. 2010. The effects of adolescent victimization on self-concept and depressive symptoms. *Child Maltreatment* 15:76–90.

U.S. Department of Health and Human Services. 2020. *Child maltreatment 2018.* Washington, DC: U.S. Department of Health and Human Services, Administration for Children and Families, Administration on Children, Youth and Families, Children's Bureau.

Vega, E. M., and K. D. O'Leary. 2007. Test-retest reliability of the revised conflict tactics scales (CTS2). *Journal of Family Violence* 22:703–708.

Visher, C., and K. McFadden. 1991. A comparison of urinalysis technologies for drug testing in criminal justice. *National Institute of Justice Research in Action.* Washington, DC: U.S. Department of Justice.

Vondracek, F. W., and E. J. Porfeli. 2006. The world of work and careers. In *Blackwell handbook of adolescence*, ed. G. R. Adams and M. D. Berzonsky, 109–128. Oxford, UK: Blackwell Publishing.

Vrana, S., and D. Lauterbach. 1994. Prevalence of traumatic events and post-traumatic stress symptoms in a nonclinical sample of college students. *Journal of Traumatic Stress* 7:289–302.

Wasserman, G. A., and A. M. Seracini. 2001. Family risk factors and interventions. In *Child delinquents: Development, interventions, and service needs*, ed. R. Loeber and D. P. Farrington, 165–189. Thousand Oaks, CA: Sage Publications, Inc.

Watts, S. J., and T. L. McNulty. 2013. Childhood abuse and criminal behavior: Testing a general strain theory model. *Journal of Interpersonal Violence* 28:3023–3040.

Weaver, A., J. A. Himle, R. J. Taylor, N. N. Matusko, and J. M. Abelson. 2015. Urban vs. rural residence and the prevalence of depression and mood disorder among African American women and non-Hispanic white women. *JAMA Psychiatry* 72:576–583.

Weems, C. F., M. Klabunde, J. D. Russell, and V. G. Carrion. 2015. Posttraumatic stress and age variation in amygdala volumes among youth exposed to trauma. *Social Cognitive and Affective Neuroscience* 10:1661–1667.

Weir, H., C. Kaukinen and A. Cameron. 2019. Diverse long-term effects of childhood exposure to intimate partner violence: Development of externalizing behaviors in males and females. *Journal of Interpersonal Violence*, published online December 18 2019, doi: 10.1177/0886260519888528.

Welsh, B. C., and S. N. Zane. 2019. Family-based programs for preventing delinquency and later offending. In *The Oxford handbook of developmental and life-course criminology*, ed. D. P. Farrington, L. Kazemian, and A. R. Piquero, 653–672. New York, NY: Oxford University Press.

Widom, C. S. 1989a. Child abuse, neglect, and adult behavior: Research design and findings on criminality, violence, and child abuse. *American Journal of Orthopsychiatry* 59:355–367.

————. 1989b. The cycle of violence. *Science* 244:160–166.

————. 2014. Long-term consequences of child maltreatment. In *Handbook of child maltreatment*, ed. J. E. Korbin and R. D. Krugman, 225–247. Dordrecht, Netherlands: Springer.

Widom, C. S., and M. G. Maxfield. 1996. A prospective examination of risk for violence among abused and neglected children. *Annals of the New York Academy of Sciences* 794:224–237.

Widom, C. S., and S. Morris. 1997. Accuracy of adult recollections of childhood victimization, Part 2: Childhood sexual abuse. *Psychological Assessment* 9:34–46.

Widom, C. S., A. M. Schuck, and H. R. White. 2006. An examination of pathways from childhood victimization to violence: The role of early aggression and problematic alcohol use. *Violence and Victims* 21:675–690.

Widom, C. S., and R. L. Shepard. 1996. Accuracy of adult recollections of childhood victimization, Part 1: Childhood physical abuse. *Psychological Assessment* 8:412–421.

Widom, C. S., B. L. Weiler, and L. B. Cottler. 1999. Childhood victimization and drug abuse: A comparison of prospective and retrospective findings. *Journal of Consulting and Clinical Psychology* 67:867–880.

Widom, C. S., and H. R. White. 1997. Problem behaviors in abused and neglected children grown up: Prevalence and co-occurrence of substance abuse, crime, and violence. *Criminal Behaviour and Mental Health* 7:287–310.

Wittchen, H. U. 1994. Reliability and validity studies of the WHO-Composite International Diagnostic Interview (CIDI): A critical review. *Journal of Psychiatric Research* 28:57–84.

Wolfe, D. A., C. V. Crooks, V. Lee, S. McIntyre-Smith, and P. G. Jaffe. 2003. The effects of children's exposure to domestic violence: A meta-analysis and critique. *Clinical Child and Family Psychology Review* 6:171–187.

Wolfe, D. A., K. Scott, C. Wekerle, and A. Pittman. 2001. Child maltreatment: Risk of adjustment problems and dating violence in adolescence. *Journal of American Academy of Child and Adolescent Psychiatry* 40:282–289.

Wolfinger, N. H. 2000. Beyond the intergenerational transmission of divorce: Do people replicate the patterns of marital instability they grew up with? *Journal of Family Issues* 21:1061–1086.

Woon, F. L., and D. W. Hedges. 2008. Hippocampal and amygdala volumes in children and adults with childhood maltreatment-related posttraumatic stress disorder. *Hippocampus* 18:729–736.

Wright, E. M., A. A. Fagan, and G. M. Pinchevsky. 2013. The effects of exposure to violence and victimization across life domains on adolescent substance use. *Child Abuse and Neglect* 37:899–909.

Yingling, J. 2016. Gender pathways to crime. In *The handbook of measurement issues in criminology and criminal justice*, ed. B. M. Huebner and T. S. Bynum, 181–201. Chichester, West Sussex, UK: Wiley Blackwell.

Zara, G. 2019. Cognitive-behavioral treatment to prevent offending and to rehabilitate offenders. In *The Oxford handbook of developmental and life-course criminology*, ed. D. P. Farrington, L. Kazemian, and A. R. Piquero, 694–725. New York, NY: Oxford University Press.

Zeller, R. A., and E. G. Carmines. 1980. *Measurement in the social sciences: The link between theory and data.* Cambridge, UK: Cambridge University Press.

Zhang, S., T. Benson, and X. Deng. 2000. A test-retest reliability assessment of the International Self-Report Delinquency instrument. *Journal of Criminal Justice* 28:283–295.

Zielinski, D. S. 2009. Child maltreatment and adult socioeconomic well-being. *Child Abuse and Neglect* 33:666–678.

Zimmerman, G. M., and M. Kushner. 2017. Examining the contemporaneous, short-term, and long-term effects of secondary exposure to violence on adolescent substance use. *Journal of Youth and Adolescence* 46:1933–1952.

Zingraff, M. T., J. Leiter, K. A. Myers, and M. C. Johnsen. 1993. Child maltreatment and youthful problem behavior. *Criminology* 31:173–202.

Zinzow, H. M., K. J. Ruggiero, R. F. Hanson, D. W. Smith, B. E. Saunders, and D. G. Kilpatrick. 2009. Witnessed community and parental violence in relation to substance use and delinquency in a national sample of adolescents. *Journal of Traumatic Stress* 22:525–533.

Zych, I., and D. P. Farrington. 2019. Developmental preschool and school programs against violence and offending. In *The Oxford handbook of developmental and life-course criminology*, ed. D. P. Farrington, L. Kazemian, and A. R. Piquero, 673–693. New York, NY: Oxford University Press.

Index

Page references for figures and tables are italicized.

About the Authors

Scott Menard (PhD, 1981, in sociology, University of Colorado, Boulder) is a retired professor of criminal justice and criminology, most recently in the Department of Criminal Justice and Criminology at Sam Houston State University in Huntsville, Texas. He is also the third and most recent principal investigator on the National Youth Survey Family Study, a national study of prosocial behavior, substance use, and criminal victimization and offending, both over the life course and across generations. His publications include books, monographs, and articles on criminological theory testing, and studies of victimization, illicit substance use, criminal behavior in adolescents and adults, and quantitative methods and statistics (particularly logistic regression and longitudinal research), among them *Applied Logistic Regression Analysis*, second edition (2002) and the *Handbook of Longitudinal Research* (2008).

Herbert C. Covey (PhD, 1979, in sociology, University of Colorado, Boulder) is the retired deputy director of the Adams County, Colorado, Human Services Department. He has worked for over forty years as an administrator in the areas of human services, criminal justice, and public policy, and as an instructor in sociology, most recently at the University of Colorado, Boulder. His scholarly work includes nineteen books and forty-seven refereed journal articles in the areas of child abuse and neglect, street gangs, gerontology, methamphetamine, criminology and criminal justice, African American history, and human services, among them *The Smallest Victims: The History of Child Maltreatment and Child Protection in America* (2018) and *The Meth Crisis* (2006).